A ROMANTIC STORYBOOK

A ROMANTIC STORYBOOK

❧ *Selected and edited by Morris Bishop*

Drawings by Alison Mason Kingsbury

Cornell University Press / ITHACA & LONDON

Copyright © 1971 by Cornell University

First published 1971 by Cornell University Press.
Published in the United Kingdom by Cornell University
Press Ltd., 2–4 Brook Street, London W1Y 1AA.

International Standard Book Number 0–8014–0658–7
Library of Congress Catalog Card Number 70–155821

Printed in the United States of America by Kingsport Press, Inc.

❧ Preface

A ROMANTIC STORYBOOK could be one of many things, as Romanticism itself is many things.

In literary usage, "Romantic" has a large meaning and a small meaning. In the large meaning, it indicates a cast of character, a state of mind, a basis of behavior and judgment. To summarize a summary of my own:* Romanticism is the prizing of emotion above reason; it is tender-mindedness versus tough-mindedness (William James); it is the desire and expectation of change rather than the desire and expectation of fixity (Jacques Barzun); it is organicism, dynamism, diversitarianism (Arthur O. Lovejoy); it is the recognition of the subconscious (F. L. Lucas); its values are change, imperfection, growth, diversity, the creative imagination, the unconscious (Morse Peckham). And long ago Walter Pater defined it as "the addition of strangeness to beauty."

In this larger sense Euripides was a Romantic; so were the medieval romancers; so was Shakespeare; and D. H. Lawrence and James Joyce. And one has no difficulty in pointing to Romantics among contemporary writers.

But in the smaller meaning Romanticism is a literary movement, a school with a doctrine, which flourished at

---

* In *A Survey of French Literature* (New York, 1965), II, 3.

the end of the eighteenth century and in the early years of the nineteenth. Its common tenets may be thus catalogued:

1. The cultivation of sensibility, emotion, passion, in opposition to classic rationality, common sense, decorum. (The opposition appears clearly in the title of Jane Austen's novel *Sense and Sensibility*, 1811.) The Romantics believed that the emotions, spontaneously released, conduce to good conduct. But the encouragement of emotional release (in "self-awareness" and "self-expression") leads to an individualism which may be admirable but which may also be inconveniently anti-social. Further, sensibility may degenerate into sentimentality; and, through excessive self-analysis, it may provoke a morbid melancholy, ending even in madness and suicide.

2. Appreciation of nature, on philosophical as well as aesthetic grounds. Eighteenth-century literature, even poetry, had been predominantly an urban literature. The predecessors of the Romantics, the pre-Romantics, opened their eyes to the beauty of wild nature, and described it with loving exactness. They found a harmony between nature and man; nature is good, and man is good insofar as he cleaves to her. Such convictions could turn into an ecstatic pantheism.

3. Respect for the simple, primitive man, representative of "the Folk." Rejecting the aristocratism of the past, the pre-Romantics and the Romantics found inspiration in the virtues, sufferings, and emotional dramas of the common man, and in those of "the noble savage," uncorrupted by civilization. A mystical regard for *das Volk*, especially in Germany, encouraged folkloristic studies, by which the Romantic writers profited.

4. Relish of medievalism. The preceding period had

been classical, looking back to Greece and Rome, and using the term "Gothic" in derision. The Romantics rediscovered the Middle Age; indeed, they turned it into a rich costume drama which still imposes itself on the historic picture of that time.

5. Taste for the mysterious, the fantastic, the supernatural. The rationalist mood of the early eighteenth century had sought scientific clarity and had scouted the miraculous, in faith and life. The Romantics restored it, perhaps more for its artistic opportunities than out of conviction, in their effort to promote what has been called "the renascence of wonder."

6. Acclaim of the exceptional man, the tragic hero, of the type soon to be known as "Byronic." The experiences of the exceptional man were bound to be exceptional; hence the Romantic writers favored plots of violent melodrama.

7. Acceptance of realism in development and detail; but the subordination of realism to spiritual purpose.

8. Contempt for the bourgeois, who is by definition materialistic, mean-minded, groveling before authority, and infuriate against the exceptional man, the poet.

It is this Romanticism that is represented in this book.

The history of literary Romanticism begins in the early eighteenth century with certain forerunners, mostly in Germany, Switzerland, and France, who displayed unmistakable Romantic qualities. We call them pre-Romantics (an unsatisfactory term, since they did not know they were *pre*-anything; they thought they were achievers of something new and great). Most influential was Rousseau, whose novel *Julie, or the New Héloïse* (1761) proclaimed the divine rights of passion in conflict with social convention. Goethe's *Sorrows of Young Werther* (1774) pushed love's despair to its logical conclusion in suicide. In this *Storybook* pre-Romanticism is represented by Prévost's *Adventure of a Desperate Man* (1734), Marmontel's *Shepherdess of the Alps* (1759), and Macpherson's *Calthon and Colmal* (1762).

The Romantic School as such was formally founded in Germany in 1798, when Ludwig Tieck, the Schlegel brothers, and others established in Jena a tendentious literary magazine, *Athenaeum*. A younger group, including Achim von Arnim, made its headquarters in Heidelberg. By about 1830 the German Romantic School lost its vigor, and yielded its dominance to the "Young Germany" movement. In England also the initial date of Romanticism proper is 1798, when the *Lyrical Ballads* of Wordsworth and Coleridge was published. The terminal date is often set at 1837, with the accession of Queen Victoria and the formulation of new literary as well as social principles. In France the Romantic Period of the textbooks begins with the publication of Lamartine's *Méditations poétiques* in 1820 and ends with the failure of Victor Hugo's drama *Les Burgraves* in 1843. Plenty of later writers can of course be called post-Romantics, but with them we have nothing to do.

The scheme of this book is to present both familiar and (it is hoped) unfamiliar, seldom-anthologized examples of Romantic prose fiction. The editor has not sought to be all-inclusive. Some writers, like Alfred de Musset, could not be brief enough to fit the anthologist's requirements. Some novelists, like Stendhal and Mary Shelley, do not lend themselves to excerpting. And some more or less famous works proved, on examination, to be dead. The examples chosen are all, in the editor's judgment, still alive.

The editor has no particular gratitude to express to any-one, except the Cornell University Libraries and Cornell University Press.

MORRIS BISHOP

Ithaca, New York
May 1971

Contents

A ROMANTIC STORYBOOK

❦ *The Adventure of a Desperate Man*

by ABBÉ PRÉVOST

Antoine-François Prévost (1697–1763), known in later life as the Abbé Prévost d'Exiles, or simply the Abbé Prévost, is generally remembered today as the author of the immortal *Manon Lescaut*. Until he was forty he led a stormy life, in and out of monasteries, the army, and jail. He then settled down to authorship; he produced altogether 112 volumes, half original fiction, half translations.

His *Aventure d'un désespéré* is undatable; it must have been written some time after 1734. It exhibits many of the qualities of the Romantic spirit—the taste for melodrama and violence, the prizing of emotion for its own sake, the exaltation of the man ruled by passion, the scorn of bourgeois values and sanctions. It is at the same time a realistic picture of eighteenth-century Paris—and a prefigurement of the Lolita theme. The translation is by Morris Bishop.

A FEW YEARS AGO two gentlemen crossing the Pont-Neuf, between eleven o'clock and midnight, heard a woman's voice. She seemed to be in some pressing danger, but fear itself, or some violent emotion, robbed her of strength to make her outcries audible at any distance. The two passers-by hastened forward in the darkness and halted in amazement at the sight that met their eyes. A feeble shaft of moonlight, appearing amidst the clouds, revealed to them a woman, who was uttering terrified moans rather than screams, mingled with half-articulate words, begging only that life be spared her. A tall man, decently dressed, was dragging her along the parapet; suddenly he bent her backward over the low wall. He seemed on the point of casting her into the Seine, when, with a shift of purpose, he thrust her into the midway of the bridge. "Enough!" he said; "you aren't worthy to die!" He leaped lightly onto the wall, and without another word plunged into the stream.

Though all these events occurred so quickly that the two companions had no time to recover from their first surprise, a natural compassion led them to run toward the steps descending to the streamside. Determining to seek the mooring-place of the river-skiffs opposite the Quatre-Nations, in the hope of using them for rescue, they reached the spot so opportunely that they saw a body floating close enough to be unmistakable. However, finding no oars in the boats, they would have reached vainly for the body had it not occurred to them to run farther downstream to the floating riverside craft of the launderers. These, moored side by side, are interconnected; the outermost ones lie almost in the middle of the current. Thereby the gentlemen advanced so far that they had only to stretch forth their hands to receive the corpse, which seemed to surrender to them.

I call him a corpse, not unfittingly, for he was no different from a lifeless body. But after the rescuers held him up by the feet, the violence with which he disgorged a great quantity of water indicated that he retained some inward vigor. Almost immediately he regained consciousness. He asked his liberators where he was and by what mercy of heaven he lay in their embrace. Then, recalling all the circumstances of his misadventure, he thanked the two warmly for the service they had rendered him. "How weak is reason!" he exclaimed, calmly enough. "How ill reason serves us in the transports of violent passion! But if you have come so nobly to my rescue after witnessing my folly, tell me what has happened to the unhappy creature who has so upset my mind, and who deserved, far more than I, the dreadful fate to which I exposed myself."

The gentlemen recounted all that they had seen, and how they had gone about saving him, without having leisure to pay the least attention to his companion. "Alas!" he sighed. "She is unworthy of the concern that still afflicts me. But no matter. If only a moment has elapsed since my plunge, you will perhaps find her still on the Pont-Neuf, and you will perhaps aid her to return to her home. I shall never see her again."

To satisfy him, one of the rescuers returned to the Pont-Neuf. Occasionally shouting to attract her attention, he sought everywhere in vain. Finding no one, he accosted some pedestrians coming from the rue Dauphine, and asked them if they had not seen a lady on foot and unattended. He learned that they had in fact seen one such in the Carrefour de la rue de Buci, escorted by the night watch. In their presence she had asked the watchmen to conduct her to her home. It was clear that she was the sought-for person. The interrogator returned immediately to the quay, being curious to discover the sense of this adventure and eager to continue rendering his services. He found the unfortunate stranger where he had been left, and sufficiently recovered to cooperate in the restoration of his normal state. Being informed that the lady was in safety, he asked the two companions to identify themselves, in order to learn if they might be as capable of discretion as of zeal, and if he might accord them confidence as great as the gratitude and affection that he owed them. One reported that he was a notary; the other that he had been the business manager of the late Duc de ———, that he had retired after the death of his master and was now living comfortably on his savings. Since these two descriptions avouched good sense and probity, the stranger did not hesitate to explain in all frankness his situation.

"I am happy," he said, "to owe an obligation to such worthy men. You can still be of service to me; and I am assured that the importance of my confidences will impose an inviolable law of secrecy." He then told them the name of the lady who had caused all his misfortune. He begged the notary to proceed immediately to her house, to inform her that he had fortunately been rescued, and to expose to her that in her own interest she should preserve eternal silence on the occurrences of the night. "Say the same to her father," he added; "for I imagine that in her first agitation of mind she will have revealed to him a part of the truth. And promise them, on my behalf, that if they are able to keep silence they will have nothing to fear from my rancor." He then appointed a nearby tavern as rendezvous, and repaired thither with the man of affairs, to dry his clothes and to fit himself to return home without giving rise to suspicious concern on the part of his family.

The notary, after capably executing his mission, rejoined the others at the designated spot. He reported that he had found father and daughter in the utmost consternation, that his words had appeared to console them vastly, and that without further ado they had promised the discretion asked of them.

"Perfidious wretch!" cried the stranger, yielding momentarily to impulse. "Should I have spared her life? What madness made me divert my purpose to myself? But let me consider no other vengeance than contempt!" Then, glancing at his two rescuers, he pursued: "I am too far in your debt to conceal from you what led me to the abyss from which you saved me. And if I venture to pray silence about all you have beheld, I must indicate to you, by my voluntary confidence, that I think you capable of preserving it. Hear then my sad and shameful story.

"I am the eldest son of a very rich family. I should have married long since in a fashion suitable to my birth had not the force of an indomitable passion rendered me insensible to all the advantages of fortune. A female monster, of whom I can henceforth speak only with horror, but whose charms compelled my adoration, seduced my heart some two years since. She was the only daughter of a physician who then dwelt in my neighborhood. I was wont to see her with my sisters, by whom she thought herself much honored to be received. I conceived for her an inexpressible tenderness. She had barcly attained her twelfth year. I was unable to conceal my feelings toward her. She did not repel me totally by her reply; but whether her heart still kept some modicum of virtue, or whether she was already sly enough to ply her advantage, she ceased to see my sisters and seemed to make a practice of avoiding me. I made such efforts to encounter her that once, having found an opportunity to speak to her in the street, I complained bitterly to her of her contrived absence. She heard me out; and if I was enchanted by her person I was the more so by her character, when she confided to me that she felt an inclination toward me, but added that it was the fear of too ready a surrender to it and her awareness of the inequality of our names and fortunes that had made her take the course of sparing needless suffering to us both. From that moment I would have sacrificed all to her. I told her plainly that a heart like mine could not be deterred by such feeble obstacles.

"She did not surrender to my persuasions. I spent several weeks in seeking new occasions to see her. Desperate at her persistent avoidance, I attempted several times to slip into her house, in spite of the resistance I met at her door, which I could attribute only to her orders. Her father, warned that I had threatened his servants with violence, complained to my father. But far from thwarting my purposes, this action gave me a double advantage, for it inspired in me the idea of dealing directly with the doctor, and it allayed my father's suspicions, which might have been aroused by various incidents that ensued.

"Thus, instead of trying to execute my threats, I decently begged permission to see the doctor. He could not refuse me this favor. I reproached him tenderly with causing me mortal pain by aligning himself against me without knowing the nature of my feelings and purposes. I was nearly thirty years old, of such an age that one might depend upon my character and upon my promises. I loved his daughter with the regard of a gentleman; I was ready to give him my word that I would marry her. Permission to see her, which I begged him to grant, would be meaningless to me without the hope of marriage. In short, I left him free to take every precaution to set his mind at rest and to make his conditions, by which he might assure the fortune of his daughter and facilitate my happiness.

"These words, uttered with all the force that honor and love can inspire, made more of an impression on the doctor than I had dared to hope. His objections were provoked merely by fear of offending my father and of bringing on himself the hostility of a man well known both for his importance and his violence of temper. But I persuaded him easily that at my age I was free to marry a girl I was enamored of, whose virtue well compensated for her lack of fortune. Though I had to show some circumspection toward my father, I could readily pay all my devoirs to him while concealing my passion and the bonds which I wished to assume. These could likewise, through secrecy, be hidden from the public eye, without loss of their effectiveness and sanctity. This sincere, straightforward language brought me the doctor's consent. He imposed only two conditions: the first that, to remove any doubt of my good faith, I should begin by marrying his daughter; the second that for two years I should renounce the rights of marriage, because the disproportion of our forces made him fear for her health.

"My emotions were so pure that, making no complaint of his conditions, which set so long a term to the achievement of my desires, I thought myself only too happy at the advantages gained. I engaged myself forthwith to execute the two articles imposed, and so I vowed at the feet of his daughter, who seemed as happy as I at an outcome so little hoped for. We agreed that to facilitate my visits and to hide my actions from my family, the doctor would remove to another quarter. I undertook to find him a suitable house. I had his daughter's apartment furnished with as much luxury as taste. The day of her entrance therein was chosen for the celebration of our marriage. Avoiding all ceremonious show, I took care that decency should be observed and that nothing essential should be wanting to the bonds destined to assure my lifelong bliss.

"You may admire my restraint, in these times when such moderation receives but little commendation. In the two years since I contracted my disastrous bond I have permitted myself no violation of my promises. Only too glad of my liberty to see constantly a woman I adored and to observe attentively the development of her charms, I awaited without impatience the term to which I had engaged myself. I gave all my study to the cultivation of her liking for me, by the gentleness of my behavior and by continual evidences of my affection. I made it even my serious occupation to keep fresh in mind all the taste, all the intellectual enlightenment I had garnered from my education and the frequentation of society, in order to form her heart and mind. I thought I recognized daily that she was profiting by my efforts. Besides, I supplied her with the best teachers; and I would have allowed her nothing but the most exquisite products of the court and the city.

"I spent two full years dwelling in this enchantment, disgusted with society, with the pleasures normal to my years, even with the cultivation of friendship, in short, thinking only of fleeing everything that could turn me aside from the abode of all my affections. My father, noticing the change in my conduct and inclinations, urged me on innumerable occasions to elucidate to him a mystery which alarmed him. He suspected even that love had made me embark on some wild enterprise; but as his suspicions merely made me augment my vigilance, I always succeeded most happily in eluding his own.

"Three days ago I spoke to the doctor about his daughter's state of health. It seemed to me vigorous enough to dissipate all his fears. I recalled to him that the date upon which he had fixed was drawing near and told him that if he had no better arguments to present to me, it was time to yield to me my well-deserved rights. She was not present at this conversation. My conviction of her innocence would have made me fearful of exposing her to suggestions which might have appeared strange and shocking. Though I had sometimes ventured in her presence some indelicate badinage, I had thought I recognized that she understood nothing of it, and, respecting her modesty, I had hastily changed the subject. However, when her father replied that he thought she had reached the stage of development he had thought desirable before totally according her to me, I made no secret of my hope soon to pass my nights as well as my days by her side. We proposed even to celebrate our pleasures by a fête, to which, I agreed, some of her near relatives should be invited. I felt no reluctance to reveal to them our secret. I gave orders for the preparation of a grand supper; it was to take place tomorrow. Having prudently given my father's household to believe that I was to depart in the morning for a week at a friend's country house, I promised myself that I would employ the time more agreeably in the first exercise of my affection.

"So, this afternoon I proceeded, with, if I may so put it, more ardor than usual, to the house of my innocent, modest charmer. I did not find her at home. Her father told me that she had asked permission to go to the Palais * to buy some jewelry, that she went off in a cab, followed by her lackey, and that, being engaged to sup with one of her aunts, she could not return before ten or eleven o'clock.

"My impatience to see her and my desire to buy, on my own part, all that might strike her fancy led me straightway to the Palais. I spent two hours vainly seeking her, and then returned to her father, distressed only by missing the pleasure I had promised myself. Unable to withdraw without seeing the sole object of my love, I determined to await her.

"While meditating on the satisfactions assured to me on the morrow, and anticipating with transport those delights, I reflected that nothing obliged me to postpone so long what I could properly obtain that very day. My undertaking to wait was merely a pretext, a formality. I communicated my ideas to the doctor; he seemed to concur with them. With this resolution in mind, I delighted in the thought of going to meet my virtuous mistress. Obtaining the address of the house where she was visiting, I had the

* Palais: the Palais de Justice, on the Ile de la Cité, locus of specialty shops.—Ed.

patience to stand for a good half hour in the street before it. I was alone, as I had sent home my lackey to offer some excuse for my absence; and I did not wish to present myself until she had taken leave of her aunt, since I was always concerned to humor her modesty.

"Finally she emerged. Her lackey had summoned a sedan chair. It started off; I was only some twenty paces away, ready to confront her. I was on the point of speaking to the chairmen, when I saw them stop of their own accord. It was the lackey who had so ordered them. He was on the opposite side of the chair from me. I heard him address his mistress and urge her to return to the Quai des Orfèvres. He assured her that it was not late, and that she could yet dispose of an hour. After evincing timidity and making some difficulties, she consented. The bearers took the course indicated to them by the lackey.

"Although nothing in the nature of fear or suspicion occurred to me, curiosity alone sufficed to make me follow her. What business could summon her to the Quai des Orfèvres at eleven o'clock of the night? Falling back against a door to let the chair go past, I followed at a certain distance, and reached the Quai almost as soon as the bearers. They stopped at the door indicated to them. The lackey introduced his mistress into the house, and ordered them to wait, and followed her within.

"As soon as I had seen her disappear I did not hesitate to advance. Without a word to the bearers, who apparently took me for a dweller in the same house, I penetrated into a dark entry, which led me to the foot of a staircase. This I mounted with some alarm, although I was guided by the sound of those who had preceded me. They were admitted to a door on the third floor; they closed it immediately behind them. I listened intently for a few minutes. Distrust was already beginning to invade my spirit; I was more alarmed by the pervading silence than I would have been by any other explanation of the situation. I was seized by impatience; but wishing to proceed reasonably, I knocked very gently, and in the same manner addressed a small servant-girl who opened the door. I asked her if Mademoiselle —— would be there long. She replied that she didn't know, but that her mistress was not accustomed to receive girls so late in her house.

"These words made me tremble. A few words of explanation, which I had control enough to elicit by my same calm manner, revealed to me the evil nature of the place. I could hardly restrain my fury from bursting forth in shouts and cries and in all the violence that this frightful adventure could provoke. Nevertheless some remainder of hope still prompted my actions. I asked the servant as a signal favor to admit me without noise to the reception-room, where she was stationed. A louis which I slipped into her hand disposed her to serve me. Imagining that I was in search of pleasure, she made some objections, to which I made no response. When I asked her merely to tell me whither the young lady had withdrawn, she made no ado about pointing to the door of a room that opened on the reception-room.

"Shall I reveal to you all my shame? I listened at the door; the imprudent ardor of the conversation within spared me the trouble of straining my ears. I was the subject of their modest colloquy. The basest of men was boasting that he had covered me with opprobrium, and was rejoicing that he had obtained what, as he complained, had been too long refused him. In a word, I learned from the words of these noble lovers that after confining themselves for more than eighteen months within certain limits imposed on them by fear, they had chosen this day to compensate themselves for their long restraint, and that they were reserving as my share only the leftovers of their offerings to love.

"You may judge of my fury. I would have stabbed the two wretches on the spot; I would have drowned them in each other's blood; but a stout, firmly fastened door protected them from my first transport of rage. I chose then to descend and to postpone their punishment until their arrival at the street door. The hour, the place, gave me assurance of total vengeance. I quitted the servant-girl, on the pretext that it was too late to linger further. Finding the chairmen waiting impatiently at the door, I paid them their due and bade them be off. The night was not too dark to hide my victims from me. I took my stand a few steps from the entrance; every moment of my wait merely redoubled my wrath.

"I heard them coming. Their approach caused me a cruel joy. I would have liked to run them both through with a single thrust. But instead of seeing them appear together, I saw only my unworthy rival, who turned his head this way and that, to discover the bearers. I would have liked to spring upon him and snatch away his life with a thousand dagger-blows. The only reason I refrained was my fear that his companion might have time to escape me. He caught sight of me and took off with such haste that I had no hope of overtaking him. I breathed my bitterness to heaven, accusing it of injustice; without further restraint I dashed to the door, to make sure at least of the main part of my vengeance. The infamous creature, who no doubt took me for her lover, awaited me at the threshold. I seized her with an inexpressible transport. Threatening to cut her throat if she made the slightest outcry, I dragged her toward some steps leading up to the bridge parapet, where-upon, I thought, I might readily climb. I had made the sudden resolution to drown her. Her initial fright and my violent action prevented her at first from recognizing me; but she could not long be deluded. She fainted in my arms. Far from being moved to pity, I felt my rage increased by the mere difficulty of dragging along her limp body. My efforts to carry her soon brought her back to consciousness. She uttered a few cries, which could hardly have been very loud in her state of weakness and distress. Finally I reached the parapet, and forced her to its top.

"Perhaps she was not yet aware of my purpose. I had not so far pronounced a single word. But when she realized, by my movements in thrusting her against the wall, that I was planning to make an end of her, her resistance became so vigorous that I began to fear that I was not the stronger of the two. She seized my arm, clutching it with such force that I could not make use of it, and expressed in a voice half-stifled with fear all that she could suppose capable of moving me. I did not answer; more resolute than ever to rid myself of my shame, I used my free arm to bend her over the wall, hoping to push her the more easily with my knee. It was at this moment that I thought I heard someone crossing the bridge. She heard it at the same time; the hope of rescue renewed her strength. In fact, I conceived that I was going to miss my revenge. Despair invaded my heart; assured that together with my rage at seeing my prey reft from me I would endure the humiliation of being recog-nized, and that of hearing on the morrow the story of my adventure retailed in every quarter of Paris, I made the fatal resolve to throw myself down. I wavered for a mo-ment, irresolute whether I should use my sword to put a quietus to her who would perhaps triumph at my death;

but I concluded that I would be better avenged by my scorn. I thrust her aside, with some words forced from me by this emotion. And then, unheeding, I cast myself into the river."

ꙮ *The Shepherdess of the Alps*

by JEAN-FRANÇOIS MARMONTEL

Jean-François Marmontel (1723–1799) was a thoroughgoing man of letters, of a type now rare. He wrote tragedies, comic operas, romances, histories, memoirs, and literary criticism; he was Secretary of the Académie Française and editor of the *Mercure de France,* a popular literary magazine. He was an indomitable socializer and a mainstay of Mme Geoffrin's famous salon.

He contributed to the *Mercure* a series of *contes moraux,* or *Moral Tales.* (But in French the connotation of *conte moral* is rather "a story on ethical themes.") *The Shepherdess of the Alps* is a good example. It first appeared in the *Mercure,* probably in 1759. It is already Romantic in its picturesque Alpine setting (previously celebrated by the Swiss Gessner, J.-J. Rousseau, and others), in its exaltation of pure, all-conquering love, in its dripping sentimentality, and in what Marmontel himself terms "a pleasing melancholy."

Our translation (anonymous) is contained in Marmontel's *Moral Tales* (London, 1810). Some slight modernizations have been made, such as the substitution of "sensitive" for "sensible."

IN THE MOUNTAINS of Savoy, not far from the road from Briançon to Modena, is a solitary valley, the sight of which inspires travellers with a pleasing melancholy. Three little hills shaping an amphitheatre, on which are scattered, at a great distance from one another, some shepherds' huts, torrents that fall from the mountains, clumps of trees here and there, pastures always green, form the ornament of this rural place.

The Marchioness of Fonrose was returning from France to Italy with her husband. The axle-tree of their carriage broke; and as the day was on the decline, they were obliged to seek in this valley for some shelter to pass the night. As they advanced toward one of the huts, they saw a flock going that way, conducted by a shepherdess whose gait astonished them. They drew nearer, and heard a heavenly voice, whose plaintive and moving accents made the echoes groan.

"How the setting sun still glitters with a gentle light! It is thus," said she, "that at the end of a painful race the exhausted soul departs to grow young again in the pure source of immortality. But alas, how distant is the period, and how long is life!" On saying these words, the shepherdess retired with her head inclined; but the negligence of her attitude seemed to give still more nobleness and majesty to her person and deportment.

Struck with what they saw, and still more with what they had just heard, the Marquis and Marchioness of Fonrose redoubled their pace, in order to overtake this shepherdess whom they admired. But what was their surprise, when under the plainest head-dress, beneath the most humble garb, they saw all the graces, all the beauties united! "Child," said the Marchioness to her, on seeing that she avoided them, "fear nothing; we are travellers whom an accident obliges to seek shelter in these huts till the day: will you be so good as to be our guide?"

"I pity you, Madam," said the shepherdess, looking down and blushing; "these huts are inhabited by poor wretches, and you will be very ill lodged."

"You lodge there without doubt yourself," replied the Marchioness; "and I can easily endure, for one night, the inconveniences which you suffer always."

"I am formed for that," said the shepherdess, with a modesty that charmed them. "No, surely," said the Marquis de Fonrose, who could no longer dissemble the emotion she had caused in him; "No, you are not formed to suffer; and Fortune is very unjust! Is it possible, lovely damsel, that so many charms are buried in this desert, under that habit?"

"Fortune, Sir," replied Adelaide (this was the name of the shepherdess), "Fortune is not cruel but when she takes from us that which she has given us. My condition has its pleasures for one who knows no other, and custom creates wants for you which shepherds do not know."

"That may be," said the Marquis, "with respect to those whom heaven has placed from their birth in this obscure condition; but you, astonishing damsel, you whom I admire, you, who enchant me, you were never born what you now are; that air, that gait, that voice, that language, everything betrays you. But two words which you have just now spoken proclaim a cultivated understanding, a noble soul. Proceed, teach us what misfortune can have reduced you to this strange abasement."

"For a man in misfortune," replied Adelaide, "there are a thousand ways to extricate himself; for a woman, you know, there is no other honest resource than servitude, and the choice of masters. They do well, in my opinion, who prefer the good. You are now going to see mine; you will be charmed with the innocence of their lives, the candour, the simplicity, the probity of their manners."

While she talked thus, they arrived at the hut. It was separated by a partition from the fold into which this *incognita* drove her sheep, telling them over with the most serious attention, and without deigning to take any further notice of the travellers, who contemplated her. An old man and his wife, such as Philemon and Baucis are described to us, came forth to meet their guests with that village honesty which recalls the golden age to our minds. "We have nothing to offer you," said the good woman, "but fresh straw for a bed, milk, fruit, and rye bread for your food; but the little that heaven gives us we will most heartily share with you." The travellers, on entering the hut, were surprised at the air of regularity which everything breathed there. The table was one single plank of walnut-tree highly polished; they saw themselves in the enamel of the earthen vessels designed for their milk. Everything presented the image of cheerful poverty and of the first wants of nature agreeably satisfied. "It is our dear daughter," said the good woman, "who takes upon her the management of our house. In the morning, before her flock ramble far into the country, and while they begin to graze round the house on the grass covered with dew, she washes, cleans, and sets everything in order with a dexterity that charms us."

"What!" said the Marchioness, "is this shepherdess your daughter?"

"Ah, Madam! Would to heaven she were!" cried the good old woman. "It is my heart that calls her so, for I have a mother's love for her; but I am not so happy as to have borne her; we are not worthy to have given her birth."

"Who is she, then? Whence comes she? And what misfortune has reduced her to such a condition?"

"All that is unknown to us. It is now four years since she came to us in the habit of a female peasant to offer herself to keep our flocks; we would have taken her for nothing, so much had her good looks and pleasing manner won upon our hearts. We doubted her being born a villager; but our questions afflicted her, and we thought it our duty to abstain from them. This respect has but augmented in proportion as we have become better acquainted with her soul; but the more we would humble ourselves to her, the more she humbles herself to us. Never had daughter more attention for her father and mother, nor officiousness more tender. She cannot obey us, because we are far from commanding her; but it seems as if she saw through us, and everything that we can wish is done before we perceive that she thinks of it. She is an angel come down among us to comfort our old age."

"And what is she doing now in the fold?" demanded the Marchioness.

"Giving the flock fresh litter; drawing the milk from the ewes and she-goats. This milk, pressed out by her hand, seems to become the more delicious for it. I who go and sell it in the town cannot serve it fast enough. They think it delicious. The dear child employs herself, while she is watching the flock, in works of straw and osier, which are admired by all. Everything becomes valuable beneath her fingers. You see, Madam," continued the good old woman, "you see here the image of an easy and quiet life: it is she that procures it to us. This heavenly daughter is never employed but to make us happy."

"Is she happy herself?" demanded the Marquis de Fonrose.

"She endeavors to persuade us so," replied the old man; "but I have frequently observed to my wife that at her return from the pasture she had her eyes bedewed with tears, and the most afflicted air in the world. The moment she sees us she affects to smile; but we see plainly that she has some grief that consumes her. We dare not ask her what it is."

"Ah, Madam," said the old woman, "how I suffer for this child, when she persists in leading out her flocks to pasture in spite of rain and frost! Many a time have I thrown myself on my knees, in order to prevail with her to let me go in her stead; but I never could prevail on her.

She goes out at sunrise, and returns in the evening benumbed with cold. 'Judge now,' says she to me, 'whether I would suffer you to quit your fireside and expose yourself at your age to the rigours of the season. I am scarce able to withstand it myself.' Nevertheless she brings home under her arm the wood with which we warm ourselves; and when I complain of the fatigue she gives herself, 'Have done, have done, good mother; it is by exercise that I keep myself from cold; labour is made for my age.' In short, Madam, she is as good as she is handsome, and my husband and I never speak of her but with tears in our eyes."

"And if she should be taken from you?" said the Marchioness.

"We should lose," interrupted the old man, "all that we hold dearest in the world; but if she herself was to be the happier for it, we would die happy in that consolation."

"Oh, ay!" replied the old woman, shedding tears. "Heaven grant her a fortune worthy of her, if it be possible! It was my hope that that hand, so dear to me, would have closed my eyes, for I love her more than my life."

Her arrival broke off their discourse. She appeared with a pail of milk in one hand, a basket of fruit in the other; and after saluting them with an ineffable grace, she directed her attention to the care of the family, as if nobody observed her.

"You give yourself a great deal of trouble," said the Marchioness.

"I endeavor, Madam," replied she, "to fulfil the intention of those I serve, who are desirous of entertaining you in the best manner they are able. You will have," continued she, spreading over the table a coarse but very white cloth, "you will have a frugal and rural repast. This bread is not the whitest in the world, but it tastes pretty well. The eggs are fresh, the milk is good; and the fruits, which I have just now gathered, are such as the season affords." The diligence, the attention, the noble and becoming grace with which this wonderful shepherdess paid them all the duties of hospitality, the respect she showed for her master and mistress, whether she spoke to them or whether she sought to read in their eyes what they wanted her to do, all these things filled the Marquis and Marchioness of Fonrose with astonishment and admiration. As soon as they were laid down on the bed of fresh straw which the shepherdess had prepared for them herself, "Our adventure has the air of a prodigy," said they one to another. "We must clear up this mystery; we must carry away this child along with us."

At break of day, one of the men, who had been up all night mending their carriage, came to inform them that it was thoroughly repaired. Madame de Fonrose, before she set out, ordered the shepherdess to be called to her. "Without wanting to pry," she said, "into the secret of your birth and the cause of your misfortune, all that I see, all that I hear, interests me in your favour. I see that your spirit has raised you above ill fortune, and that you have suited your sentiments to your present condition; your charms and your virtues render it respectable, but yet it is unworthy of you. I have it in my power, amiable stranger, to procure you a happier lot; my husband's intentions agree entirely with mine. I have a considerable estate at Turin; I want a friend of my own sex; and I shall think I bear away from this place an invaluable treasure, if you will accompany me. Separate from the proposal, from the suit I now make you, all notion of servitude; I do not think you made for that condition. But though my prepossessions in your favour should deceive me, I had rather raise you above your birth than leave you beneath it. I repeat to you, it is a friend of my own sex that I want to attach to me. For the rest, be under no concern for the fate of these good people; there is nothing which I would not do to make them amends for your loss. At least they shall have wherewith to spend the remainder of their lives happily, according to their condition; and it is from your hand that they shall receive the benefits I intend them."

The old folks, who were present at this discourse, kissing the hands of the Marchioness and throwing themselves at her feet, begged the young *incognita* to accept of these generous offers. They represented to her with tears that they were on the brink of the grave, that she had no other consolation than to make them happy in their old age, and that at their death, when left to herself, their habitation would become a dreadful solitude. The shepherdess, embracing them, mingled her tears with theirs; she returned thanks to the Marquis and Marchioness, with a sensibility that made her still more beautiful. "I cannot," said she, "accept of your courtesies. Heaven has marked out my place, and its will is accomplished; but your goodness has made impressions on my soul which will never be effaced. The respectable name of Fonrose shall ever be present to my imagination. I have but one favour more to ask of you," said she, blushing and looking down. "That is to be so good as to bury this adventure in eternal silence, and to leave the world forever ignorant of the lot of an unknown wretch, who wants to live and die in oblivion." The Marquis and Marchioness of Fonrose, moved with pity and grief, redoubled a thousand times their instances; she was immovable, and the old people, the travellers, and the shepherdess separated, with tears in their eyes.

During the journey the Marquis and his lady were taken up with nothing but this adventure. They thought they had been in a dream. Their imaginations being filled with this kind of romance, they arrive at Turin. It may easily be imagined that they did not keep silence, and this was an inexhaustible subject for reflections and conjectures. The young Fonrose, being present at these discourses, lost not one circumstance. He was at that age wherein the imagination is most lively and the heart most susceptible; but he was one of those characters whose sensibility displays not itself outwardly, and who are so much the more violently agitated, when they are so at all, as the sentiment which affects them does not weaken itself by any sort of dissipation. All that Fonrose hears said of the charms, virtues, and misfortunes of the shepherdess of Savoy kindles in his soul the most ardent desire of seeing her. He forms to himself an image of her which is always present to him. He compares her to everything that he sees, and everything that he sees vanishes before her. But the more his impatience redoubles, the more care he takes to conceal it. Turin becomes odious to him. The valley which conceals from the world its brightest ornament attracts his whole soul. It is there that happiness awaits him. But if his project is known, he foresees the greatest obstacles. They will never consent to the journey he meditates; it is the folly of a young man, the consequences of which they will be apprehensive of; the shepherdess herself, affrighted at his pursuits, will not fail to withdraw herself from them; he loses her, if he should be known. After all these reflections, which employed his thoughts for three months, he takes a resolution to quit everything for her sake, to go, under the habit of a shepherd, to seek her in her solitude, and to die there, or draw her out of it.

He disappears; they see him no more. His parents become alarmed at his absence. Their fear increases every day; their expectations disappointed throw the whole family into affliction. The fruitlessness of their inquiries completes their despair. A duel, an assassination, everything that is most unfortunate presents itself to their imagination; and these unhappy parents ended their researches by lamenting the death of their son, their only hope. While his family are in mourning, Fonrose, under the habit of a shepherd, presents himself to the inhabitants of the hamlet adjoining to the valley, which they had but too well described to him. His ambition is accomplished; they trust him with the care of their flocks.

The first days after his arrival he left them to wander at random, solely attentive to discover the places to which the shepherdess led hers. "Let us treat with caution," said he, "the timidity of this solitary fair one. If she is unfortunate, her heart has need of consolation; if it be nothing but a desire to banish herself from the world, and the pleasure of a tranquil and innocent life that holds her here, she will feel some dull moments, and wish for company to amuse or console her. If I succeed so far as to render that agreeable to her, she will soon find it necessary; then I shall take counsel from the situation of her soul. After all, we are here alone, as it were, in the world, and we shall be everything to each other. From confidence to friendship the passage is not long; and from friendship to love, at our age, the road is still easier." And what was Fonrose's age when he reasoned thus? Fonrose was eighteen; but three months' reflection on the same object unfolds a number of ideas!

While he was thus giving himself up to his imagination, with his eyes wandering over the country, he hears at a distance that voice, the charms of which had been so often extolled to him. The emotion it excited in him was as lively as if it had been unexpected. "It is here," said the shepherdess in her plaintive strains, "it is here that my heart enjoys the only happiness that remains to it. My grief has a luxury in it for my soul; I prefer its bitterness to the deceitful sweets of joy."

These accents rent the sensitive heart of Fonrose. "What," said he, "can be the cause of the chagrin that consumes her? How pleasing would it be to console her!" A hope still more pleasing presumed, not without difficulty, to flatter his desires. He feared to alarm the shepherdess if he resigned himself imprudently to his impatience of seeing her near, and for the first time it was sufficient to have heard her. The next day he went out again to lead his sheep to pasture; and after observing the route which she had taken, he placed himself at the foot of a rock, which the day before repeated to him the sounds of that touching voice. I forgot to mention that Fonrose to the handsomest demeanour had joined those talents which the young nobility of Italy do not neglect. He played on the oboe like Besuzzi, of whom he had taken his lessons, and who formed at that time the delight of Europe. Adelaide, buried in her own afflicting ideas, had not yet made her voice heard, and the echoes kept silence. All of a sudden this silence was interrupted by the plaintive sounds of Fonrose's oboe. These unknown sounds excited in the soul of Adelaide a surprise mingled with anxiety. The keepers of the flocks that wandered on the hills had never caused her to hear aught before but the sound of rustic pipes. Immovable and attentive, she seeks with her eyes who it was that could cause such harmonious sounds. She perceives at a distance a young shepherd seated in the cavity of a rock, at the foot of which he fed his flock; she draws near, to hear him the better. "See," said she, "what the mere instinct of nature can do! The ear teaches this shepherd all the refinements of the art. Can anyone breathe purer sounds? What delicacy in his inflections! What variety in his gradations! Who can say, after this, that taste is not a gift of nature?" Ever since Adelaide had dwelled in this solitude, this was the first time that her grief, suspended by an agreeable distraction, had delivered up her soul to the sweet emotion of pleasure.

Fonrose, who saw her approach and seat herself at the foot of a willow to hear him, pretended not to perceive her. He seized, without seeming to affect it, the moment of her retreat, and managed the course of his own flock in such a manner as to meet her on the declivity of a hill, where the roads crossed. He cast only one look on her, and continued his route, as if taken up with nothing but the care of his flock. But what beauties had that one look run over! What eyes! What a divine mouth! How much more ravishing still would those features be, which are so noble and touching in their languor, if love reanimated them! He saw plainly that grief alone had withered in their spring the roses on her lovely cheeks; but of so many charms that which had moved him most was the noble elegance of her person and her gait. In the ease of her motions he thought he saw a young cedar, whose straight and flexible trunk yields gently to the zephyrs. This image, which love had just engraven in flaming characters on his memory, took up all his thoughts. "How feebly," said he, "have they painted to me this beauty unknown to the world, whose adoration she merits! And it is a desert that she inhabits! And it is thatch that covers her! She who ought to see kings at her feet employs herself in tending an humble flock! Beneath what garments has she presented herself to my view! She adorns everything, and nothing disfigures her. Yet what a life for a frame so delicate! Coarse food, a savage climate, a bed of straw, great gods! And for whom are the roses made? Yes, I will draw her out of this state, so much too hard and too unworthy of her." Sleep interrupted his reflections, but effaced not her image.

Adelaide, on her side, sensibly struck with the youth, the beauty of Fonrose, ceased not to admire the caprices of Fortune. "Where is nature going," said she, "to reassemble together so many talents and so many graces? But alas! those gifts which to him are here but useless would be perhaps his misfortune in a more elevated state. What evils does not beauty create in the world! Unhappy as I am, is it for me to set any value on it?" This melancholy reflection began to poison in her soul the pleasure she had tasted; she reproached herself for having been sensible of it, and resolved to deny it herself for the future.

The next day Fonrose thought he perceived that she avoided his approach; he fell into a profound melancholy. "Could she suspect my disguise?" said he. "Should I have betrayed it myself?" This uneasiness possessed him all the livelong day, and his oboe was neglected. Adelaide was not so far but she could easily have heard it, and his silence astonished her. She began to sing herself. "It seems," said the song, "that everything around me partakes of my heaviness. The birds send forth none but sorrowful notes, echo replies to me in complaints, the zephyrs moan amidst these leaves, the sound of the brooks imitates my sighs, one might say that they flowed with tears." Fonrose, softened by these strains, could not help replying to them. Never was concert more moving than that of his oboe with Adelaide's voice. "O heaven!" said she; "it is enchantment! I dare not believe my ears; it is not a shepherd; it is a god whom I have heard. Can the natural sense of harmony inspire such concord of sounds?" While she was speaking thus a rural, or rather a celestial, melody made the valley resound. Adelaide thought she saw those prodigies realising which Poetry attributes to her sprightly sister Music. Astonished, confounded, she knew not whether she ought to take herself away or resign herself up to this enchantment. But she perceived the shepherd whom she had just heard reassembling his flock in order to regain his hut. "He knows not," says she, "the delight he diffuses around him; his undisguised soul is not in the least vain of it; he waits not even for the praises I owe him. Such is the power of music; it is the only talent that places its happiness in itself; all the others require witnesses. This gift of heaven was granted to man in his innocence; it is the purest of all pleasures. Alas! It is the only one I still relish; and I consider this shepherd as a new echo who is come to answer my grief."

The following days Fonrose affected to keep at a distance in his turn; Adelaide was affected at it. "Chance," said she, "seemed to have procured me this feeble consolation; I gave myself up to it too easily, and to punish me, she has deprived me of it." At last, one day when they happened to meet on the declivity of the hill, "Shepherd," she said to him, "are you leading your flocks far off?" These first words of Adelaide caused an emotion in Fonrose which almost deprived him of the use of his voice. "I do not know," said he, hesitating; "it is not I who lead my flock, but my flock that leads me. These places are better known to it than to me; I leave to it the choice of the best pastures."

"Whence are you then?" said the shepherdess to him.

"I was born beyond the Alps," replied Fonrose.

"Were you born among shepherds?" continued she.

"As I am a shepherd," said he, looking down, "I must have been born to be one."

"I doubt it," replied Adelaide, viewing him with attention. "Your talents, your language, your very air, all tell me that fate had placed you in a better situation."

"You are very obliging," said Fonrose; "but ought you, of all persons, to believe that nature refuses everything to shepherds? Were you born to be a queen?"

Adelaide blushed at this answer; and changing the subject: "The other day," said she, "by the sound of an oboe you accompanied my songs with an art that would be a prodigy in a simple shepherd."

"It is your voice that is so," replied Fonrose, "in a simple shepherdess."

"But has nobody instructed you?"

"I have, like yourself, no other guides than my heart and my ear. You sing; I was melted; what my heart feels, my oboe expresses; I breathe my soul into it. This is the whole of my secret; nothing in the world is easier."

"That is incredible," said Adelaide.

"I said the very same on hearing you," replied Fonrose. "But I was forced to believe it. What will you say? Nature and love sometimes take a delight in assembling their most precious gifts in persons of the most humble fortune, to show that there is no condition which cannot ennoble."

During this discourse, they advanced toward the valley; and Fonrose, whom a ray of hope now animated, began to make the air resound with those sprightly notes which pleasure inspires. "Ah, prithee now," said Adelaide, "spare my soul the troublesome image of a sentiment which she cannot relish. This solitude is consecrated to grief; her echoes are not used to repeat the accents of a profane joy. Here everything groans in concert with me."

"I also have cause to complain," replied the young man; and these words, pronounced with a sigh, were followed by a long silence.

"You have cause to complain!" replied Adelaide. "Is it of mankind? Is it of Fortune?"

"No matter," said he. "But I am not happy; ask me no more."

"Hear me," said Adelaide. "Heaven gives us to each other as a consolation in our troubles. Mine are like an overwhelming load which weighs down my heart. Whoever you may be, if you know misfortune you ought to be compassionate, and I believe you worthy of my confidence. But promise me that it shall be mutual."

"Alas!" said Fonrose, "my misfortunes are such that I shall perhaps be condemned never to reveal them." This mystery but redoubled the curiosity of Adelaide. "Repair tomorrow," said she to him, "to the foot of that hill, beneath that old tufted oak where you have heard me moan. There I will teach you things that will excite your pity."

Fonrose passed the night in the utmost emotion. His fate depended on what he was going to hear. A thousand alarming ideas agitated him by turns. He dreaded, above all, being driven to despair by the communication of an unsuccessful and faithful love. "If she is in love," said he, "I am undone."

He repairs to the appointed place. He sees Adelaide arrive. The day was overcast with clouds, and Nature, mourning, seemed to forebode the sadness of their conversation. As soon as they were seated at the foot of the oak, Adelaide spoke thus: "You see these stones which the grass begins to cover; they are the tomb of the most tender, the most virtuous of men, whom my love and my imprudence have cost his life. I am a Frenchwoman, of a family of distinction, and, to my misfortune, too rich. The Count d'Orestan conceived the tenderest passion for me; I was sensible to it, sensible to excess. My parents opposed the inclination of our hearts, and my frantic passion made me consent to a marriage sacred to virtuous souls, but disallowed by the laws. Italy was at that time the theatre of war. My husband went thither to join the corps which he was to command. I followed him as far as Briançon. My foolish tenderness retained him there two days, in spite of himself; for he, a young man, full of honour, prolonged his stay there with the greatest reluctance. He sacrificed his duty to me; but what would not I have sacrificed to him? In a word, I required it of him, and he could not withstand my tears. He took leave with a foreboding which alarmed me. I accompanied him as far as this valley, where I received his adieus; and in order to wait to hear from him, I returned to Briançon. A few days after, a report was spread of a battle. I doubted whether d'Orestan had got thither; I wished it for his honour, I dreaded it for my love; when I received a letter from him, which I thought very consoling. 'I shall be such a day, at such an hour,' said he, 'in the valley, and under the oak where we parted. I shall repair there alone. I conjure you to go there, and expect me likewise alone. I live yet but for you.' How great was my mistake! I perceived in this billet nothing more than an impatience to see me again, and this impatience made me happy.

"I repaired then to this very oak. D'Orestan arrives, and after the tenderest reception, 'You would have it so, my dear Adelaide,' said he. 'I have failed in my duty at the most important moment of my life. What I feared is come to pass. A battle has happened. My regiment charged; it performed prodigies of valour, and I was not there. I am dishonoured, lost without resource. I reproach not you with my misfortune, but I have now but one sacrifice more to make you, and my heart is come to accomplish it.' At this discourse, pale, trembling, and scarce breathing, I took my husband into my arms. I felt my blood congeal in my veins, my knees bent under me, and I fell down senseless. He availed himself of my fainting to tear himself from my bosom, and in a little time I was recalled to life by the report of a shot, which killed him. I will not describe to you the situation I was in. It is inexpressible; and the tears which you now see flowing, the sighs that stifle my voice, are but a feeble image of it.

"After passing a whole night beside his bloody corpse, in a grief that stupefied me, my first care was to bury along with him my shame. My hands dug out his grave. I seek not to move you, but the moment in which the earth was to separate me from the sorrowful remains of my husband was a thousand times more dreadful to me than that can be which is to separate my body from my soul. Spent with grief, and deprived of nourishment, my enfeebled hands took up two whole days in hollowing out this tomb with inconceivable labour. When my strength forsook me, I reposed myself on the livid and cold bosom of my husband. In short, I paid him the rites of sepulture, and my heart promised him to wait in these parts till death reunites us. In the meantime, cruel hunger began to devour my exhausted entrails. I thought it criminal to refuse nature the supports of a life more grievous than death. I changed my garments for the plain habit of a shepherdess, and I embraced that condition as my only refuge.

"From that time my only consolation has been to come here and weep over this grave, which shall be my own. You see," continued she, "with what sincerity I open my soul to you. With you I may henceforth weep at liberty; it is a consolation I had need of. But I expect the same confidence from you. Do not think that you have deceived me.

I see clearly that the state of a shepherd is as foreign, and newer, to you than to me. You are young, perhaps sensitive; and if I may believe my conjectures, our misfortunes have the same source, and you have loved as well as I. We shall only feel the more for one another. I consider you as a friend, whom heaven, touched by my misfortunes, deigns to send me in my solitude. Do you also consider me as a friend, capable of giving you, if not salutary counsel, at least a consolatory example."

"You pierce my very soul," said Fonrose, overcome with what he had just heard. "And whatever sensibility you may attribute to me, you are very far from conceiving the impression that the recital of your misfortunes has made on me. Alas! Why cannot I return it with that confidence which you testify toward me, and of which you are so worthy? But I warned you of it; I foresaw it. Such is the nature of my sorrows that an eternal silence must shut them up in the bottom of my heart. You are very unhappy," added he, with a profound sigh. "I am still more unhappy; this is all I can tell you. Be not offended at my silence; it is terrible to me to be condemned to it. The companion of all your steps, I will soften your labours; I will partake of all your griefs. I will see you weep over this grave; I will mingle my tears with yours. You shall not repent of having deposited your woes in a heart, alas! but too tender."

"I repent me of it from this moment," said she, with confusion. And both, with downcast eyes, retired in silence from each other. Adelaide, on quitting Fonrose, thought she saw in his countenance the impression of a profound grief. "I have revived," said she, "the sense of his sorrows; and what must be their horror, when he thinks himself still more wretched than I!"

From that day more sighing and more conversation followed between Fonrose and Adelaide. They neither sought nor avoided one another; looks of consternation formed almost their only language. If he found her weeping over the grave of her husband, his heart was seized with pity, jealousy, and grief; he contemplated her in silence, and answered her sighs with deep groans.

Two months had passed away in this painful situation, and Adelaide saw Fonrose's youth wither as a flower. The sorrow which consumed him afflicted her so much the more deeply as the cause of it was unknown to her. She had not the most distant suspicion that she was the object of it. However, as it is natural, when two sentiments divide a soul, for one to weaken the other, Adelaide's regret on account of the death of d'Orestan became less lively every day, in proportion as she delivered herself up to the pity with which Fonrose inspired her. She was very sure that this pity had nothing but what was innocent in it; it did not even come into her head to defend herself from it. And the object of this generous sentiment, being continually present to her view, awakened it every instant. The languor into which this young man was fallen became such that she thought it her duty not to leave him any longer to himself. "You are dying," said she to him, "and you add to my griefs that of seeing you consumed with sorrow under my eye, without being able to apply any remedy. If the recital of the imprudences of my youth has not inspired you with a contempt for me; if the purest and tenderest friendship be dear to you; in short, if you would not render me more unhappy than I was before I knew you, confide to me the cause of your griefs. You have no person in the world but myself to assist you in supporting them. Your secret, though it were more important than mine, fear not that I shall divulge. The death of my husband has placed a gulf betwixt the world and me; and the confidence which I require will soon be buried in this grave, to which grief is with slow steps conducting me."

"I hope to go before you," said Fonrose, bursting into tears. "Suffer me to finish my deplorable life without leaving you afterwards the reproach of having shortened its course."

"O heavens, what do I hear!" cried she, with distraction. "What! Can I have contributed to the evils which overwhelm you? Go on, you pierce my soul! What have I done? What have I said? Alas, I tremble! Good heaven, hast thou sent me into the world only to create wretches? Speak, nay speak! You must no longer conceal who you are; you have said too much to dissemble any longer."

"Well, then, I am . . . I am Fonrose, the son of those travellers whom you filled with admiration and respect. All that they related of your virtues and your charms inspired me with the fatal design of coming to see you in this disguise. I have left my family in the deepest sorrow, thinking they have lost me and lamenting my death. I have seen you, I know what attaches you to this place, I know that the only hope that is left me is to die here adoring you. Give me no useless counsel or unjust reproaches. My resolution is as firm, as immovable as your own. If, in betraying my secret, you disturb the last moments of a life almost at an end, you will to no purpose injure me, who would never offend you."

Adelaide, confounded, endeavoured to calm the despair into which this young man was plunged. "Let me," said she, "do to his parents the service of restoring him to life; let me save their only hope. Heaven presents me with this opportunity of acknowledging their favours." Thus, far from making him furious by a misplaced rigour, all the tenderness of pity and consolation of friendship was put in practice in order to soothe him.

"Heavenly angel," cried Fonrose, "I see all the reluctance that you feel to make anyone unhappy. Your heart is with him who reposes in this grave. I see nothing can detach you from him; I see how ingenious your virtue is to conceal your woe from me. I perceive it in all its extent; I am overwhelmed by it. But I pardon you. It is your duty never to love me; it is mine ever to adore you."

Impatient of executing the design which she had conceived, Adelaide arrives at her hut. "Father," said she to her old master, "do you think you have strength to travel to Turin? I have need of somebody whom I can trust, to give the Marquis and Marchioness of Fonrose the most interesting intelligence." The old man replied that his zeal to serve them inspired him with courage. "Go," resumed Adelaide. "You will find them bewailing the death of their only son. Tell them that he is living, and in these parts, and that I will restore him to them; but that there is an indispensable necessity for their coming here themselves to fetch him."

He sets out, arrives at Turin, sends in his address as the old man of the valley of Savoy. "Ah!" cried Madame de Fonrose; "some misfortune perhaps has happened to our shepherdess."

"Let him come in," added the Marquis. "He will tell us perhaps that she consents to live with us."

"After the loss of my son," said the Marchioness, "it is the only comfort I can taste in this world."

The old man is introduced. He throws himself at their feet; they raise him. "You are lamenting the death of your son," said he. "I come to tell you that he lives. Our dear child has discovered him in the valley; she sends me to inform you of it. But yourselves only, she says, can bring him back." As he spoke this, surprise and joy deprived the Marchioness of Fonrose of her senses. The Marquis, distracted and amazed, calls out for help for his lady, recalls her to life, embraces the old man, publishes to the whole house that their son is restored to them. The Marchioness resuming her spirits, "What shall we do?" said she, taking the old man by the hands, and pressing them with tenderness, "What shall we do in gratitude for this benefit, which restores life to us?"

Everything is ordered for their departure. They set out with the good man; they travel night and day, and repair to the valley, where their only good awaits them. The shepherdess was out at pasture. The old woman conducts them to her; they approach. How great is their surprise! Their son, that well-beloved son, is by her side in the habit of a simple shepherd. Their hearts sooner than their eyes acknowledge him. "Ah, cruel child!" cried his mother, throwing herself into his arms, "what sorrow have you occasioned us! Why withdraw yourself from our tenderness? And what is it you come here for?"

"To adore," said he, "what you yourself admired."

"Pardon me, Madam," said Adelaide, while Fonrose embraced his father's knees, who raised him with kindness; "pardon me for having left you so long in grief. If I had known it sooner, you should have been sooner consoled." After the first emotions of nature, Fonrose relapsed into the deepest affliction. "Let us go," said the Marquis, "let us go rest ourselves in the hut, and forget all the pain that this young madman has caused us."

"Yes, sir, I have been mad," said Fonrose to his father, who led him by the hand. "Nothing but the loss of my reason could have suspended in my heart the emotions of nature, so as to make me forget the most sacred duties, in short, to detach myself from everything that I held dearest in the world. But this madness you gave birth to, and I am but too severely punished for it. I love without hope the most accomplished person in the world. You see nothing, you know nothing of this incomparable woman. She is honesty, sensibility, virtue itself. I love her even to idolatry, I cannot be happy without her, and I know that she cannot be mine."

"Has she confided to you," said the Marquis, "the secret of her birth?"

"I have learned enough of it," said Fonrose, "to assure you that it is in no respect beneath my own. She has even renounced a considerable fortune to bury herself in this desert."

"And do you know what has induced her to it?"

"Yes, Sir; but it is a secret which she alone can reveal to you."

"She is married, perhaps?"

"She is a widow; but her heart is not the more disengaged; her ties are but too strong."

"Daughter," said the Marquis, on entering the hut, "you see that you turn the heads of the whole family of Fonrose. The extraordinary passion of this young man cannot be justified but by such a prodigy as you are. All my wife's wishes are confined to having you for a companion and a friend; this child here will not live unless he obtains you for his wife; I desire no less to have you for my daughter. See how many persons you will make unhappy by a refusal."

"Ah, Sir," said she, "your goodness confounds me. But hear and judge for me." Then Adelaide, in the presence of the old man and his wife, made a recital of her deplorable adventure. She added the name of her family, which was not unknown to the Marquis de Fonrose, and ended by calling on himself to witness the inviolable fidelity she owed her spouse. At these words, consternation spread over every countenance. Young Fonrose, choked with sobs, threw himself into a corner of the hut in order to give them free scope. The father, moved at the sight, flew to the assistance of his son. "See," said he, "my dear Adelaide, to what a condition you have reduced him." Madame de Fonrose, who was near Adelaide, pressed her in her arms, bathing her at the same time with her tears. "Alas, why, my daughter," said she, "why will you a second time make us mourn the death of our dear child?" The old man and his wife, their eyes filled with tears and fixed upon Adelaide, waited her speaking. "Heaven is my witness," said Adelaide, rising, "that I would lay down my life in gratitude for such goodness. It would heighten my misfortunes to have occasion to reproach myself with yours; but I am willing that Fonrose himself should be my judge. Suffer me, if you please, to speak to him for a moment." Then, retiring with him alone, "Fonrose," said she, "you know what sacred ties retain me in this place. If I could cease to love and lament a husband who loved me but too well, I should be the most despicable of women. Esteem, friendship, gratitude, are the sentiments I owe you; but none of these can cancel love. The more you have conceived for me, the more you should expect from me. It is the impossibility of fulfilling that duty that hinders my imposing it on myself. At the same time, I see you in a situation that would move the least sensitive heart. It is shocking to me to be the cause; it would be still more shocking to me to hear your parents accuse me with having been your destruction. I will forget myself then for the present, and leave you, as far as in me lies, to be the arbiter of our destiny. It is for you to choose that of the two situations which appears to you least painful: either to renounce me, to subdue yourself, and to forget me; or to possess a woman whose heart, being full of another object, can only grant you sentiments too feeble to satisfy the wishes of a lover."

"That is enough," said Fonrose. "And, in a soul like yours, friendship should take place of love. I shall be jealous, without doubt, of the tears which you shall bestow to the memory of another husband; but the cause of that jealousy, in rendering you more respectable, will render you also more dear in my eyes."

"She is mine!" said he, coming and throwing himself into the arms of his parents. "It is to her respect for you, to your goodness, that I owe her, and it is owing you a second life." From that moment their arms were chains from which Adelaide could not disengage herself.

Did she yield only to pity, to gratitude? I would fain believe it, in order to admire her the more. Adelaide believed so herself. However it be, before she set out she would revisit the tomb, which she had quitted but with regret. "O my dear d'Orestan!" said she; "if from the bosom of the dead thou canst read the bottom of my soul, thy shade has no cause to murmur at the sacrifice I make; I owe it to the generous sentiments of this virtuous family—but my heart remains thine forever. I go to endeavour to make them happy, without any hope of being myself so." It was not without some sort of violence that they forced her from the place; but she insisted that they should erect a monument there to the memory of her husband, and that the hut of her old master and mistress, who accompanied them to Turin, should be converted into a country-house, as plain as it was solitary, where she proposed to come sometimes to mourn the errors and misfortunes of her youth. Time, the assiduities of Fonrose, the fruits of her second marriage, have since opened her soul to the impressions of a new affection; and they cite her as an example of a woman remarkable and respectable, even in her infidelity.

ꙮ Calthon and Colmal

by JAMES MACPHERSON

James Macpherson (1736–1796), a Highland Scot, published
in 1760 his *Fragments of Ancient Poetry Collected in the High-
lands of Scotland;* in 1762, *Fingal, an Ancient Epic Poem* (from
which volume our story of Calthon and Colmal is taken); and
finally, in 1765, *The Works of Ossian.* Macpherson alleged that
all these were translations of ancient Gaelic poems by the
blind harp-strumming bard Ossian (see his "Argument" of the
story), but he never produced the originals. Modern critical
opinion holds that the works are his own creations, based on
legends and ballads persisting among Gaelic-speakers.

The Ossianic poems caused a great literary sensation. The
tales of doomed love and savage battles in a dim heroic north-
ern world stirred imaginations sated with classic good sense.
The poems introduced a new mythology and a new background of wild and somber nature, bare mountains, misted
lakes, ancient ruins, and gray seas, suffused with poetic melancholy. The style too was new—brief, simple sentences, abundant repetitions, far-fetched similes, a choice of vague, suggestive
words. The influence of the Ossianic poems was enormous, in
all western Europe, in Russia, even in America. Thomas
Jefferson could quote them at length. (And your editor's
grandfather grew up in Ossian, New York, in the 1830's.)

ARGUMENT

[By James Macpherson]

This piece, as many more of Ossian's compositions, is addressed to one of the first Christian missionaries. The story of
the poem is handed down, by tradition, thus: In the country of
the Britons between the walls, two chiefs lived in the days of
Fingal—Dunthalmo, lord of Teutha, supposed to be the
Tweed; and Rathmor, who dwelt at Clutha, well known to be

the river Clyde. Rathmor was not more renowned for his generosity and hospitality than Dunthalmo was infamous for his
cruelty and ambition. Dunthalmo, through envy, or on account
of some private feuds which subsisted between the families,
murdered Rathmor at a feast; but being afterwards touched
with remorse, he educated the two sons of Rathmor, Calthon
and Colmar, in his own house. They growing up to man's
estate, dropped some hints that they intended to revenge the
death of their father, upon which Dunthalmo shut them up in
two caves on the banks of Teutha, intending to take them off
privately. Colmal, the daughter of Dunthalmo, who was
secretly in love with Calthon, helped him to make his escape
from prison, and fled with him to Fingal, disguised in the habit
of a young warrior, and implored his aid against Dunthalmo.
Fingal sent Ossian with three hundred men to Colmar's relief.
Dunthalmo, having previously murdered Colmar, came to a
battle with Ossian; but he was killed by that hero, and his army
totally defeated.

Calthon married Colmal, his deliverer; and Ossian returned
to Morven.

PLEASANT is the voice of thy song, thou lonely dweller
of the rock! It comes on the sound of the stream, along
the narrow vale. My soul awakes, O stranger! in the midst
of my hall. I stretch my hand, to the spear, as in the days
of other years. I stretch my hand, but it is feeble; and the
sigh of my bosom grows. Wilt thou not listen, son of the
rock! to the song of Ossian? My soul is full of other times;
the joy of my youth returns. Thus the sun appears in the
west, after the steps of his brightness have moved behind a
storm: the green hills lift their dewy heads; the blue stream
rejoices in the vale. The aged hero comes forth on his staff;
his grey hair glitters in the beam. Dost thou not behold,
son of the rock! a shield in Ossian's hall? It is marked with

the strokes of battle; and the brightness of its bosses has failed. That shield the great Dunthalmo bore, the chief of streamy Teutha. Dunthalmo bore it in battle, before he fell by Ossian's spear. Listen, son of the rock! to the tale of other years!

Rathmor was a chief of Clutha. The feeble dwelt in his hall. The gates of Rathmor were never shut; his feast was always spread. The sons of the stranger came. They blessed the generous chief of Clutha. Bards raised the song, and touched the harp: joy brightened on the face of the sad! Dunthalmo came, in his pride, and rushed into the combat of Rathmor. The chief of Clutha overcame: the rage of Dunthalmo rose. He came, by night, with his warriors; the mighty Rathmor fell. He fell in his halls, where his feast was often spread for strangers.

Colmar and Calthon were young, the sons of car-borne Rathmor. They came in the joy of youth, into their father's hall. They behold him in his blood; their bursting tears descend. The soul of Dunthalmo melted, when he saw the children of youth. He brought them to Alteutha's walls: they grew in the house of their foe. They bent the bow in his presence; and came forth to his wars. They saw the fallen walls of their fathers; they saw the green thorn in the hall. Their tears rushed forth in secret. At times their faces were sad. Dunthalmo beheld their grief; his darkening soul designed their death. He closed them in two caves, on the echoing banks of Teutha. The sun did not come there with his beams; nor the moon of heaven by night. The sons of Rathmor remained in darkness, and foresaw their death.

The daughter of Dunthalmo wept in silence, the fair-haired, blue-eyed Colmal. Her eye had rolled in secret on Calthon; his loveliness swelled in her soul. She trembled for her warrior; but what could Colmal do? Her arm could not lift the spear; nor was the sword formed for her side. Her white breast never rose beneath a mail. Neither was her eye the terror of heroes. What canst thou do, O Colmal! for the falling chief? Her steps are unequal; her hair is loose: her eyes look wildly through her tears. She came by night, to the hall. She armed her lovely form in steel; the steel of a young warrior, who fell in the first of his battles. She came to the cave of Calthon, and loosed the thong from his hands.

"Arise, son of Rathmor," she said, "arise, the night is dark! Let us fly to the king of Selma,* chief of fallen Clutha! I am the son of Lamgal, who dwelt in thy father's hall. I heard of thy dark dwelling in the cave, and my soul arose. Arise, son of Rathmor, arise, the night is dark!" "Blest voice!" replied the chief, "comest thou from the clouds to Calthon? The ghost of his fathers have often descended in his dreams, since the sun has retired from his eyes, and darkness has dwelt around him. Or art thou the son of Lamgal, the chief I often saw in Clutha? But shall I fly to Fingal, and Colmar my brother low? Will I fly to Morven, and the hero closed in night? No; give me that spear, son of Lamgal, Calthon will defend his brother!"

"A thousand warriors," replied the maid, "stretch their spears round car-borne Colmar. What can Calthon do against a host so great? Let us fly to the king of Morven, he will come with war. His arm is stretched forth to the unhappy; the lightning of his sword is round the weak. Arise, thou son of Rathmor! the shadows will fly away. Arise, or thy steps may be seen, and thou must fall in youth!"

The sighing hero rose; his tears descend for car-borne

* King of Selma: Fingal.—Ed.

Colmar. He came with the maid to Selma's hall; but he knew not that it was Colmal. The helmet covered her lovely face. Her bosom heaved beneath the steel. Fingal returned from the chase, and found the lovely strangers. They were like two beams of light in the midst of the hall of shells.* The king heard the tale of grief; and turned his eyes around. A thousand heroes half-rose before him; claiming the war of Teutha. I came with my spear from the hill; the joy of battle rose in my breast; for the king spoke to Ossian in the midst of a thousand chiefs.

"Son of my strength," began the king, "take thou the spear of Fingal. Go to Teutha's rushing stream, and save the car-borne Colmar. Let thy fame return before thee like a pleasant gale; that my soul may rejoice over my son, who renews the renown of our fathers. Ossian, be thou a storm in war; but mild when the foe is low! It was thus my fame arose, O my son! be thou like Selma's chief. When the haughty come to my halls, my eyes behold them not. But my arm is stretched forth to the unhappy. My sword defends the weak."

I rejoiced in the words of the king. I took my rattling arms. Diaran rose at my side, and Dargo king of spears. Three hundred youths followed our steps; the lovely strangers were at my side. Dunthalmo heard the sound of our approach. He gathered the strength of Teutha. He stood on a hill with his host. They were like rocks broken with thunder, when their bent trees are singed and bare, and the streams of their chinks have failed. The stream of Teutha rolled, in its pride, before the gloomy foe. I sent a bard to Dunthalmo, to offer the combat on the plain, but he smiled in the darkness of his pride. His unsettled host

* Shells: used as drinking-vessels.—Ed.

moved on the hill; like the mountain-cloud, when the blast has entered its womb, and scatters the curling gloom on every side.

They brought Colmar to Teutha's bank, bound with a thousand thongs. The chief is sad, but stately. His eye is on his friends; for we stood, in our arms, whilst Teutha's waters rolled between. Dunthalmo came with his spear, and pierced the hero's side: he rolled on the bank in his blood. We heard his broken sighs. Calthon rushed into the stream: I bounded forward on my spear. Teutha's race fell before us. Night came rolling down. Dunthalmo rested on a rock, amidst an aged wood. The rage of his bosom burned against the car-borne Calthon. But Calthon stood in his grief; he mourned the fallen Colmar; Colmar slain in youth before his fame arose!

I bade the song of woe to rise, to soothe the mournful chief; but he stood beneath a tree, and often threw his spear on earth. The humid eye of Colmal rolled near in a secret tear; she foresaw the fall of Dunthalmo, or of Clutha's war-like chief. Now half the night had passed away. Silence and darkness were on the field. Sleep rested on the eyes of the heroes: Calthon's settling soul was still. His eyes were half-closed, but the murmur of Teutha had not yet failed in his ear. Pale, and showing his wounds, the ghost of Colmar came: he bent his head over the hero, and raised his feeble voice!

"Sleeps the son of Rathmor in his night, and his brother low? Did we not ride in the chase together? Pursued we not the dark-brown hinds? Colmar was not forgot till he fell: till death had blasted his youth. I lie pale beneath the rock of Lona. O let Calthon rise! the morning comes with its beams; Dunthalmo will dishonour the fallen." He passed away in his blast. The rising Calthon saw the steps of his departure. He rushed in the sound of his steel. Unhappy Colmal rose. She followed her hero through night, and dragged her spear behind. But when Calthon came to Lona's rock, he found his fallen brother. The rage of his bosom rose; he rushed among the foe. The groans of death ascend. They close around the chief. He is bound in the midst, and brought to gloomy Dunthalmo. The shout of joy arose; and the hills of night replied.

I started at the sound: and took my father's spear. Diaran rose at my side; and the youthful strength of Dargo. We missed the chief of Clutha, and our souls were sad. I dreaded the departure of my fame. The pride of my valour rose! "Sons of Morven!" I said, "it is not thus our fathers fought. They rested not on the field of strangers, when the foe was not fallen before them. Their strength was like the eagles of heaven; their renown is in the song. But our people fall by degrees. Our fame begins to depart. What shall the king of Morven say if Ossian conquers not at Teutha? Rise in your steel, ye warriors! follow the sound of Ossian's course. He will not return, but renowned, to the echoing walls of Selma."

Morning rose on the blue waters of Teutha. Colmal stood before me in tears. She told of the chief of Clutha: thrice the spear fell from her hand. My wrath turned against the stranger; for my soul trembled for Calthon. "Son of the feeble hand," I said, "do Teutha's warriors fight with tears? The battle is not won with grief; nor dwells the sigh in the soul of war. Go to the deer of Carmun, to the lowing herds of Teutha. But leave these arms, thou son of fear! A warrior may lift them in fight."

I tore the mail from her shoulders. Her snowy breast appeared. She bent her blushing face to the ground. I looked in silence to the chiefs. The spear fell from my hand; the sigh of my bosom rose! But when I heard the name of the maid, my crowding tears rushed down. I blessed the lovely beam of youth, and bade the battle move!

Why, son of the rock, should Ossian tell how Teutha's warriors died? They are now forgot in their land; their tombs are not found on the heath. Years came on with their storms. The green mounds are mouldered away. Scarce is the grave of Dunthalmo seen, or the place where he fell by the spear of Ossian. Some grey warrior, half blind with age, sitting by night at the flaming oak of the hall, tells now my deeds to his sons, and the fall of the dark Dunthalmo. The faces of youth bend sidelong towards his voice. Surprise and joy burn in their eyes! I found Calthon bound to an oak; my sword cut the thongs from his hands. I gave him the white-bosomed Colmal. They dwelt in the halls of Teutha.

❧ The Runenberg

by JOHANN LUDWIG TIECK

A group of young literary men, including the Schlegel brothers, Novalis, and Johann Ludwig Tieck, assembled in Jena at the end of the eighteenth century, denounced the prevailing classic spirit of utilitarian rationalism, and proclaimed a new Romanticism. Tieck (1773–1853), an enthusiast for Shakespeare and his contemporaries, contributed dramas in the Elizabethan manner. Later, in Dresden and Berlin, he was known chiefly as a critic, editor, and translator. His specialty was *Volksmärchen,* based on popular stories, and animated by an artful simplicity, somber, fantastic imaginations, a ready acceptance of the supernatural, and a sometimes cloudy symbolism. In them, said Thomas Carlyle, "low tones of plaintiveness and awe flit around us."

The Runenberg (1803) was translated by Carlyle in his *German Romance* (Edinburgh, 1827).

A YOUNG HUNTER was sitting in the heart of the mountains, in a thoughtful mood, beside his fowling-floor,* while the noise of the waters and the woods was sounding through the solitude. He was musing on his destiny; how he was so young, and had forsaken his father and mother, and accustomed home, and all his comrades in his native village, to seek out new acquaintances, to escape from the circle of returning habitude; and he looked up with a sort of surprise that he was here, that he found himself in this valley, in this employment. Great clouds were passing over him, and sinking behind the mountains; birds were singing from the bushes, and an echo was replying to them. He slowly

* Fowling-floor: area arranged for catching birds with nets or snares.—Ed.

descended the hill; and seated himself on the margin of a brook, that was gushing down among the rocks with foamy murmur. He listened to the fitful melody of the water; and it seemed to him as if the waves were saying to him, in unintelligible words, a thousand things that concerned him nearly; and he felt an inward trouble that he could not understand their speeches. Then again he looked aloft, and thought that he was glad and happy; so he took new heart, and sang aloud this hunting song:

> Blithe and cheery through the mountains
> Goes the huntsman to the chase,
> By the lonesome shady fountains,
> Till he finds the red-deer's trace.
>
> Hark! his trusty dogs are baying
> Through the bright green solitude;
> Through the groves the horns are playing:
> O, thou merry gay green wood!
>
> In some dell, when luck hath blest him,
> And his shot hath stretch'd the deer,
> Lies he down, content, to rest him,
> While the brooks are murmuring clear.
>
> Leave the husbandman his sowing,
> Let the shipman sail the sea;
> None, when bright the morn is glowing,
> Sees its red so fair as he,
>
> Wood, and wold, and game that prizes,
> While Diana loves his art;
> And, at last, some bright face rises:
> Happy huntsman that thou art!

Whilst he sung, the sun had sunk deeper, and broad shadows fell across the narrow glen. A cooling twilight glided over the ground; and now only the tops of the trees, and the round summits of the mountains, were gilded by the glow of evening. Christian's heart grew sadder and sadder: he could not think of going back to his bird-fold, and yet he could not stay; he felt himself alone, and longed to meet with men. He now remembered with regret those old books, which he used to see at home, and would never read, often as his father had advised him to it: the habitation of his childhood came before him, his sports with the youth of the village, his acquaintances among the children, the school that had afflicted him so much; and he wished he were again amid these scenes, which he had wilfully forsaken, to seek his fortune in unknown regions, in the mountains, among strange people, in a new employment. Meanwhile it grew darker; and the brook rushed louder; and the birds of night began to shoot, with fitful wing, along their mazy courses. Christian still sat disconsolate, and immersed in sad reflection; he was like to weep, and altogether undecided what to do or purpose. Unthinkingly, he pulled a straggling root from the earth; and on the instant, heard, with affright, a stifled moan under ground, which winded downwards in doleful tones, and died plaintively away in the deep distance. The sound went through his inmost heart: it seized him as if he had unwittingly touched the wound, of which the dying frame of Nature was expiring in its agony. He started up to fly; for he had already heard of the mysterious mandrake-root, which, when torn, yields such heart-rending moans, that the person who has hurt it runs distracted by its wailing. As he turned to go, a stranger man was standing at his back, who looked at him with a friendly countenance, and asked him whither he was going. Christian had been longing for society, and yet he started in alarm at this friendly presence.

"Whither so fast?" said the stranger again.

The young hunter made an effort to collect himself, and told how all at once the solitude had seemed so frightful to him, he had meant to get away; the evening was so dark, the green shades of the wood so dreary, the brook seemed uttering lamentations, and his longing drew him over to the other side of the hills.

"You are but young," said the stranger, "and cannot yet endure the rigour of solitude: I will accompany you, for you will find no house or hamlet within a league of this; and in the way we may talk, and tell each other tales, and so your sad thoughts will leave you: in an hour the moon will rise behind the hills; its light also will help to chase away the darkness of your mind."

They went along, and the stranger soon appeared to Christian as if he had been an old acquaintance. "Who are you?" said the man; "by your speech I hear that you belong not to this part."

"Ah!" replied the other, "upon this I could say much, and yet it is not worth the telling you, or talking of. There was something dragged me, with a foreign force, from the circle of my parents and relations; my spirit was not master of itself: like a bird which is taken in a net, and struggles to no purpose, so my soul was meshed in strange imaginations and desires. We dwelt far hence, in a plain, where all round you could see no hill, scarce even a height: a few trees adorned the green level; but meadows, fertile corn-fields, gardens stretched away as far as the eye could reach; and a broad river glittered like a potent spirit through the midst of them. My father was gardener to a nobleman, and meant to breed me to the same employment. He delighted in plants and flowers beyond aught else, and could unweariedly pass day by day in watching them and tending them. Nay, he went so far as to maintain, that he could almost speak with them; that he got knowledge from their growth and spreading, as well as from the varied form and colour of their leaves. To me, however, gardening was a tiresome occupation; and the more so that my father kept persuading me to take it up, or even attempted to compel me to it with threats. I wished to be a fisherman, and tried that business for a time; but a life on the waters would not suit me: I was then apprenticed to a tradesman in the town; but soon came home from this employment also. My father happened to be talking of the Mountains, which he had travelled over in his youth; of the subterranean mines and their workmen; of hunters and their occupation; and that instant, there arose in me the most decided wish; the feeling that at last I had found out the way of life which would entirely fit me. Day and night I meditated on the matter; representing to myself high mountains, chasms, and pine forests: my imagination shaped wild rocks; I heard the tumult of the chase, the horns, the cry of the hounds and the game; all my dreams were filled with these things, and they left me neither peace nor rest any more. The plain, our patron's castle, and my father's little hampered garden, with its trimmed flower-beds; our narrow dwelling; the wide sky which stretched above us in its dreary vastness, embracing no hill, no lofty mountain, all became more dull and odious to me. It seemed as if the people about me were living in most lamentable ignorance; that every one of them would think and long as I did, should the feeling of their wretchedness but once arise within their souls. Thus did I bait my heart with restless fancies; till one morning I resolved on leaving my father's house directly, and for ever. In a book, I had found some notice of the nearest mountains; some charts of the neighbouring districts, and by them I shaped my course. It was early in spring, and I felt myself cheerful, and altogether light of heart. I hastened on, to get away the faster from the level country: and one evening, in the distance, I descried the dim outline of the mountains, lying on the sky before me. I could scarcely sleep in my inn, so impatient did I feel to have my foot upon the region which I regarded as my home: with the earliest dawn I was awake, and again in motion. By the afternoon, I had got among my beloved hills; and here, as if intoxicated, I went on, then stopped a while, looked back; and drank, as in inspiring draughts, the aspect of these foreign, yet well-known objects. Ere long, the plain was out of sight; the forest streams were rushing down to meet me; the oaks and beeches sounded to me from their steep precipices with wavering boughs; my path led me by the edge of dizzy abysses; blue hills were standing vast and solemn in the distance. A new world was opened to me; I was never weary. Thus, after some days, having roamed over great part of the mountains, I reached the dwelling of an old forester, who consented, at my urgent request, to take me in, and instruct me in the business of the chase. It is now three months since I entered his service. I took possession of the district where I was to live, as my kingdom. I got acquainted with every cliff and dell among the mountains; in my occupation, when at dawn of day we moved to the forest, when felling trees in the wood, when practising my fowling-piece, or training my trusty attendants, our dogs, to do their feats, I felt completely happy. But for the last eight days I have staid up here at the fowling-floor, in the loneliest quarter of the hills; and to-night I grew so sad as I was never in my life before; I seemed so lost, so utterly unhappy; and even yet I cannot shake aside that melancholy humour."

The stranger had listened with attention, while they

both wandered on through a dark alley of the wood. They now came out into the open country, and the light of the moon, which was standing with its horns over the summit of the hill, saluted them like a friend. In undistinguishable forms, and many separated masses, which the pale gleam again perplexingly combined, lay the cleft mountain-range before them; in the background a steep hill, on the top of which an antique weathered ruin rose ghastly in the white light. "Our roads part here," said the stranger; "I am going down into this hollow; there, by that old mine-shaft, is my dwelling: the metal ores are my neighbours; the mine streams tell me wonders in the night; thither thou canst not follow me. But look, there stands the Runenberg, with its wild ragged walls; how beautiful and alluring the grim old rock looks down on us! Wert thou never there?"

"Never," said the hunter. "Once I heard my old forester relating strange stories of that hill, which I, like a fool, have forgotten; only I remember that my mind that night was full of dread and unearthly notions. I could like to mount the hill some time; for the colours there are of the fairest, the grass must be very green, the world around one very strange; who knows, too, but one might chance to find some curious relic of the ancient time up there?"

"You could scarcely fail," replied the stranger: "whoever knows how to seek, whoever feels his heart drawn towards it with a right inward longing, will find friends of former ages there, and glorious things, and all that he wishes most." With these words the stranger rapidly descended to a side, without bidding his companion farewell; he soon vanished in the tangles of the thicket, and after some few instants, the sound of his footsteps also died away. The young hunter did not feel surprised, he but went on with quicker speed towards the Runenberg: thither all things seemed to beckon him; the stars were shining towards it; the moon pointed out as it were a bright road to the ruins; light clouds rose up to them; and from the depths, the waters and sounding woods spoke new courage into him. His steps were as if winged; his heart throbbed; he felt so great a joy within him, that it rose to pain. He came into places he had never seen before; the rocks grew steeper; the green disappeared; the bald cliffs called to him, as with angry voices, and a lone moaning wind drove him on before it. Thus he hurried forward without pause; and late after midnight he came upon a narrow footpath, which ran along by the brink of an abyss. He heeded not the depth which yawned beneath, and threatened to swallow him for ever; so keenly was he driven along by wild imaginations and vague wishes. At last his perilous track led him close by a high wall, which seemed to lose itself in the clouds; the path grew narrower every step; and Christian had to cling by projecting stones to keep himself from rushing down into the gulf. Ere long, he could get no farther; his path ended underneath a window: he was obliged to pause, and knew not whether he should turn or stay. Suddenly he saw a light, which seemed to move within the ruined edifice. He looked towards the gleam; and found that he could see into an ancient spacious hall, strangely decorated, and glittering in manifold splendour, with multitudes of precious stones and crystals, the hues of which played through each other in mysterious changes, as the light moved to and fro; and this was in the hand of a stately female, who kept walking with a thoughtful aspect up and down the apartment. She seemed of a different race from mortals; so large, so strong was her form, so earnest her look; yet the enraptured huntsman thought he had never seen or fancied such surpassing beauty. He trembled, yet secretly wished she might come

near the window and observe him. At last she stopped; set
down the light on a crystal table; looked aloft, and sang
with a piercing voice:

> What can the Ancient keep
> That they come not at my call?
> The crystal pillars weep,
> From the diamonds on the wall
> The trickling tear-drops fall;
> And within is heard a moan,
> A chiding fitful tone:
> In these waves of brightness,
> Lovely changeful lightness,
> Has the Shape been form'd,
> By which the soul is charm'd,
> And the longing heart is warm'd.
> Come, ye Spirits, at my call,
> Haste ye to the Golden Hall;
> Raise, from your abysses gloomy,
> Heads that sparkle; faster
> Come, ye Ancient Ones, come to me!
> Let your power be master
> Of the longing hearts and souls,
> Where the flood of passion rolls,
> Let your power be master!

On finishing the song, she began undressing, laying her
apparel in a costly press. First, she took a golden veil from
her head; and her long black hair streamed down in curling
fulness over her loins: then she loosed her bosom-dress; and
the youth forgot himself and all the world, in gazing at that
more than earthly beauty. He scarcely dared to breathe, as
by degrees she laid aside her other garments: at last she
walked about the chamber naked; and her heavy waving
locks formed round her, as it were, a dark billowy sea, out

of which, like marble, the glancing limbs of her form beamed forth, in alternating splendour. After a while, she went forward to another golden press; and took from it a tablet, glittering with many inlaid stones, rubies, diamonds, and all kinds of jewels; and viewed it long with an investigating look. The tablet seemed to form a strange inexplicable figure, from its individual lines and colours; sometimes, when the glance of it came towards the hunter, he was painfully dazzled by it; then, again, soft green and blue playing over it, refreshed his eye: he stood, however, devouring the objects with his looks, and at the same time sunk in deep thought. Within his soul, an abyss of forms and harmony, of longing and voluptuousness, was opened: hosts of winged tones, and sad and joyful melodies flew through his spirit, which was moved to its foundations: he saw a world of Pain and Hope arise within him; strong towering crags of Trust and defiant Confidence, and deep rivers of Sadness flowing by. He no longer knew himself: and he started as the fair woman opened the window; handed him the magic tablet of stones, and spoke these words: "Take this in memory of me!" He caught the tablet; and felt the figure, which, unseen, at once went through his inmost heart; and the light, and the fair woman, and the wondrous hall, had disappeared. As it were, a dark night, with curtains of cloud, fell down over his soul: he searched for his former feelings, for that inspiration and unutterable love; he looked at the precious tablet, and the sinking moon was imaged in it faint and bluish.

He had still the tablet firmly grasped in his hands, when the morning dawned; and he, exhausted, giddy, and half-asleep, fell headlong down the precipice.

The sun shone bright on the face of the stupefied sleeper; and, awakening, he found himself upon a pleasant hill. He looked round, and saw far behind him, and scarce discernible at the extreme horizon, the ruins of the Runenberg; he searched for his tablet, and could find it nowhere. Astonished and perplexed, he tried to gather his thoughts, and connect together his remembrances; but his memory was as if filled with a waste haze, in which vague irrecognisable shapes were wildly jostling to and fro. His whole previous life lay behind him, as in a far distance; the strangest and the commonest were so mingled, that all his efforts could not separate them. After long struggling with himself, he at last concluded that a dream, or sudden madness, had come over him that night; only he could never understand how he had strayed so far into a strange and remote quarter.

Still scarcely waking, he went down the hill; and came upon a beaten way, which led him out from the mountains into the plain country. All was strange to him: he at first thought that he would find his old home; but the country which he saw was quite unknown to him; and at length he concluded that he must be upon the south side of the mountains, which, in spring, he had entered from the north. Towards noon, he perceived a little town below him: from its cottages a peaceful smoke was mounting up; children, dressed as for a holiday, were sporting on the green; and from a small church came the sound of the organ, and the singing of the congregation. All this laid hold of him with a sweet, inexpressible sadness; it so moved him, that he was forced to weep. The narrow gardens, the little huts with their smoking chimneys, the accurately-parted corn-fields, reminded him of the necessities of poor human nature; of man's dependence on the friendly Earth, to whose benignity he must commit himself; while the singing, and the music of the organ, filled the stranger's heart with a devoutness it had never felt before. The desires and emotions of the bygone night seemed reckless and wicked; he wished once more, in childlike meekness, helplessly and humbly to unite himself to men as to his brethren, and fly from his ungodly purposes and feelings. The plain, with its little river, which, in manifold windings, clasped itself about the gardens and meadows, seemed to him inviting and delightful: he thought with fear of his abode among the lonely mountains amid waste rocks; he wished that he could be allowed to live in this peaceful village; and so feeling, he went into its crowded church.

The psalm was just over, and the preacher had begun his sermon. It was on the kindness of God in regard to harvest; how His goodness feeds and satisfies all things that live; how marvellously He has, in the fruits of the Earth, provided support for men; how the love of God incessantly displays itself in the bread He sends us; and how the humble Christian may, therefore, with a thankful spirit, perpetually celebrate a Holy Supper. The congregation were affected; the eyes of the hunter rested on the pious priest, and observed, close by the pulpit, a young maiden, who appeared beyond all others reverent and attentive. She was slim and fair; her blue eye gleamed with the most piercing softness; her face was as if transparent, and blooming in the tenderest colours. The stranger youth had never been as he now was; so full of charity, so calm, so abandoned to the stillest, most refreshing feelings. He bowed himself in tears, when the clergyman pronounced his blessing; he felt these holy words thrill through him like an unseen power; and the vision of the night drew back before them to the deepest distance, as a spectre at the dawn. He issued from the church; stopped beneath a large lime-tree; and thanked God, in a heart-felt prayer, that He had saved him, sinful and undeserving, from the nets of the Wicked Spirit.

The people were engaged in holding harvest-home that day, and every one was in a cheerful mood; the children, with their gay dresses, were rejoicing in the prospect of the sweetmeats and the dance; in the village square, a space encircled with young trees, the youths were arranging the preparations for their harvest sport; the players were seated, and essaying their instruments. Christian went into the fields again, to collect his thoughts and pursue his meditations; and on his returning to the village, all had joined in mirth, and actual celebration of their festival. The fair-haired Elizabeth was there, too, with her parents; and the stranger mingled in the jocund throng. Elizabeth was dancing; and Christian, in the meantime, had entered into conversation with her father, a farmer, and one of the richest people in the village. The man seemed pleased with his youth and way of speech; so, in a short time, both of them agreed that Christian should remain with him as gardener. This office Christian could engage with; for he hoped that now the knowledge and employments, which he had so much despised at home, would stand him in good stead.

From this period, a new life began for him. He went to live with the farmer, and was numbered among his family. With his trade, he likewise changed his garb. He was so good, so helpful and kindly; he stood to his task so honestly, that ere long every member of the house, especially the daughter, had a friendly feeling to him. Every Sunday, when he saw her going to church, he was standing with a fair nosegay ready for Elizabeth; and then she used to thank him with blushing kindliness: he felt her absence, on days when he did not chance to see her; and at night, she would tell him tales and pleasant histories. Day by day they grew more necessary to each other; and the parents, who observed it, did not seem to think it wrong; for Christian was the most industrious, and handsomest youth in the village. They themselves had, at first sight, felt a touch of love and friendship for him. After half a year, Elizabeth became his wife. Spring was come back; the swallows and the singing birds had revisited the land; the garden was standing in its fairest trim; the marriage was celebrated with abundant mirth; bride and bridegroom seemed intoxicated with their happiness. Late at night, when they retired to their chamber, the husband whispered to his wife. "No, thou art not that form which once charmed me in a dream, and which I never can entirely forget; but I am happy beside thee, and blessed that thou art mine."

How delighted was the family, when, within a year, it became augmented by a little daughter, who was baptized Leonora. Christian's looks, indeed, would sometimes take a rather grave expression as he gazed on the child; but his youthful cheeriness continually returned. He scarcely ever thought of his former way of life, for he felt himself entirely domesticated and contented. Yet, some months afterwards, his parents came into his mind; and he thought how much his father, in particular, would be rejoiced to see his peaceful happiness, his station as husbandman and gardener; it grieved him that he should have utterly forgotten his father and mother for so long a time; his own only child made known to him the joy which children afford to parents; so at last he took the resolution to set out, and again revisit home.

Unwillingly he left his wife; all wished him speed; and the season being fine, he went off on foot. Already at the distance of a few miles, he felt how much the parting grieved him; for the first time in his life, he experienced the pains of separation; the foreign objects seemed to him almost savage; he felt as if he had been lost in some unfriendly solitude. Then the thought came on him, that his youth was over; that he had found a home to which he now belonged, in which his heart had taken root; he was almost ready to lament the lost levity of younger years; and his mind was in the saddest mood, when he turned aside into a village inn to pass the night. He could not understand how he had come to leave his kind wife, and the parents she had given him; and he felt dispirited and discontented, when he rose next morning to pursue his journey.

His pain increased as he approached the hills: the distant ruins were already visible, and by degrees grew more distinguishable; many summits rose defined and clear amid the blue vapour. His step grew timid; frequently he paused, astonished at his fear; at the horror which, with every step, fell closer on him. "Madness!" cried he, "I know thee well, and thy perilous seductions; but I will withstand thee manfully. Elizabeth is no vain dream; I know that even now she thinks of me, that she waits for me, and fondly counts the hours of my absence. Do I not already see forests like black hair before me? Do not the glancing eyes look to me from the brook? Does not the stately form step towards me from the mountains?" So saying, he was about to lay himself beneath a tree, and take some rest; when he perceived an old man seated in the shade of it, examining a flower with extreme attention; now holding it to the sun, now shading it with his hands, now counting its leaves; as if striving in every way to stamp it accurately in his memory. On approaching nearer, he thought he knew the form; and soon no doubt remained that the old man with the flower was his father. With an exclamation of the liveliest joy, he rushed into his arms; the old man seemed delighted, but not much surprised, at meeting him so suddenly.

"Art thou with me already, my son?" said he: "I knew

that I should find thee soon, but I did not think such joy had been in store for me this very day."

"How did you know, father, that you would meet me?"

"By this flower," replied the old gardener; "all my days I have had a wish to see it; but never had I the fortune; for it is very scarce, and grows only among the mountains. I set out to seek thee, for thy mother is dead, and the loneliness at home made me sad and heavy. I knew not whither I should turn my steps; at last I came among the mountains, dreary as the journey through them had appeared to me. By the road, I sought for this flower, but could find it nowhere; and now, quite unexpectedly, I see it here, where the fair plain is lying stretched before me. From this I knew that I should meet thee soon; and, lo! how true the fair flower's prophecy has proved!"

They embraced again, and Christian wept for his mother; but the old man grasped his hand, and said: "Let us go, that the shadows of the mountains may be soon out of view; it always makes me sorrowful in the heart to see these wild steep shapes, these horrid chasms, these torrents gurgling down into their caverns. Let us get upon the good, kind, guileless level ground again."

They went back, and Christian recovered his cheerfulness. He told his father of his new fortune, of his child and home: his speech made himself as if intoxicated; and he now, in talking of it, for the first time truly felt that nothing more was wanting to his happiness. Thus, amid narrations sad and cheerful, they returned into the village. All were delighted at the speedy ending of the journey; most of all, Elizabeth. The old father stayed with them, and joined his little fortune to their stock; they formed the most contented and united circle in the world. Their crops were good, their cattle throve; and in a few years Christian's house was among the wealthiest in the quarter; Elizabeth had also given him several other children.

Five years had passed away in this manner, when a stranger halted from his journey in their village; and took up his lodging in Christian's house, as being the most respectable the place contained. He was a friendly, talking man; he told them many stories of his travels; sported with the children, and made presents to them: in a short time, all were growing fond of him. He liked the neighbourhood so well, that he proposed remaining in it for a day or two; but the days grew weeks, and the weeks months. No one seemed to wonder at his loitering; for all of them had grown accustomed to regard him as a member of the family. Christian alone would often sit in a thoughtful mood; for it seemed to him as if he knew this traveller of old, and yet he could not think of any time when he had met with him. Three months had passed away, when the stranger at last took his leave, and said: "My dear friends, a wondrous destiny, and singular anticipations, drive me to the neighbouring mountains; a magic image, not to be withstood, allures me: I leave you now, and I know not whether I shall ever see you any more. I have a sum of money by me, which in your hands will be safer than in mine; so I ask you to take charge of it; and if within a year I come not back, then keep it, and accept my thanks along with it for the kindness you have shown me."

So the traveller went his way, and Christian took the money in charge. He locked it carefully up; and now and then, in the excess of his anxiety, looked over it; he counted it to see that none was missing, and in all respects took no little pains with it. "This sum might make us very happy," said he once to his father; "should the stranger not return, both we and our children were well provided for."

"Heed not the gold," said the old man; "not in it can happiness be found: hitherto, thank God, we have never wanted aught; and do thou put away such thoughts far from thee."

Christian often rose in the night to set his servants to their labour, and look after everything himself: his father was afraid lest this excessive diligence might harm his youth and health; so one night he rose to speak with him about contracting such unreasonable efforts; when, to his astonishment, he found him sitting with a little lamp at his table, and counting, with the greatest eagerness, the stranger's gold. "My son," said the old man, full of sadness; "must it come to this with thee? Was this accursed metal brought beneath our roof to make us wretched? Bethink thee, my son, or the Evil One will consume thy blood and life out of thee."

"Yes," replied he; "it is true, I know myself no more; neither day nor night does it give me any rest: see how it looks on me even now, till the red glance of it goes into my very heart! Hark how it clinks, this golden stuff! It calls me when I sleep; I hear it when music sounds, when the wind blows, when people speak together on the street; if the sun shines, I see nothing but these yellow eyes, with which it beckons to me, as it were, to whisper words of love into my ear: and therefore I am forced to rise in the night time, though it were but to satisfy its eagerness; and then I feel it triumphing and inwardly rejoicing when I touch it with my fingers; in its joy, it grows still redder and lordlier. Do but look yourself at the glow of its rapture!" The old man, shuddering and weeping, took his son in his arms; he said a prayer, and then spoke: "Christel, thou must turn again to the Word of God; thou must go more zealously and reverently to church, or else, alas! my poor child,

thou wilt droop and die away in the most mournful wretchedness."

The money was again locked up; Christian promised to
take thought and change his conduct, and the old man
was composed. A year and more had passed, and no tidings
had been heard of the stranger: the old man at last gave in
to the entreaties of his son; and the money was laid out in
land, and other property. The young farmer's riches soon
became the talk of the village; and Christian seemed contented and comfortable, and his father felt delighted at beholding him so well and cheerful; all fear had now vanished
from his mind. What then must have been his consternation,
when Elizabeth one evening took him aside; and told him,
with tears, that she could no longer understand her husband; how he spoke so wildly, especially at night; how he
dreamed strange dreams, and would often in his sleep walk
long about the room, not knowing it; how he spoke strange
things to her, at which she often shuddered. But what terrified her most, she said, was his pleasantry by day; for his
laugh was wild and hollow, his look wandering and strange.
The father stood amazed, and the sorrowing wife proceeded: "He is always talking of the traveller, and maintaining that he knew him formerly, and that the stranger
man was in truth a woman of unearthly beauty; nor will he
go any more into the fields or the garden to work, for he
says he hears underneath the ground a fearful moaning,
when he but pulls out a root; he starts and seems to feel a
horror at all plants and herbs."

"Good God!" exclaimed the father, "is the frightful
hunger in him grown so rooted and strong, that it is come
to this? Then is his spell-bound heart no longer human, but
of cold metal; he who does not love a flower, has lost all
love and fear of God."

Next day the old man went to walk with his son, and told him much of what Elizabeth had said; calling on him to be pious, and devote his soul to holy contemplations. "Willingly, my father," answered Christian; "and I often do so with success, and all is well with me: for long periods of time, for years, I can forget the true form of my inward man, and lead a life that is foreign to me, as it were, with cheerfulness: but then on a sudden, like a new moon, the ruling star, which I myself am, arises again in my heart, and conquers this other influence. I might be altogether happy; but once, in a mysterious night, a secret sign was imprinted through my hand deep on my soul; frequently the magic figure sleeps and is at rest; I imagine it has passed away; but in a moment, like a poison, it darts up and lives over all its lineaments. And then I can think or feel nothing else but it; and all around me is transformed, or rather swallowed up, by this subduing shape. As the rabid man recoils at the sight of water, and the poison in him grows more fell; so too it is with me at the sight of any cornered figure, any line, any gleam of brightness; anything will then rouse the form that dwells in me, and make it start into being; and my soul and body feel the throes of birth; for as my mind received it by a feeling from without, she strives in agony and bitter labour to work it forth again into an outward feeling, that she may be rid of it, and at rest."

"It was an evil star that took thee from us to the mountains," said the old man; "thou wert born for calm life, thy mind inclined to peace and the love of plants; then thy impatience hurried thee away to the company of savage stones: the crags, the torn cliffs, with their jagged shapes, have overturned thy soul, and planted in thee the wasting hunger for metals. Thou shouldst still have been on thy guard, and kept thyself away from the view of mountains;

so I meant to bring thee up, but it has not so been to be. Thy humility, thy peace, thy childlike feeling, have been thrust away by scorn, boisterousness, and caprice."

"No," said the son; "I remember well that it was a plant which first made known to me the misery of the Earth; never, till then, did I understand the sighs and lamentations one may hear on every side, throughout the whole of Nature, if one but give ear to them. In plants and herbs, in trees and flowers, it is the painful writhing of one universal wound that moves and works; they are the corpse of foregone glorious worlds of rock, they offer to our eye a horrid universe of putrefaction. I now see clearly it was this, which the root with its deep-drawn sigh was saying to me; in its sorrow it forgot itself, and told me all. It is because of this that all green shrubs are so enraged at me, and lie in wait for my life; they wish to obliterate that lovely figure in my heart; and every spring, with their distorted death-like looks, they try to win my soul. Truly it is piteous to consider how they have betrayed and cozened thee, old man; for they have gained complete possession of thy spirit. Do but question the rocks, and thou wilt be amazed when thou shalt hear them speak."

The father looked at him a long while, and could answer nothing. They went home again in silence, and the old man was as frightened as Elizabeth at Christian's mirth; for it seemed a thing quite foreign; and as if another being from within were working out of him, awkwardly and ineffectually, as out of some machine.

The harvest-home was once more to be held; the people went to church, and Elizabeth, with her little ones, set out to join the service; her husband also seemed intending to accompany them, but at the threshold of the church he turned aside; and with an air of deep thought, walked out of the village. He set himself on the height, and again looked over upon the smoking cottages; he heard the music of the psalm and organ coming from the little church; children, in holiday dresses, were dancing and sporting on the green. "How have I lost my life as in a dream!" said he to himself: "years have passed away since I went down this hill to the merry children; they who were then sportful on the green, are now serious in the church; I also once went into it, but Elizabeth is now no more a blooming childlike maiden; her youth is gone; I cannot seek for the glance of her eyes with the longing of those days; I have wilfully neglected a high eternal happiness, to win one which is finite and transitory."

With a heart full of wild desire, he walked to the neighbouring wood, and immersed himself in its thickest shades. A ghastly silence encompassed him; no breath of air was stirring in the leaves. Meanwhile, he saw a man approaching him from a distance, whom he recognised for the stranger; he started in affright, and his first thought was that the man would ask him for his money. But as the form came nearer, he perceived how greatly he had been mistaken; for the features, which he had imagined known to him, melted into one another; an old woman of the utmost hideousness approached; she was clad in dirty rags; a tattered clout bound up her few grey hairs; she was limping on a crutch. With a dreadful voice she spoke to him, and asked his name and situation; he replied to both inquiries, and then said, "But who art thou?"

"I am called the Woodwoman," answered she; "and every child can tell of me. Did'st thou never see me before?" With the last words she whirled about, and Christian thought he recognised among the trees the golden veil, the lofty gait, the large stately form which he had once beheld of old. He turned to hasten after her, but nowhere was she to be seen.

Meanwhile, something glittered in the grass, and drew his eye to it. He picked it up; it was the magic tablet with the coloured jewels, and the wondrous figure, which he had lost so many years before. The shape and the changeful gleams struck over all his senses with an instantaneous power. He grasped it firmly, to convince himself that it was really once more in his hands, and then hastened back with it to the village. His father met him. "See," cried Christian, "the thing which I was telling you about so often, which I thought must have been shown to me only in a dream, is now sure and true."

The old man looked a long while at the tablet, and then said: "My son, I am struck with horror in my heart when I view these stones, and dimly guess the meaning of the words on them. Look here, how cold they glitter, what cruel looks they cast from them, bloodthirsty, like the red eye of the tiger! Cast this writing from thee, which makes thee cold and cruel, which will turn thy heart to stone:

> See the flowers, when morn is beaming,
>   Waken in their dewy place;
> And, like children roused from dreaming,
>   Smiling look thee in the face.
>
> By degrees, that way and this,
>   To the golden Sun they're turning,
> Till they meet his glowing kiss,
>   And their hearts with love are burning:
>
> For, with fond and sad desire,
>   In their lover's looks to languish,
> On his melting kisses to expire,
>   And to die of love's sweet anguish:

This is what they joy in most;
　To depart in fondest weakness;
In their lover's being lost,
　Faded stand in silent meekness.

Then they pour away the treasure
　Of their perfumes, their soft souls,
And the air grows drunk with pleasure,
　As in wanton floods it rolls.

Love comes to us here below,
　Discord harsh away removing;
And the heart cries: "Now I know
　Sadness, Fondness, Pain of Loving."

"What wonderful incalculable treasures," said the other, "must there still be in the depths of the Earth! Could one but sound into their secret beds and raise them up, and snatch them to oneself! Could one but clasp this Earth like a beloved bride to one's bosom, so that in pain and love she would willingly grant one her costliest riches! The Wood-woman has called me; I go to seek for her. Near by is an old ruined shaft, which some miner has hollowed out many centuries ago; perhaps I shall find her there!"

He hastened off. In vain did the old man strive to detain him; in a few moments Christian had vanished from his sight. Some hours afterwards, the father, with a strong effort, reached the ruined shaft: he saw footprints in the sand at the entrance, and returned in tears: persuaded that his son, in a state of madness, had gone in, and been drowned in the old collected waters, and horrid caves of the mine.

From that day his heart seemed broken, and he was incessantly in tears. The whole neighbourhood deplored the fortune of the young farmer. Elizabeth was inconsolable, the children lamented aloud. In half a year the aged gardener died; the parents of Elizabeth soon followed him;

and she was forced herself to take charge of everything. Her multiplied engagements helped a little to withdraw her from her sorrow; the education of her children, and the management of so much property, left little time for mourning. After two years, she determined on a new marriage; she bestowed her hand on a young light-hearted man, who had loved her from his youth. But, ere long, everything in their establishment assumed another form. The cattle died; men and maid-servants proved dishonest; barns full of grain were burnt; people in the town, who owed them sums of money, fled and made no payments. In a little while, the landlord found himself obliged to sell some fields and meadows; but a mildew, and a year of scarcity, brought new embarrassments. It seemed as if the gold, so strangely acquired, were taking speedy flight in all direction. Meanwhile, the family was on the increase; and Elizabeth, as well as her husband, grew reckless and sluggish in this scene of despair: he fled for consolation to the bottle, he was often drunk, and therefore quarrelsome and sullen; so that frequently Elizabeth bewailed her state with bitter tears. As their fortune declined, their friends in the village stood aloof from them more and more; so that after some few years they saw themselves entirely forsaken, and were forced to struggle on, in penury and straits, from week to week.

They had nothing but a cow and a few sheep left them; these Elizabeth herself, with her children, often tended at their grass. She was sitting one day with her work in the field, Leonora at her side, and a sucking child on her breast, when they saw from afar a strange-looking shape approaching towards them. It was a man with a garment all in tatters, barefoot, sunburnt to a black brown colour in the face, deformed still farther by a long matted beard: he wore no covering on his head; but had twisted a garland of green branches through his hair, which made his wild appearance still more strange and haggard. On his back he bore some heavy burden in a sack, very carefully tied, and as he walked, he leaned upon a young fir.

On coming nearer, he put down his load, and drew deep draughts of breath. He bade Elizabeth good-day; she shuddered at the sight of him, the girl crouched close to her mother. Having rested for a little while, he said: "I am getting back from a very hard journey among the wildest mountains of the Earth; but to pay me for it, I have brought along with me the richest treasures which imagination can conceive, or heart desire. Look here, and wonder!" Thereupon he loosed his sack, and shook it empty: it was full of gravel, among which were to be seen large bits of chuckstone, and other pebbles. "These jewels," he continued, "are not ground and polished yet, so they want the glance and the eye; the outward fire, with its glitter, is too deeply buried in their inmost heart; yet you have but to strike it out and frighten them, and show that no deceit will serve, and then you see what sort of stuff they are." So saying, he took a piece of flinty stone, and struck it hard against another, till they gave red sparks between them. "Did you see the glance?" cried he. "Ay, they are all fire and light; they illuminate the darkness with their laugh, though as yet it is against their will." With this he carefully repacked his pebbles in the bag, and tied it hard and fast. "I know thee very well," said he then, with a saddened tone. "Thou art Elizabeth." The woman started.

"How comest thou to know my name?" cried she, with a forecasting shudder.

"Ah, good God!" said the unhappy creature, "I am

Christian, he that was a hunter: Dost thou not know me, then?"

She knew not, in her horror and deepest compassion, what to say. He fell upon her neck and kissed her. Elizabeth exclaimed: "O Heaven! my husband is coming!"

"Be at thy ease," said he; "I am as good as dead to thee: in the forest, there, my fair one waits for me; she that is tall and stately, with the black hair, and the golden veil. This is my dearest child, Leonora. Come hither, darling: come, my pretty child; and give me a kiss, too; one kiss, that I may feel thy mouth upon my lips once again, and then I leave you."

Leonora wept; she clasped close to her mother, who, in sobs and tears, half held her towards the wanderer, while he half drew her towards him, took her in his arms, and pressed her to his breast. Then he went away in silence, and in the wood they saw him speaking with the hideous Woodwoman.

"What ails you?" said the husband, as he found mother and daughter pale and melting in tears. Neither of them answered.

The ill-fated creature was never seen again from that day.

❧ The Strange Story of a Young
Englishman by JOHANN PETER HEBEL

Johann Peter Hebel (1760–1826) was born in Basel, Switzerland, and was brought up, in poverty, in a village of the German Black Forest. He took Protestant orders and taught school. Drawing on his experience of country life, he wrote many bucolic poems in the Black Forest dialect, and, taking the name Der rheinische Hausfreund, or Family Friend of the Rhineland, contributed short stores and anecdotes to local journals. He has always been widely popular in Germany, thanks to his intimate, friendly style and his often whimsical humor. He is Romantic, perhaps, chiefly in his taste for gruesome melodrama.

His *Strange Story of a Young Englishman* first appeared in 1809. The translation is by Morris Bishop.

O NCE A YOUNG ENGLISHMAN came by the mail-coach (his first such experience) to the great city of London. He knew none of its inhabitants except a brother-in-law, whom he proposed to visit; and also his sister, obviously the brother-in-law's wife. The only other occupant of the mail-coach was the guard, that is, the conductor, who had to supervise everything and properly receive and deliver letters and packages. The two fellow-travelers had no idea where they would see each other again, if ever.

The mail-coach reached London late in the evening. The traveler could not remain overnight in the post-house, for the postmaster was a high and mighty man, no innkeeper; and the poor young man knew no more how to find his brother-in-law's house in the pitch-black night of the gigantic city than how to find a needle in a cartload of hay.

Then up spoke the guard: "Young gentleman, come with me. I don't live here, in fact, but for my stops in London I keep a little room with a relative; and there are two beds in it. My cousin will put you up, and tomorrow you can inquire about your brother-in-law's house; you will find it more easily then."

The young man did not need to be asked twice. With the lady cousin they drank a jug of English beer (not their first), which must be better than even Donaueschingen or Säckingen brews, which aren't bad either; and they ate a saveloy sausage and then went to bed. But in the night the traveler felt an urgent call of nature, and he had to go out. Then he was worse off than before. For in his tiny quarters he was as unaware of his surroundings as, a couple of hours before, he had been of the great city. Fortunately the guard waked up and told him how to go—left, right, and left again. "When you come to the right place," he added, "the door is in fact locked, and we have lost the key. But take the big knife out of my great-coat pocket, and shove it between the door and the doorpost, and you can lift up the latch inside. Just follow your ears; you will hear the Thames rushing below. And put something on; it's a cold night." In his haste and in the darkness the young man picked up the guard's jacket instead of his own, pulled it on, and arrived gratefully at the right place. He hardly noticed that on his way he had made too sharp a turn, so that his nose struck against a corner and bled freely, thanks to all the heady beer he had drunk. What with his loss of blood and his chilling, he was overcome by weakness and fell asleep in the privy.

Meanwhile the guard, aroused, waited and waited, and could not imagine why his companion lingered so long, until he heard a noise in the street. Half asleep, he thought:

"What's up? The poor devil must have been coming to the house door; he was out in the street and he has been pressed!" (For when the English need crews for their ships, gangs of strong men are picked to go by night to common taverns and questionable resorts, and they even scour the streets; and if anyone falls into their hands who looks fit for service, they don't waste time saying: "Comrade, who are you?" They work very snappily, put him, willing or unwilling, aboard ship, and good-bye forever! These midnight man hunters are called press gangs; that is why the guard said: "What's up? The poor devil has been pressed!") In great anxiety and haste he sprang up, cast his great-coat about him, and ran out into the street, to rescue, if possible, the poor wretch. But when he had gotten one or two streets away from the noise, he himself fell into the hands of the press-gang. He was dragged, much against his will, on board a ship. The rest later. Enough now that he was far away.

Afterwards the young man in the privy came to himself, hurried back to his bed without missing his companion, and slept till dawn. Meanwhile the guard was due at the posting-station at eight o'clock. As he didn't come and didn't come, an employee was sent after him. He found no guard, but instead a man with a bloody garment lying in bed, and in the passage a great bared knife, a trail of blood all the way to the privy, and below the rushing Thames. So the blood-stained newcomer fell under the dark suspicion that he had murdered the guard and thrown him into the water. He was haled before a summary court. He was searched; and when the police found in the pocket of the jacket, which he was still wearing, a leather money-bag with the well-known silver seal-ring of the post attached to the belt, it was all up with the poor young man. He tried to make appeal to his brother-in-law; no one had ever heard of him; to his sister; she was unknown. He told the whole story of his misadventure as it had occurred. But the judges said: "A lot of fairy tales! You will be hanged!" And what they ordered was executed that very afternoon, according to English law and custom. For this is the English usage: since there are so many criminals in London, short shrift is given to hangbirds, and few pay much attention to them, since they so abound. The condemned are assembled, put in a big cart, and transported under the gallows. There the halter is attached to the fatal hook, and the cart is driven off, leaving the jolly boys to kick and dance in air. But in England hanging is not so shameful as with us; it is merely a way of dying. Therefore after the hanging the nearest relatives of the criminal come and pull on his legs until the good cousin up above is thoroughly choked.* But no one performed this gruesome service of love and friendship for our young man, until in the evening a young married couple strolled arm in arm past the place of execution and glanced up at the gallows. Then with a scream of horror the wife fell into her husband's arms, crying: "Merciful heaven, there is our brother hanging!" But her shock increased when, at the well-known voice of his sister, the young man opened his eyes and rolled them in a ghastly manner, for he was still alive. The brother-in-law was a man of decision. He did not lose his wits; he conceived of a rescue. The square was vacant and unfrequented; with money and blandishments he won over a couple of trusty, stout-hearted fellows. They took down the hanged man coolly enough, as if they had every right to do so, and brought him safe and sound to the brother-in-law's house.

* This curious custom of the English is attested even in the sixteenth century. See René Graziani, "Non-Utopian Euthanasia," in *Renaissance Quarterly*, Winter 1969.—Ed.

There he was restored in a few hours. He had a little fever, but under the tender care of his devoted sister he soon regained his health.

But one evening the brother-in-law said to him: "Brother, you can't stay longer in this country. If you are discovered, you may well be hanged again, and I with you. And even if not, you are wearing a collar that bodes evil for you and your relatives. You must go to America. I will arrange for you there."

The young man agreed. At the first opportunity he sailed in a safe ship, and in eighty days came securely to harbor in Philadelphia. With a heavy heart he set foot on this foreign shore, thinking: "Ah, if God would only grant me the sight of one single man who knows me!" And lo, there appeared, in rough sailor's costume, the guard! But however great, in general, is the pleasure of an unexpected reunion in a far land, in this case the first greeting was far from pleasant. One can imagine a series of pictures: first, the guard, shaking his fist and exploding, "Where did the devil bring you from, you damned night-prowler? Do you know that you got me pressed?" And second, one sees the young Englishman, whose hands also were ready for action, answering, "Goddam, you cursed meddler, do you know that on account of you I was hanged!" But third, one sees the Inn of the Three Crowns in Philadelphia. There the two met next day, recounted their adventures and became again the best of friends. The young Englishman entered a business house and prospered. He did not rest until he could buy out his good friend and send him back to England. He became in time a rich merchant in America; now he lives in the city of Washington, on the new extension of Lord Street, number 46.

❧ An Unexpected Reunion

by JOHANN PETER HEBEL

For a word about Hebel see the headnote of the preceding story. The present one is dated 1811; it is translated by Morris Bishop.

A GOOD FIFTY and more years ago a young miner in Falun, Sweden, kissed his young, pretty, affianced bride and said to her: "On St. Lucy's Day our love will be blessed by the hand of the preacher. Then we shall be man and wife, and we shall set to building our own little nest."

"And peace and love shall dwell therein," said the lovely bride, with a winsome smile, "for you are my one and all; without you I would rather lie in the grave than anywhere else."

But before St. Lucy's Day, when the preacher had for the second time proclaimed in church: "If any man can show just cause why they may not lawfully be joined together, let him now speak," Death answered the summons. For when next morning the young man passed her house in his black miner's clothes (miners are always dressed for death), he knocked once at her window and gave her good morning, but good evening he gave her never. He never returned from the mine. That very morning she sewed for him, all for nothing, a black scarf with a red border for his wedding day. But as he did not come, she laid it aside, wept for him, and never forgot him.

Meanwhile the city of Lisbon in Portugal was destroyed by an earthquake, and the Seven Years' War came and went, and Emperor Francis I died, and the Jesuit order was banned, and Poland divided, and Empress Maria Theresa died, and Struensee was beheaded, America was liberated, and the united French and Spanish forces were unable to capture Gibraltar. The Turks confined General Stein in Veterans' Cave in Hungary, and Emperor Joseph died in his turn. King Gustav of Sweden invaded Russian Finland, the French Revolution and the long war began, and Emperor Leopold II likewise descended to the grave. Napoleon overran Prussia, the English bombarded Copenhagen; and the peasants sowed and harvested. The millers ground their grain, the smiths hammered, and the miners probed the veins of ore in their underground workshops. But when, in 1809, about St. John's Day, the miners of Falun started to hew out an opening between two shafts, a good two hundred yards below ground, they dug out of the rubble and vitriolic water the body of a young man. He was totally impregnated with iron-vitriol but otherwise uncorrupted and unaltered, so that one could readily recognize his features and his age, as if he had died only an hour before, or as if he had just fallen asleep at his work. But when they brought him up into the light his father and mother, friends and acquaintances were already long dead, and no one could identify the sleeping youth or reveal anything about his mishap, until arrived the former betrothed of the miner who had gone down long since into the gallery and had never returned. Gray and shriveled, she came clumping on a crutch to the mine-head and recognized her bridegroom; and rather with rejoicing than with distress she sank down upon the beloved body. And after a long emotional crisis she said: "It is my betrothed, whom I have mourned for fifty long years, and whom God has permitted me to see once more before my end. A week before the wedding he went down into the pit and never emerged."

Then the spirits of all the bystanders were racked with grief and tears, as they saw the former bride in the aspect of withered, impotent old age and the former bridegroom in all the luster of youth, and as they perceived how the flame of young love woke again in her breast after fifty years. But he opened not his lips in a smile or his eyes in a gleam of recognition. They saw him borne by the miners into her little room, as she was the only person who was bound to him and who had a right to him, until his grave should be made ready in the cemetery. Next day, when the grave was dug and the miners came to fetch him, she opened a little casket, tied about his neck a black silk scarf with a red border, and accompanied him in her Sunday best, as if it were her wedding day and not his funeral. For as he was laid in the churchyard grave she said: "Now sleep well for another day or a dozen in the cool wedding bed, and may the time not be long. I have still only a little to do; I will come soon, and soon it will be day again. What the earth has once surrendered it won't hold fast a second time." Thus she departed, and turned once to look back.

❧ Monsieur Charles

by JOHANN PETER HEBEL

See the headnote to the next-to-last story. This one was
written evidently in 1817. The translation is by Morris Bishop.

A MERCHANT in Petersburg, born a Frenchman, was
dandling his wonderful baby boy on his knee, and
making a grimace to indicate that the child would be a
wealthy and fortunate man, and that he should take his
good luck to be a sign of God's favor. Thereupon a
stranger, a Pole, entered the room with four sick, half-
frozen children. "I'm bringing you the children," he said.

The merchant looked at the Pole with surprise. "What
should I do with these children?" he said. "Whom do they
belong to? Who sent you to me?"

"They don't belong to anyone," said the Pole. "Or
rather to a dead woman in the snow, seventy hours' journey
away towards Vilna. Do what you like with them."

"You've come to the wrong address," said the merchant.
(And the author, the Family Friend, corroborates him.)

The Pole was not at all disconcerted. "If you are Mon-
sieur Charles, I'm at the right place," he replied. (The
Family Friend agrees with that too. He was Monsieur
Charles, right enough.)

Now a Frenchwoman, a widow, had long lived a comfortable and blameless life in Moscow. But when the French
were in Moscow five years ago, she treated her fellow-
countrymen in a more friendly manner than the native
inhabitants liked. For blood is not to be denied. And after
she had lost her little house and property and had saved

only her five children, she fell under suspicion and had to flee not only the city but the whole country. Otherwise she would have betaken herself to Petersburg, where she hoped to find a rich cousin. But when, fleeing in insufferable cold and unspeakable torment, she had reached Vilna, sick and destitute of all necessities and conveniences for so long a journey, she encountered there a noble Russian prince and to him she exposed her need. The noble prince advanced to her three hundred rubles; and when he learned that she had a cousin in Petersburg, he proposed the choice of continuing her journey to France or of turning back with a pass to Petersburg. She looked dubiously at her eldest boy, the most intelligent, as well as the most seriously ill, of the lot.

"Son," she said, "where do you want to go?"

"Wherever you go, mother," said the boy. And he was telling the truth; for even before their departure he was heading for the grave. So she did what was necessary and made an agreement with a Pole that for five hundred rubles he would take them to her cousin in Petersburg (for she thought that he would promptly make up the full sum). But she grew steadily weaker on the long, difficult journey, and on the sixth or seventh day she died. "Wherever you go, mother," the boy had said, and he kept his word.

The poor Pole inherited the four children from her; they could communicate as well as a Pole can understand a French child talking Russian, or as a French child when someone tries to talk to him in Polish. Few kind readers would have liked to be in his place. "Now what to do?" he said to himself. "If I turn back, where can I leave the children? If I go ahead, where can I deliver them?" And finally some inner voice spoke: "Do your duty. Will you rob the poor children of their last and only inheritance

from their mother—your promise, which you gave her?"
So he knelt down with the unhappy orphans around the
body and recited the Lord's prayer in Polish. "And lead us
not into temptation." Then each let fall a handful of snow
on the cold breast of the mother, to indicate that they
would gladly have performed the last duties of interment,
had it been possible, and that they were now wretched forsaken children.

Then, somewhat comforted, the Pole continued with
them on the Petersburg road, for he wouldn't admit that
the person who had entrusted the children to him could
leave him in the lurch. When the great city took shape
before his eyes, like any coachman who asks on arrival at
the gate where he is to proceed, he tried to learn from the
children, as well as he could make himself understood,
where the cousin lived. And as nearly as he could understand, they replied: "We don't know."

"Well then, what is his name?"

"We don't know that either."

"Well, what is your own family name?"

"Charles."

The amiable reader will mark this; and if the Family
Friend had been in control of events, he would have made
Monsieur Charles the cousin, the children would have been
succored, and the story would have come to a stop. But
truth is often more ingenious than fiction. No, Monsieur
Charles is not the cousin, but another man of the same
name; and even to this hour no one knows the name of the
genuine cousin, or if he lives in Petersburg, and if so, where.
So in great distress of mind the poor driver roamed for two
days around the city, trying to dispose of his little Frenchmen. Monsieur Charles didn't want them as a gift; he was
not willing to take even one of them. But as one word led

to another and as the Pole straightforwardly and humanely described their fate and his own necessity, he thought: "Well, I'll take one of them from him." Then a kindly warmth welled up in his bosom, and he thought: "No, I'll take two of them." And finally, when the children clung to him and, thinking he was their cousin, began to cry in French (for the intelligent reader will have already noticed that French children cry differently from others), Monsieur Charles recognized this national characteristic. God moved his heart, so that he felt like a father seeing his own children weep and complain. "In God's name," he said, "if this is my fate, I won't try to dodge it." And he accepted all the children. He said to the Pole: "Sit down for a while. I'll have some soup cooked for you all."

The Pole, with a good appetite and a much lightened heart, ate the soup and laid down his spoon. He laid down the spoon and remained seated. He stood up and remained standing. "Be so good," he said finally, "as to let me be on my way. It's a long journey to Vilna. The lady made a deal with me for five hundred rubles."

· Then over the face of that kindly gentleman, Monsieur Charles, passed a shadow like that of a spring cloud over a sunny meadow. "My good friend," he said, "you seem to me rather peculiar. Is it not enough that I have taken the children off your hands? Must I also pay you their fare?" For it can befall the best and most honest person, a merchant or another also, that automatically he must at first bargain and haggle, even if only with himself. The Pole answered: "My good sir, I won't tell you to your face how you look to me. Isn't it enough that I bring you your children? Should I also have brought them free of charge? Times are hard and money is scarce."

"That is just why I am complaining," said Monsieur

Charles. "Do you think I am so rich that I buy foreign children, or so impious that I would make money from them? Do you want them back?" Some discussion followed, and the Pole now first learned, to his amazement, that Monsieur Charles was not the cousin, but had accepted the orphans only out of pity. "If that's the way of it," he said, "I am no rich man, and your countrymen, the French, have done me no good; but if that's the way of it, I can't demand anything of you. Treat the poor little things well; that will be my pay." So with the worthy man, and in his eye stood a tear, which seemed to come from an overmastered heart; at least it overmastered that of Monsieur Charles. He said to himself: "Monsieur Charles—and a poor Polish drosky-driver!" The Pole began to kiss the children one after the other in farewell, and exhorted them, in Polish, to obedience and piety. "My good friend," said Monsieur Charles, "wait here a little longer. I am not so poor that I can't pay your well-earned fee, now that I have relieved you of your passengers." With that he gave the driver five hundred rubles.

Thus the children are now cared for, the fare is paid. When they entered the gates of the great city any gentle reader might well have doubted whether the cousin could be found and would assume the charge, but divine Providence took care of all.

❧ The Sandman

by E. T. A. HOFFMANN

Our author was born in Königsberg, East Prussia, in 1776, and was christened Ernst Theodor Wilhelm Hoffman. (In maturity he dropped the Wilhelm from his name and substituted Amadeus, as a tribute to Mozart.) He studied law and later practiced, but his heart was in music and letters. He discovered Tieck and others of the Romantic school, wrote operas and many musical compositions. After precarious years trying to survive in the war-troubled literary-musical world, he received in 1814 a legal appointment in Berlin, and drank himself into an early grave in 1822.

The mark of his literary work is a grotesque and ghoulish imagination evoking diabolical horrors, combined with a sardonic humor. *The Sandman* was written in 1815 and published in 1816. Many will recognize it as an episode in Offenbach's *Tales of Hoffman*. The translation, by Frederick McCurdy Atkinson, was published by George G. Harrap & Company Ltd., London, in 1933, and is reprinted by permission of the publisher.

NATHANAEL TO LOTHAR

I AM SURE you must all be very uneasy at not hearing from me for so very long. My mother will be cross, and Clara perhaps imagines that I am living in a whirl of dissipation and forgetting her angel image that is so deeply imprinted on my heart and mind. But it is nothing of the sort: every day and every minute I think of you all, and my Clara's lovely face comes to me in my dreams, and smiles on me as she used to do when we were all together. But how could I have written to you in the wretched mood that has perturbed my mind until now? Something terrible

has invaded my life! Dark forebodings of some dreadful impending fate have wrapped me round with thick black clouds impervious to any cheerful ray of sunshine. Must I tell you what has happened to me? I can see that I must indeed, but even at the thought of it I break into an involuntary laugh as though I had gone crazy. My dear Lothar, how can I put it so that you will understand that what happened a few days ago could really have such a fatal effect on my life? If you were here you could see for yourself, but now you will certainly think me a ridiculous ghost-seer. In a word, the terrible experience the impression of which I struggle in vain to overcome was simply that a few days ago, on the 20th of October at twelve o'clock midday, a seller of barometers came into my room to offer me his wares. I did not buy, and threatened to fling him downstairs, upon which he took himself off. But before telling you of the hideous relations fate was to establish between myself and this accursed pedlar, I had better recount to you some details of my early childhood.

In those years my sister and I hardly ever saw our father except at meals. His business seemed to engross all his energies. But after supper every evening we used to go with our mother and sit about a round table in his study. My father would light his pipe, fill a huge beer glass to the brim, and tell us a host of marvellous tales, during which his pipe would go out, to my great joy, for it was my job to light it again each time. Often when he was in a less expansive mood he would let us have fine books full of marvellous engravings; while we were eagerly poring over their treasures of illustration he would lie back in his big oak arm-chair and puff hard at his pipe till he disappeared in a thick fog of smoke. On those evenings my mother was sad, and when the clock struck nine, "Come now," she would say, "off to bed with you quickly, here comes the *sandman!*" And thereupon I would indeed hear a noise of heavy steps on the stair—they must be the mysterious sandman's.

One night this fantastic sound had frightened me more than usual; I asked my mother who was this nasty person she threatened us with, and who was always driving us away from our father's room. "There is no sandman, my dear boy," replied my mother; "when I say 'here's the sandman!' it only means you are sleepy and keep shutting your eyes as if somebody had thrown sand in them." My mother's answer failed to satisfy me, and my childish mind was convinced that she only denied the sandman's existence to prevent us from being afraid of him, for I still could hear him mounting the stairs. Eager and curious to learn something more definite about this sandman and his connexion with us children, I finally asked the old woman who had charge of my little sister who he was. "Ah, Thanelchen," she said, "don't you know that yet? He is a bad man who comes for children when they refuse to go to bed; he throws big handfuls of sand in their eyes, then he bundles them into a bag and carries them off to the moon for his young ones to eat. They have hooky beaks, like owls, to eat the eyes of children who don't behave themselves."

From that moment the image of the cruel sandman was imprinted upon my mind under a horrible guise. When in the evening I heard the noise he made coming up the stairs I shivered with terror. My mother could get nothing out of me but the cry I stammered through my sobs—"the sandman, the sandman!" I would rush away for refuge to the bedroom, and all night through I would be tormented by the dreadful apparition. I grasped the idea that the old servant's tale of the sandman and his brood of children in

the moon might not be altogether gospel; but the sandman remained a dreadful spectre in my eyes, and I was
seized with terror every time I heard him come up the
stair and the sharp sound of his opening the door of my
father's study and shutting it behind him. Sometimes he
let several days go by without coming, and then his visits
would continue without a break. This went on for several
years, and I could never get used to the idea of this odious
spectre; his relations with my father filled my imagination
more and more. The sandman had transported me into the
realm of the marvellous, the fantastic, the idea of which
sprouts so easily in children's minds. Nothing pleased me
more than to hear or read tales about spirits, about witches,
about dwarfs; but over everything there hovered the sandman, whom I used to draw with chalk or charcoal on the
tables, on the cupboard doors, on the walls, in the strangest
and most horrible shapes.

When I reached the age of ten my mother took me from
the nursery bedroom and installed me in a little room opening into a corridor not far from my father's study. We
were still bound to retire when on the stroke of nine the
unknown was heard in the house. From my little room I
knew the moment when he entered my father's study, and
it seemed to me that very soon after a vapour with a
strange odour spread through the house. Along with curiosity I felt rising within me also the courage to make the
acquaintance of the sandman one way or another. Often I
slipped quietly out of my room into the corridor after my
mother had left me, but without success; for the sandman
had always gone in when I had reached the point from
which I might have seen him pass. At length; yielding to
an irresistible impulse, I determined to hide in my father's
room itself, and wait for the sandman's arrival. One day I

guessed from my father's silence and my mother's low spirits that the sandman was coming; I pretended to be very tired so that I might get away from the others a little before nine o'clock, and I hid myself in a corner. Soon after, the house door opened noisily, then was shut again. A slow, heavy, echoing tread passed through the hall and made towards the stairs. My mother passed by me swiftly with my sister. Very gently I opened the door of my father's study. He was sitting as usual, silent and motionless, with his back to the door, and did not notice me. In a trice I was hidden away in a wardrobe behind the curtain that served as its door. The sound of steps came nearer and nearer. Outside could be heard a cough, a murmur, and a strange sort of shuffling. My heart beat wildly with fear: the bell rang violently, the door was thrust open. I plucked up courage with an effort and very cautiously parted the curtains slightly. The sandman was before my father, in the middle of the room; the light of the candles fell full on his face; the sandman, the terrible sandman, was —the old lawyer Coppelius, who occasionally dined at our house. But the most abominable face could not have roused in me a deeper horror than that of Coppelius.

Imagine a tall man with broad shoulders, a misshapen head, an earthy yellow face, very thick eyebrows under which there gleamed two cat's eyes, and a long nose hooked down above the upper lip. His crooked mouth often contracted into a sardonic laugh; and at that moment two dark red spots sprang up on his cheek-bones, and an extraordinary whistling sound came through his clenched teeth. Coppelius habitually wore an ashen grey coat of ancient cut, with vest and breeches to match, black stockings, and little jewelled buckles on his shoes. His little wig barely covered the top of his head, the curls did not nearly come down to his big red ears, a broad stitched bag stood out from the nape of his neck and disclosed the silver buckle that held his crumpled cravat in place. His whole person, in short, was horrible and repulsive. But what we hated worst about him were his big bony hairy fingers, so badly that we could not bear anything he had touched. He had observed this, and when our mother had slipped a piece of tart or a preserved fruit on to our plates he took a delight in putting a hand to it under some pretext or other, so that we used to reject with tears in our eyes the dainties that should have filled us with joy. He would do the same when our father had poured us out a little glass of sweet wine on festive occasions; he would quickly pass a hand over it, or even sometimes put the glass to his bluish lips, and laugh with a truly diabolical air to see our mute repugnance and the stifled sobs that betrayed our disgust. He never called us anything else than *his little animals*, and we were forbidden to complain or even to open our mouths before him for any cause or reason whatsoever. Our mother seemed to dread this horrible Coppelius no less than we did. As for my father, he behaved in his presence with all the signs of the utmost deference.

At once the idea came to my mind that the sandman could not be any other creature than this odious Coppelius; and instead of the fantastic being of the nurse's tales, I saw in him something satanic and infernal that was fated to bring some dreadful misfortune upon us.

But the dread of being caught made me suppress any outward manifestation of my fears, and I hid away closer than ever at the back of the wardrobe, only leaving enough space to let me see everything through the curtains.

My father received Coppelius with all ceremony. "Come," cried the visitor in a harsh voice, "come, to work!"

As he spoke he pulled off his coat. My father did so too, and both put on long dark robes taken from a recess in the wall, at the back of which I caught sight of a stove. Coppelius went to this, and almost at once a blue flame shot up under his fingers, filling the room with a diabolical light. Chemical vessels and utensils were lying here and there about the floor. When my father bent over the crucible on the fire, his face all at once took on a strange expression; his features, contracted with some violent inner pang, had something of the hateful mask of Coppelius. The latter was puddling in the burning mass with tongs, and he drew out ingots of metal and hammered them on the anvil. I imagined I saw human heads leaping all round him, but eyeless. "Eyes! eyes!" roared Coppelius. I heard no more; I was so agitated that I began to lose consciousness and tumbled out on the floor. The noise of my downfall made my father start, while Coppelius leapt upon me and picked me up, gnashing his teeth, and held me above the flames of the stove, which were already beginning to scorch my hair. "Ah! here are eyes, child's eyes!" cried Coppelius, raking red-hot coals out of the fire and making to put them on my eyelids. My father struggled to stop him. "Master, Master!" he cried, "leave my Nathanael his eyes!" "Be it so," said Coppelius; "then I shall study the mechanism of his feet and his hands." He then began to twist and turn my joints so rudely that they all felt as though they were dislocated. Then everything went black and silent about me, and I ceased to feel anything. When I came out of this second fainting fit, my mother's gentle breath was warming my frozen lips. "Is the sandman there still?" I stammered. "No, my darling boy," said my mother, "he is gone, and he shall never harm you. Do not be afraid of him, for I shall never leave you now!" And she hugged me to her breast with the convulsive embrace of mingled love and fear.

Can you understand, Lothar, the true inwardness of this adventure? A raging fever took hold of me, and for six weeks I hovered between life and death; in my delirious fits I always imagined I saw the sandman in the shape and features of Coppelius. But that is not the most terrible part of my story. Listen again. For a year nobody had seen Coppelius, and everyone thought he had left the town. Little by little my father had recovered his cheerful spirits and his customary ways of tranquillity and paternal affection. But one night, as nine o'clock struck from the neighbouring belfry, we heard the door of the house creak on its hinges, and footsteps as heavy as a hammer on the anvil began to come upstairs. "It is Coppelius!" said my mother, turning pale. "Yes, it is Coppelius," repeated my father brokenly, and sinister visions flocked upon me on every hand.

Tears ran down my mother's face. "My dear, my dear!" she exclaimed, "must this be?" "For the last time," replied my father. "He has come for the last time, I swear to you. Go, go with your children, and good night!"

I was as though turned to stone, I could not breathe. Seeing me motionless, my mother took me by the arm. "Come, Nathanael!" she said. I let her draw me along to my room. "Be very quiet and go to sleep. Sleep!" said she as she left me. But I was filled with a terror I could not master, and could not shut my eyes. I saw before me that horrible, odious Coppelius with his shining eyes; he smiled at me with a hypocritical air, and vainly did I seek to drive away his image. It was on the stroke of midnight when a violent noise was heard, like the report of a fire-arm. The whole house shook, someone ran by outside my room, and the door shut with a loud bang. I sprang out of bed, dashed along the corridor; heart-rending cries came from my father's room, out of which a black foul smoke was surging in great whirls; the servant was screaming, "Ah, my master, my poor master!"

In front of the flaring hearth lay my father's body, blackened and mutilated in horrible fashion. My mother and my sister were bending over him, uttering lamentable cries. "Coppelius, Coppelius," I exclaimed, "you have killed my father!" and I fell almost lifeless.

Two days after, when my poor father had been laid in his coffin, his features had recovered, in spite of the ravages of death, the peace and tranquillity of the old days; we hoped that, in spite of his relations with Coppelius, God had pardoned his soul and had called it to Himself.

The explosion had roused the neighbours. The affair made a sensation, and the authorities tried to lay hold of Coppelius, but the wretch had disappeared, and nobody knew where he had gone.

And now, my dear Lothar, when I tell you that the barometer-seller who visited me was no other than this accursed Coppelius, you will understand the overwhelming horror this apparition of an enemy brought upon me. He was dressed differently, but the features of Coppelius are too strongly printed in my soul for me to mistake them. He is passing himself off as a Piedmontese mechanic, and has given himself the name of Giuseppe Coppola.

I am determined to avenge my father whatever may happen. Do not speak of this horrible encounter to my mother. Greet dear Clara from me; I shall write to her when I am in a calmer mood.

CLARA TO NATHANAEL

Although you have not written to me for a long time, I am still convinced that you have not yet banished me from your heart and mind; for when you wrote the other day to my brother you put my name on the envelope. And so I opened your letter, but perceived my mistake with the first line. Of course I ought to have read not another word, and should have taken your letter to my brother. But the beginning of the tale you had to tell him had so filled me with curiosity that it almost made me dizzy. Your Coppelius is a terrifying person. Till now I never knew the nature of the dreadful accident that deprived you of your dear father. This accursed barometer-monger you call Giuseppe Coppola, and who, you say, is so fatally like Coppelius, has pursued me for a whole day like a threatening spectre. I dreamed of him in my sleep, and awoke more than once with terrified cries. Still you must not be annoyed, my dear, if Lothar's reply tells you that next day I had recovered my usual serenity and had driven away the phantoms of my imagination. I confess that this matter does not appear to me to have anything supernatural about it. Coppelius might be the most repulsive creature in the world, and I can conceive your childish aversion for his ugly face. You made him into a personification of the sandman. That was the working of a youthful mind infected by an old nurse's tales. Coppelius's nocturnal interviews with your father had certainly no other object than experiments in alchemy. Your mother was distressed because these things must entail great expenditure with no return; and besides, your father, being absorbed in this passion for making gold and hunting for the philosopher's stone, was neglecting his household affairs and his family ties. Your father's death seems to me to have resulted from some piece of carelessness. Certain combinations of substances in fusion can produce an explosion of greater or less violence; this I have ascertained from a chemist, who filled my ears with a great number of strange names that I shall spare you, since I have clean forgotten them myself.

I know you will be sorry for your poor Clara, who has no belief in the fantastic, and who only sees the world through very ordinary eyes. Ah! my dear Nathanael, is there really an occult power endowed with such an ascendancy over our nature that it can drag us along a path of disaster and misfortune? No, God has given us the light of the spirit and the touchstone of conscience that by their help we may recognize at any point and under any guise the enemy that prowls about our destiny. If we proceed with steady steps, and eyes fixed on heaven, along the path of virtue, this occult power seeks in vain to draw us into its snares. It may happen that at moments our imagination lets itself be fascinated by deceiving ghosts that to our senses put on the appearance of a menacing reality; but these ghosts are but our own thoughts, transformed by a kind of fever, which lends them strange shapes borrowed, according to our momentary mood, from the notions we have made for ourselves of heaven or of hell. There, my dear Nathanael, is the way my brother and I look at these high questions of occult powers. You see that mysteries don't frighten everybody, and that there are even girls bold enough to reason instead of trembling. So I beg you to put clear away from your memory the ugly faces of Coppelius and the barometer-monger Giuseppe Coppola. If your letter did not in every line betray signs of the utmost agitation I would take delight in telling you all the comical things that floated through my mind about the sandman and Coppelius, the lawyer-barometer-pedlar. But that will be for another occasion.

If your fears seize upon you again, come and shelter under my wing; I will be your good fairy. I know nothing so good as a jolly spell of laughing to put fantastic monsters to flight for ever.

Always yours, my dearest Nathanael.

NATHANAEL TO LOTHAR

I was greatly put out, my dear friend, to think that, thanks to my foolish slip, Clara had read the letter I wrote to you. The lively girl made fun of me to her heart's content; and yet, in spite of all her arguments about what she regards as my obsession, I am sure of what my own eyes have seen.

In any event I have realized that the seller of barometers and the lawyer Coppelius are two quite different persons. I am attending the lectures of the celebrated physicist Spalanzani, who is an Italian. This man has for a long time known Giuseppe Coppola, who as a matter of fact has a Piedmontese accent. Coppelius was German, extremely German. And now your sister and you, my friend, may both look on me as a morbid dreamer, but I cannot shake off my first impression of that fatal likeness. I am glad he has left the town, as Spalanzani tells me. This professor is a singular person, rotund, with high cheek-bones, a pointed nose and eyes shining like carbuncles. The other day as I went up to his flat I noticed that the green curtain, usually drawn over a glass door, was a little open. I hardly know how I came to look through the glass. A splendid beauty, in richest attire, was sitting in the room, with her folded hands lying on a small table in front of her. She was facing me, and I could see her eyes. I observed with astonishment, mingled with a secret fear, that they were utterly lifeless and vacant. She seemed to be asleep with her eyes open. In a whirl of emotions I slipped into the lecture-room, where a full class was waiting for the professor. Someone told me that the mysterious lady was Olympia, Spalanzani's daughter, whom he keeps in almost cloistered seclusion. Perhaps this lovely person is astray in her wits, or he may have some other good reason for his conduct. I intend to find out the truth. But why need I go on wearying you with my mare's nests? We shall soon be able to talk face to face. In a fortnight at the most I shall be with you all, with my dear Clara, and my poor imagination will be soothed under the happy influence of her kind eyes, and so farewell, my friend.

I

The narrative of the strange adventures of the student Nathanael might very well begin at the point where he sends the barometer-seller to the devil. The three letters shown me by my friend Lothar are like three strokes of the brush laid at random on the canvas. The outlines must be sketched in and then the colouring done later. Let us set to work.

Not long after the death of Nathanael's father, Clara and Lothar, the children of a distant relation, were received in the house of our hero's mother. Clara and Nathanael grew up together, conceived a mutual affection, and were betrothed when Nathanael went away to the city of G., where he was to finish his studies, and where we have just seen him attending the physics lectures of Professor Spalanzani.

Clara was not beautiful in the common sense of the

word. A painter would have found in the lines of her figure, her shoulders, and her bust, merely an exaggerated maidenliness, but he would have been obliged to admire her magnificent Magdalen-like hair with which she could cover herself like an all-enveloping veil, and the sheen of her satin skin eclipsed the whitest snow. A devotee of beauty compared Clara's eyes to the blue lakes of Ruysdael, whose limpid mirror reflects with so pure a charm the woods, the meadows, and the flowers, all the poetic elements of the most smiling landscape. To these natural graces the girl added a vivid imagination, a sensitive and affectionate heart that was by no means incompatible with clear and positive powers of reasoning, as her letter has shown us. Romantic spirits were never to her taste; she held little conversation with light and presumptuous persons; her sparkling eye and ironical smile seemed to say to them, "Poor shadows that you are, do you hope to pass yourselves off to me as noble figures, full of life and sap?" And hence some accused Clara of being cold and prosaic, while others, who knew more of life, admired her exquisite sense of delicacy and purity under that cool exterior. Yet no one loved her like Nathanael, who cultivated science and the arts assiduously, and Clara returned his affection with all her heart. With what joy did she throw herself into his arms when he came home from G. at the time he had said in his letter to Lothar! And as Nathanael had hoped, from that day the young man was entirely rid of all thoughts of Coppelius and Coppola alike.

Yet Nathanael had been right when he told his friend Lothar that the appearance of the accursed pedlar Giuseppe Coppola had cast a fatal spell upon his destiny. His disposition had undoubtedly altered, and his humour, hitherto so cheerful, had given way to melancholy. His mystical broodings, from which nothing now availed to draw him, gave poor Clara much distress; all her wise arguments were insufficient to cope with the moral malady that was killing her friend. One day when Nathanael was complaining very seriously that the monster Coppelius was the evil principle that had fastened upon him from the moment he had hidden behind a curtain to watch him, and that his demon antagonist would poison their happy love, Clara suddenly became serious, and said, "Yes, Nathanael, Coppelius is a hostile principle that will trouble our happiness if you do not banish him from your mind: his power lies only in your credulity." This clash of minds irritated Nathanael without curing him of his dismal preoccupations; little by little, in his vexation, he came to place Clara among those inferior creatures whose eye, lacking in *second sight*, cannot penetrate the secrets of invisible nature. Next morning he bent himself to the task of converting her to his ideas, and read treatises of occult philosophy to her while she was busily preparing breakfast. "But, my dear Nathanael," said Clara after a few minutes' attention, "what would you say if I were to call you the bad genius of my coffee, for if I were to spend my time listening to you reading and holding forth, my coffee would boil over on the ashes and you would all have to go without breakfast!" Nathanael shut his book with a bang, and buried himself in his room, and no one saw him again all day. Uneasiness fell upon the family gatherings, and a discord grew up between the hearts of two people who had been born to adore each other and make each other happy. Yet time went on, and took with it some of poor Nathanael's eccentricities, and he found the detestable image of Coppelius gradually recede into a distant haze. He found in poetry a distraction for his fatal thoughts. One day he hastened to Clara, a bulky manuscript in his hand: it was a whole poem, into which he had lavishly poured all his impressions, all his dreams, all the sufferings of his fevered brain. He began to read it under the arbour in the garden; the air was scented with the warm breath of evening; the setting sun gilded the tree-tops with its mild rays. Nathanael opened his book, Clara went on knitting, promising herself to turn a deaf ear to a work that she expected to be dull and tiresome, but when the first pages were finished she felt a singular agitation; her work fell from her hands; she remained fixed in contemplation of Nathanael, who was completely carried away by his frenzied poetry. When he had come to an end of his reading the young man flung his manuscript from him, and, eyes filled with tears, breast strained with sobs, leaned over to Clara, pressing her hands with a convulsive clasp and crying out in despairing tones, "Ah, Clara! Clara!" The kind girl looked at him with tender pity. "My darling," she said, "your poem is absurd, do throw the dreadful thing in the fire!" Nathanael leaped to his feet. "Foolish creature," he said, eyeing her darkly. "An automaton with no life and no soul!" and he left her, running away. Clara remained behind in tears. "Alas!" she said to herself, "he never loved me, for he is unable to understand me and scorns me!"

At that moment Lothar made his appearance in the arbour; he forced his unhappy sister to tell him why she was weeping, for he loved her with boundless affection. Two minutes after he was on Nathanael's heels, and reproached him bitterly; the other made violent reply. They exchanged dreadful provocations, and finally agreed to meet in a duel at daybreak next morning behind the wall of the garden. All the rest of the day they remained dark and speechless in each other's presence. But Clara had guessed everything, she had seen the duelling swords being furbished; she trembled to think of the danger that might tear from her

her brother and her betrothed as well. At the appointed hour the naked swords lay on the sward they were meant to redden with blood. Lothar and Nathanael had already thrown aside their coats, their eyes flashed fire and their mouths were filled with threats; they were on the point of engaging when Clara flung herself all dishevelled between them, crying, "Kill me, since it is for me you are going to murder one another; and whichever of you may be the one to fall in this dreadful duel, I swear I will not survive him!" Her brother hurled his sword away, and Nathanael threw himself at Clara's feet. "Dear angel, forgive me," he said, weeping, "you too, Lothar, forgive me; I am in fault towards both of you! But you know whether I love you, my tears and my repentance are full proof!" The brother and sister joined in raising him up, and they all three mingled their tears and their renewed vows of eternal affection.

From this day, Nathanael felt his heart eased to some extent. The affection of those he loved had driven from his brain part of the fumes and vapours that vexed it. He spent three days more with them before returning to G. for his final year of study at the university, after which he was to settle down permanently in his native town at the side of his beloved.

Nathanael's mother knew nothing of the disorder wrought by the memory of Coppelius in her son's mind. This unhappy secret had been sedulously concealed from her to spare her distress, for she had never ceased to grieve for her husband's death; and the mere name of Coppelius uttered in her presence would have been an agony to her.

II

Nathanael on his return to G. found the house where he had lodged burned to the ground; there was nothing of it left but two or three stumps of walls blackened and calcined by the flames. The fire had broken out in an apothecary's workshop. A number of Nathanael's friends, who lived close to the scene of disaster, had saved his clothes, his scientific instruments, his papers, and deposited them under lock and key in another room which they hired in his name. This room was situated over against the apartment of Professor Spalanzani. From its window the eye could readily see into the room where, when the curtains were open, Olympia might often be observed, silent and sitting in an unchanging posture. Nathanael was at first astonished at this immobility she maintained for hours together at her little table. The contemplation of this magnificent creature had an electric effect on Nathanael. But the faithful love of Clara filled his soul and preserved him against the charms of the austere Olympia; and thus it was only at intervals that our friend threw a few almost casual glances in the direction of the retreat occupied by that lovely statue. He was writing a long letter to his betrothed, when he suddenly became aware of the unpleasant figure of Coppola. A nervous shudder ran through him; but presently, recalling Clara's arguments and the details he had heard from Professor Spalanzani with regard to Coppola, he was almost ashamed of his first dismay, and in a voice as calm as he could contrive he said to his unwelcome visitor: "My friend, I never buy barometers; will you kindly go to the deuce."

But Coppola, taking no notice of this dismissal, entered the room, and fixing eyes full of sinister fire on the student replied: "I have not only barometers, I have also eyes, lovely eyes!" "What, eyes!" cried Nathanael, "accursed madman, how can you have eyes?" "There you are," replied the hawker, opening his pack, and taking out a collection of spectacles of all sizes and all colours. He went on laying out more and more till the table was covered with them. Poor Nathanael imagined thousands of fantastic eyes staring at him on every hand; the more spectacles Coppola produced, as though bringing them out from an inexhaustible store, the greater was our poor student's agitation. Suddenly he could contain himself no longer, and sprang upon the hawker, who fell back in terror, huddled all his spectacles back into his bundle, crying, "For pity's sake, my dear sir, what are you doing? If these glasses are not what you want, that's no reason to throttle me. Perhaps you would rather have lorgnettes. Here are some for every taste." As soon as the spectacles had gone back in the bag, Nathanael became calm once more as though by magic. The new articles that Coppola showed him had no disturbing influence on him whatever. Vexed at his loss of self-control, he determined to buy something from the hawker to make up for his violence; he chose a very small lorgnette of exquisite workmanship, and to try it levelled it at the room in which Olympia Spalanzani was seated in her usual place. For the first time he saw her features close at hand; the sight threw him into a long trance, from which he was roused only by the noise Coppola made tapping his foot on the floor. *"Tre zecchini"* (three ducats) repeated the prosaic mechanic *ad nauseam*. Nathanael made haste to pay him, and Coppola backed out of the room with innumerable bowings and thankings, but no sooner had he reached the stairs than he gave vent to a gross burst of laughter. "This thieving dog," said Nathanael to himself, "has made me pay ten times too much for his lorgnette, and is laughing at his victim." He tossed the thing aside to finish his letter to Clara, but hardly had he resumed his pen when the image of Olympia intervened to distract his mind to an excessive degree; he got up once more and fixed his eyes on the window of her room. And so he continued in a kind of daze till the moment when his friend Siegmund came to fetch him to Professor Spalanzani's lecture.

From that moment the curtains of Olympia's room remained closely drawn; the love-sick student lost his time and his trouble in two whole days spent like a sentry at watch, lorgnette in hand, in his window. On the third his brain was on fire. Seized by a kind of delirium, he ran out of the city. Olympia's figure seemed to multiply itself around him as though by enchantment; he saw it hovering in air like a snowy mist, gleaming through the flowery hedges and mirrored in the crystal brooks. Poor Clara was utterly forgotten! Nathanael went along at random, eyes uplifted to the sky, and with sobs in his voice he cried, "O my star of love, why dost thou leave me thus alone on earth? Far from thee my days turn drab and my life withers like a flower under the desert sun!"

When Nathanael returned to his lodging, there was a great to-do in Spalanzani's. The doors were opened, the windows had been taken off their hinges; many workmen were coming and going, carrying furniture, nailing up hangings and plying hammers with extraordinary activity. His friend Siegmund informed our hero that Professor Spalanzani was giving a great ball next day to all the *élite* of the university, and that on this occasion Miss Olympia would make her first appearance in society.

Nathanael found an invitation awaiting him in his lodgings. How great was his joy when at the appointed hour he made his way into the brilliantly lighted drawing-room, where the best society of the little city was already gathered around the learned professor. Olympia was dressed with exquisite taste and magnificence. Everybody admired her beauty, and no one could find any fault with her admirable shape, except for a slightly exaggerated curve in the waist, which seemed to be due to an excess of pressure by her corset. This beautiful person had a stately way of walking; but there was a touch of stiffness in it that was put down to her natural shyness. She took her place at the harpsichord, and sang a national song then very popular, with a sonorous and vibrant tone like that of a harmonica.*

Nathanael gazed on her in a kind of ecstasy; but as he had come a little late, or had not been able to make his way into the front of the crowd, he took from his pocket Coppola's little lorgnette and discreetly levelled it at the charming features of Olympia. Immediately a sort of delirium took hold upon him. It seemed to him that Spalanzani's lovely daughter fixed upon him looks filled with voluptuous languor; her singing assumed in his ear all the sublime inflexions of an echo from heaven; then a cloud passed before his eyes; his imagination lost itself in the most distant spheres of the ideal; for a moment he fancied he felt about his neck the warm clasp of two amorous arms, and exclaimed, "Olympia! Olympia!" Some of the guests who were near Nathanael turned and laughed in his face; but he took no heed. After the concert came the ball. To dance with this masterpiece of beauty would be the highest possible peak of happiness. But how was he to dare to invite her? How indeed? I cannot tell; but the fact is that after a very few moments Nathanael was seen bowing very low before Miss Olympia. A cold perspiration bedewed his brow when with the tips of his fingers he lightly touched those of Olympia. The girl's hand was icy like the hand of a corpse. Nathanael lifted his eyes to hers, and found in

* Harmonica: a set of glass or metal pieces, played by striking with a mallet.—Ed.

them the same languorous fixity; he forgot his impression of timid surprise, and placing a supple arm about the waist of the queen of the ball he took the floor among the crowd of the waltzers, turning about with infinite grace. Miss Olympia waltzed with a rhythm and precision that shamed all the girls of the little city. When he had brought her back to her place, Nathanael, like a lovesick hero, would willingly have sought a quarrel with anyone who might have taken into his head to invite her to dance, but the gravity of the place and of the people present happily restrained him. He had sat down beside Olympia, and taking her hand in his own he spoke to her of his love in delicate but burning words. The virtuous young lady made him no answer save with a guttural monosyllable sufficiently hard to reproduce, "Ach! ach! ach!" and that was all. And Nathanael, losing his head, said to her, "O woman, worthy of the love of the angels! Chaste reflection of the happiness of the blessed! Let your gentle eyes fall on me!" But to all that Miss Olympia replied only with her eternal "Ach! ach! ach!"

During this remarkable conversation Professor Spalanzani several times passed before our lovers, smiling strangely on them the while. Gradually, despite his preoccupation, Nathanael perceived that the blaze of the lights was decreasing. The tapers in the drawing-room were one after another dying out; the music and dancing had long since ceased; the guests had gone. "O God!" said Nathanael, "must we leave one another already, and shall I be allowed to see you again, my angel?" He bowed over Olympia's hands to cover them with kisses. But the chill of death met his lips—he shivered from head to foot. "Olympia," he said in a broken voice, "Olympia, do you love me?" Olympia rose up as though moved by a spring, and answered as always, "Ach! ach! ach!" And she began to walk away, followed by Nathanael, who ceaselessly repeated his emphatic declarations. Olympia stopped in front of Spalanzani, who said to the student, "My dear sir, since you take so much pleasure in my daughter's conversation, your visits will always be very welcome to us." Nathanael thought the heavens had opened upon him, and went away wild with love and joy.

Long was Doctor Spalanzani's ball the theme of all gossiping, and in particular the object of severe criticism. Some found fault with numbers of solecisms that had not escaped them, and which betrayed the Professor's ignorance of good society; the others, the great majority, discussed the imperfections of Miss Olympia; all agreed in finding her stupid, which offered sufficient justification for the care Spalanzani had taken to keep her out of sight so long. Nathanael heard this sort of talk with great wrath, but dared not burst out with it, for fear of compromising his beloved, and seeing her door shut in his face. One day Siegmund said to him: "My dear brother, how can a reasonable man fall in love, as you have done, with a doll that can't say a word?" Nathanael replied with outward calm: "How can a young man with such excellent eyes have failed to see all the visible and hidden charms and treasures in the person of Olympia? All the better, my brother, that you have not seen all this, for you would love the lady with a fervour like mine; and I feel that I could not live alongside a rival, were he my best friend!"

Siegmund grasped that Nathanael's head was gravely affected, and accordingly sought to bring him back to less aggressive notions. "Beauty," he said, "is a matter of convention: caprice often has more to say to it than any reality. But does it not seem strange to you that all our comrades pass the same judgment on Olympia? Even if this woman has a great many beautiful features and physical attractions, can it be denied, when one has examined her closely, that her eye is empty and that every movement seems the effect of a mechanism? She sings, she plays with perfect rhythm; but it is always the same song with the same accompaniment; her dancing is mechanical and uniform. That is what I have seen, what we have all seen; I conclude from it that your Olympia is a supernatural creature whose secret will one day be revealed to us." Nathanael made a fresh effort to contain himself. "You are all," he said to Siegmund, "nothing but prosaic creatures; all the loveliness and charm in Olympia is revealed to me alone, because I am the only one with sufficiently sensitive faculties to appreciate the treasure fate offered to me. I can conceive that she may not please you; for she has no part or lot in your insipid conversations. The few words she lets fall from her lips are to me like hieroglyphs from the inner world where souls reside; but you know nothing of all that." "Quite true," replied Siegmund, "and so I leave you to your dreams; but if ever you come to need, in the real world to which you will descend sooner or later, the services of a friend, remember me. Adieu!" Nathanael seemed touched by his friend's last words, and the two young men, before parting, exchanged a cordial grasp of the hand.

Clara, kind good Clara, was as much forgotten as though she had never existed. Lothar had likewise vanished from Nathanael's memory. The poor fellow spent all his days at Olympia's side; he came and recited to her verses, poems, ballads, treatises of psychology, without end. The beauty listened to it all with a patience and impassiveness that were fantastic. She looked at her lover with her two black eyes that never changed; when Nathanael, carried away by passion, fell on his knees and kissed her hands or her lips, she always said "Ach! ach! ach!" and when he was leaving to go home she would add, "Good night, my beloved!" These few words opened to Nathanael the whole world of Platonic loves; he imagined that he thought and acted and felt for Olympia, and he admired the power of love that had drawn to itself the soul and the faculties of Olympia. Sometimes he had lucid moments, and then he would think of the strange immobility of the girl; but he would say to himself immediately, "What are words? Empty sounds that break upon the ear and vanish; Olympia's look says more than all the eloquence of men!"

Professor Spalanzani seemed to take an extraordinary interest in his daughter's relations with Nathanael; he lavished signs of the most cordial goodwill on the student. One day our hero, armed with all his resolution to strike a decided blow, determined that he would, without further delay, and with all suitable gravity, request the honour of aspiring to Olympia's hand. To be more sure of his hopes, he thought it necessary in the first place to address a positive declaration to the lady of his thoughts; and to set the seal of greater ceremony upon it, he looked through a casket for a gold ring, a gift from his mother, which he wished to place on Olympia's finger as a betrothal pledge. First of all in the casket he came upon the letters of Lothar and Clara, tossed them aside impatiently, found the ring and hastened to the professor's house.

When he had reached the head of the stair he heard a terrific hubbub in Spalanzani's apartment. Through the trampling of feet, the clinking of metal, the noise of violent battering against the walls of the house, he distinguished two voices bellowing dreadful imprecations.

"Let go, scoundrel!" "Would you dare to rob me of my

blood and my life?" "It is my best-loved handiwork!" "It was I who made the eyes!" "And I made the springs of the works!" "Go to the devil, accursed clock-maker!" "Satan, stop! Hell-hound, give me my own!" "Ha! ha! ha!" These two dreadful voices belonged to Spalanzani and Coppelius. Nathanael, quite beside himself, drove in the door with a kick, and dashed into the room in the thick of the fray. The professor had hold of the shoulders, the Italian Coppola had hold of the legs, of a woman they were furiously tugging at between them.

"Horror!" cried Nathanael, "it is Olympia!" He was leaping at the throat of Coppola, when the latter, as strong as Hercules, with a last convulsive tug forced his antagonist to let go; picking up the woman in his powerful arms, he let fly so fierce a blow with her on the professor's head that the poor man, almost stunned, fell his whole length on the floor ten paces away, smashing in his fall a table covered with a mass of flasks, retorts, alembics, and instruments. Profiting by this disorder Coppola threw Olympia across his shoulders and disappeared, laughing like a devil; all the way downstairs they could hear Olympia's legs clattering on the steps with a sound like castanets.

Olympia's head had remained on the battlefield. With terror Nathanael perceived a wax face, the enamel eyes were broken. The wretched Spalanzani was lying in the midst of splinters of glass that had cut his arms and his face and his breast to pieces. "Coppelius! Coppelius!" he cried in a voice of agonized distress. "Accursed thief! you are robbing me of the fruit of twenty years' study and work! But no matter, I have taken the eyes! Yes, there they are!" Thereupon Nathanael saw at his feet two blood-stained eyes staring fixedly at him. Spalanzani picked them up and threw them full in his breast. Immediately Nathanael,

seized with a fit of madness, began to cry out the most incoherent nonsense, and hurling himself at the professor
would have choked him to death if the neighbours had not
rushed in and seized the student. They had to tie him up
tight to avert a disaster. They took him away to the hos-
pital for the insane, and his friend Siegmund accompanied
him in tears.

The famous Professor Spalanzani recovered in a short
time, for none of his hurts was at all serious. But directly
he could travel he was obliged to leave the city; all the
students of the university who had been witnesses to the
hoax played on Nathanael had sworn to wreak a terrible
vengeance on the Italian mechanic who had had the im-
pertinence to employ a mannequin to make fools of real
persons so estimable as the inhabitants and the students of
the good town of G. A number of legal minds had proposed to bring a criminal action against Spalanzani as responsible for the madness that had torn Nathanael from the
bosom of society. But the professor had gone away in time,
and no one ever again saw Giuseppe Coppola, the seller of
barometers, spectacles, and lorgnettes.

When after anxious nursing Nathanael came back to
sound mind, he seemed to himself to be awakened out of a
long nightmare. He found himself in his paternal home;
his mother, kind Clara, and Lothar were all weeping round
his bed. The moment his eyes opened Clara was the first
to speak. "You are restored to us, my beloved! you have
been healed by our care of a dreadful malady." "Clara!
Clara!" murmured Nathanael, sending an astonished look
round all the objects in the room, as if he were endeavouring to remember something. Siegmund, who had refused
to leave his sick friend, came into the room and clasped
him by the hand. A few days of peaceful convalescence

completed the cure. When the student was perfectly recovered he was informed that an old uncle, who while he
was alive had always seemed wretchedly poor and miserly,
had just died, leaving his heirs a considerable property in
the country not far from the town, with a comfortably
furnished strong-box. The whole family proposed to go
and take up its abode here in serene retirement. The day
was fixed for this new installation, and before departing
they went here and there in the city to make the last pur-
chases, so that they need not come back for a long time.
As they were crossing the square before the church, "My
dearest beloved," said Clara, "would you not like us to go
up the tower to look once again at the view over the mountains and the distant forests?" Nathanael thought it a
charming idea, and the pair went up by themselves; the
old mother took her way back to their house, and Lothar,
not so eager to clamber up two or three hundred steps,
waited for them at the bottom of the tower.

The two lovers, leaning over the balustrade of the belfry, intoxicated themselves with the poetic spectacle that
was spread before their eyes. The tops of the great trees
were bending like waves of a green sea, and the mountains
stood out on the deep blue of the sky like silhouettes of
grey ghosts.

"Look," cried the girl, "do look at that grey clump
yonder; you would say it is moving, coming in our direction." Nathanael, less keen of eye, mechanically felt in his
pocket for Coppola's lorgnette. No sooner had he directed
it towards the plain beneath than he sprang up like a tiger
with a hoarse cry of fury: Olympia had been in front of
the lens of the fatal lorgnette. Nathanael's brain seemed to
burn. He stared fixedly at Clara; then his eyes rolled all
bloodshot in their sockets. "Mannequin! Mannequin from

hell!" he shrieked, "go back to the devil that created you!" Then he seized Clara with convulsive strength and made to fling her down from the tower. The poor child, half dead with terror, clung to the balustrade with the strength of despair. Fortunately, Lothar heard her screams; conjecturing some terrible mishap, he darted up the twisting stairway and reached the platform at the very moment when Clara had fainted and was being thrust out overy the abyss. He was just in time to snatch his sister back, and in order to make Nathanael loosen his hold he fetched him a furious blow on the head that made him stagger and spin round like a top. Lothar went down the stairs with his precious burden, seemingly deserted by life. As for Nathanael, he began to run round the platform like a maniac, leaping and dancing in the most dangerous fashion and uttering wild yells that collected a terror-stricken crowd. Among the curious spectators there suddenly appeared the lawyer Coppelius, who had just entered the town. A few of the people prepared to climb the tower and take hold of the madman, whose wild agitation made the onlookers tremble. "Pooh!" said Coppelius, "leave him alone: he will come down by himself all right!" And as he watched, openmouthed, the gyrations of Nathanael, the latter, who at that moment leaned over the balustrade, caught sight of him, and uttering a wild yell of diabolical laughter flung himself headlong.

He was taken up with his head shattered to pieces. Coppelius disappeared in the crowd.

✹ The Mad Veteran of Fort Ratonneau

by ACHIM VON ARNIM

Ludwig Joachim (abbreviated to Achim) von Arnim was born in Berlin in 1781. At Halle and Göttingen he studied law and natural science, but he fell in with the Romantic poet Clemens Brentano, married his blue-stocking sister, and was diverted to literature. Still popular is his collection of folk-poetry, *Des Knaben Wunderhorn.* He died in 1831.

Our example, *Der tolle Invalide des Fort Ratonneau* (1818), is probably his best-known short story. It is based on an actual occurrence in 1765. The real Fort Ratonneau stands on one of a group of islands offshore from Marseilles. But von Arnim's fort, in defiance of the topographical facts, is placed on an eminence in the city, commanding a navigable river. The translation is by Morris Bishop.

ONE COLD, STORMY OCTOBER EVENING Count Durand, the good old commandant of Marseilles, sat alone and freezing before an ill-furnished hearth in his splendid official quarters. He kept edging closer and closer to the fire, while in the street below carriages were rattling on their way to some great ball, and in the anteroom his orderly, Basset, who was at the same time his dearest companion, was loudly snoring. "Even in southern France it isn't always warm," thought the old gentleman, shaking his head. "And people here don't remain always young; and the social whirl has as little concern for old age as architecture has for winter." What should he do at a ball with his wooden leg, though he was commander of all the veterans garrisoning Marseilles and its forts? (All this was during the Seven Years' War.) Even the lieutenants of his regiment were too old and unfit for dancing. On the other hand, here at the hearth, it seemed to him, his wooden leg was very useful, as without rousing Basset he could use it to poke into the fire, bit by bit, the supply of green olive branches laid at his side. Such a fire has great charm; the crackling flames are as if interwoven with green foliage; the leaves, half green, half burned, look like hearts consumed with love. The old gentleman thought thereupon of his blooming youth; and he meditated on the construction of the fireworks which, long before, he had devised for the Court; and he speculated on new, variegated devices of color and movement, with which he proposed to dazzle the Marseillais on the king's birthday. He seemed as distraught as if he had attended the ball. But in the joy of creation, seeing everything flash, bang, crackle, then all blaze forth again in silent immensity, he had kept putting more and more olive branches on the fire and had not noticed that his wooden leg had caught fire and that already a third of it had been consumed. Only now, when he was stirred to spring up because the grand finale, the bursting of a thousand rockets, inflamed his soaring imagination, did he realize, as he fell back in his easy chair, that his wooden leg was shortened and the stump was a prey to eager flames. Unable, at need, to rise, with his blazing leg he propelled the chair backward like a sled into the middle of the room, and shouted first for his servant and then for water.

At this moment a woman sprang forward to bring him aid and to take charge. She had been admitted to the room, and had tried to attract the commandant's attention with timid coughs, but without success. She tried to beat out the flames with her apron, but the glowing cinders of the leg set her apron afire. The commandant, now in a real emergency, called out for someone to come to his aid.

Some passers-by rushed in from the street, and Basset awoke. The burning leg and burning apron roused a general laugh; but with the first bucket of water that Basset fetched from the kitchen all the fire was extinguished, and the people from the street departed. The poor woman was dripping wet; she could not recover immediately from her fright. The commandant had her draped in his warm greatcoat and ordered a glass of strong wine for her. But she would take nothing; she merely sobbed over her mishap, and begged the commandant to accord her a few words in private. So he dismissed his negligent servant and sat down cautiously beside her.

"Oh, my husband will be out of his wits when he hears this story!" she exclaimed in a strange German-accented French. "Oh, my poor husband! Now certainly the devil is playing him another of his tricks!" The commandant inquired about him; the woman told him that precisely on account of her dear husband she had come to him, bearing a letter from the colonel of the Picardy regiment. The commandant put on his spectacles, recognized the crest of his friend, and ran through the letter. Then he said: "So, you are this Lilie, born Demoiselle Rosalie in Leipzig, who married Sergeant Francoeur, when he lay a prisoner with a head-wound in Leipzig? I must say, that's an unusual love story! What were your parents like? Didn't they put any obstacles in the way? And what kind of peculiar kinks did he get from his head wound that made him unfit for active service, though he was regarded as the bravest and most competent sergeant, the very soul of the regiment?"

"Your Honor," replied the woman, in a new access of grief, "my love is responsible for all his misfortune. It is I who made my husband unhappy; it was not the wound.

My love brought the devil into him, to plague him and disturb his wits. Sometimes, instead of drilling the soldiers, he begins to take tremendous jumps before them, with the devil's aid, and wants them to imitate him. Or he makes terrible faces at them that frighten them to death, and insists that they must remain perfectly unmoved. And lately the last straw was that in a certain action the commanding general gave the order for the regiment to retreat, and my husband pushed the general off his horse, took his place, and led the regiment to capture a battery."

"A devil of a fellow!" cried the commandant. "If we had such a devil to inspire all our commanding generals, we shouldn't fear another defeat like that of Rossbach! If your love works such deviltry, I only wish you were in love with our whole army!"

"Alas, my love bears my mother's curse," sighed the woman. "I never knew my father. My mother had many men around her. I had to wait on them; that was all I had to do. I was a dreamy girl; I paid no attention to the advances of these men; my mother protected me against their importunities. The war scattered most of the men who visited my mother and gambled secretly in her house. We led a solitary life, much to her annoyance. She hated friend and foe equally; I was not allowed to give anything to those who passed, wounded and hungry, before our house. This made me very sorry. And once I was alone in the house, getting our lunch ready, when many carts full of wounded passed below. I knew by their talk that they were Frenchmen, captured by the Prussians. I longed to take down the prepared food to them, but I was afraid of my mother. However, when I saw Francoeur lying with a bandaged head in the last cart, I don't know how it happened, but I forgot my mother, took a bowl of stew and a spoon, and without locking our door, I ran after the cart to Pleissenburg. I found him; he had already descended. I addressed myself boldly to the warden, and promptly succeeded in getting the best straw bed for the wounded man. When he was settled upon it, what bliss it was to hand the sufferer his stew! His eyes brightened; he swore to me that I had a radiance about my head. I answered that it was my coif, which had become disarranged and had touched him. He said that the holy radiance came out of my eyes! Oh, I could never forget those words, and if he hadn't already possessed my heart, for that I would have had to offer it to him."

"That was a very true and pretty remark," said the commandant.

Rosalie continued: "It was the sweetest hour of my life. I looked at him ever more ardently, because he insisted that it did him good. And when finally he put a little ring on my finger I felt richer than I had ever been before. In this happy moment of silence my mother came in, scolding and cursing. I can't repeat the names she called me, but I felt no shame, for I knew well that I was guiltless and that he would believe nothing evil of me. She tried to drag me away, but he held me fast and told her that we were engaged. I was already wearing his ring. How my mother's face was distorted! It looked to me as if fire were coming out of her throat; her eyes contracted till they seemed all white; she cursed me and consigned me solemnly to the devil. And as a brilliant light had gleamed in my eyes in the morning when I had caught sight of Francoeur, so now it seemed that a black bat had spread its transparent wings over my eyes. The world was half hidden from me; I was no longer in possession of myself. My heart despaired, and yet I was forced to laugh. 'Listen to that! The devil is already laughing within you!' said my mother. She went out in triumph, while I fell back in a faint. When I came to myself I did not dare to go to her and leave the wounded man, who had been badly shaken by the incident; indeed I was inwardly furious with my mother for the setback she had caused the wretched fellow.

"Not till three days later did I slip out by night to our house, without a word to Francoeur. I did not dare to knock; but finally a woman who had worked for us came out. She told me that my mother had sold off all her goods in haste and had gone off, no one knew where, with a strange gentleman, presumably a gambler. So now I was cast off by everyone, and I was quite pleased to be thus relieved of all concern and free to fall into Francoeur's arms. My girl friends in the city, even, would have nothing more to do with me, and so I could nurse him and live for him alone. I worked for him; till then I had played with lace-bobbins merely for my own adornment; now I was not ashamed to sell my handiwork. This brought him some comfort and refreshment. But I couldn't help thinking of my mother, except when he diverted me with his vivid stories. My mother kept appearing to my imagination, black, with blazing eyes, forever cursing; and I couldn't get rid of her. I wouldn't say anything to my Francoeur, in order not to distress him. I complained of headaches which I didn't have, of toothaches which I didn't feel, in order to give vent to my pressing tears. Oh, if I had only trusted him more, I wouldn't have caused his misfortune! But whenever I tried to tell him that I thought I was possessed by the devil through my mother's curse, the devil shut my mouth. Also I was afraid that then he would no longer be able to love me, that he would leave me; I could hardly survive the mere thought of it. This inward torment, perhaps also overwork, finally broke down my health. Dreadful spasms, which I concealed from him, threatened to choke me; and medicines just seemed to make my illness worse. As soon as he was on his feet again he arranged our wedding. An old cleric made a solemn little speech, in which he impressed on my Francoeur all that I had done for him, and recalled how I had sacrificed for him fatherland, well-being, and friends, and had even brought my mother's curse upon me; he concluded that Francoeur must share all these burdens with me, and that we must bear all mischance together. My man shuddered at these words, but he said, 'I do' sharp and clear, and we were married.

"Our first weeks were happy; I felt relieved of half my sorrows, and I didn't immediately realize that half of the curse had been transferred to my husband. But soon he complained that that preacher in his black gown was always present in his thoughts, threatening him, so that he conceived such a violent anger and hostility against clergy, churches, and holy images that he felt bound to curse them, he didn't know why; and to quench these thoughts he yielded to every whim, dancing and drinking, to find relief in this stirring up of the blood. I blamed everything on his captivity, although I suspected indeed that it was the devil who was plaguing him. He was exchanged, thanks to the intervention of his colonel, who sadly missed him in his regiment, for Francoeur is an exceptional soldier.

"With light hearts we left Leipzig and in our talk constructed a bright future. But hardly had we escaped from the deficiency of our daily needs to the comfort of a well-cared-for army in winter quarters, when my husband began to grow more violent. To divert himself he beat a drum all day long, picked quarrels, and brawled. The colonel could not make head or tail of it. Only with me he was gentle as a child. I was delivered of a son when the army again took the field, and with the pains of childbirth the devil who harried me seemed to be entirely conjured away. Francoeur became ever more unruly and violent. The colonel wrote me that he was as foolhardy as a madman, but so far he had always been lucky. His comrades thought that he was sometimes out of his head; the colonel feared he would have to put him on sick leave or on the retired list. The colonel had a certain regard for me; he listened to my pleas, until finally my husband's insurrection against the commanding general of the division, which I have already related, put him under arrest. Then the surgeon reported that he was suffering from mental derangement caused by the head wound, which had been neglected during his captivity, and he must spend at least two years in a warm climate in one of the veterans' corps, to see if perhaps his affliction would pass away. He was told that in punishment for his offense he was being transferred to the veterans; he left his regiment with curses. I begged the colonel for this letter, and I decided to tell you everything frankly, so that he might not be judged according to the rigor of the law, but in consideration of his misfortune, which was caused solely by my love, and in the hope that you might put him, for his own good, in some small isolated place, so that he won't cause talk among the people in this big city. But, your Honor, a woman who has done you a small service today must ask your word of honor that you will keep inviolate this secret of his illness, which he himself does not suspect, and which would only offend his pride."

"My hand on it!" cried the commandant, who had listened to the devoted wife with a kindly spirit. "And what

is more, I will listen to your petition three times, if Francoeur plays any more of his stupid tricks. But the best
thing is to avoid them, and therefore I am sending him immediately as relief to a fort which needs a garrison of only
three men. You will have there comfortable quarters for
you and your child; and he will find little inducement for
follies, and those he does commit will be kept quiet."

The woman thanked the old gentleman for all his kind
dispositions. She kissed his hand, and in return he lighted
her way as, with many curtseys, she descended the stairs.
This surprised Basset, the old orderly; he wondered what
had got into the old man, whether he could possibly have
conceived for the fire-extinguishing lady some attachment
which might be prejudicial to his own influence. Now the
old gentleman had the habit of reviewing aloud all the
events of the day, when he could not sleep at night, as if
he had to make his confession to his bed. And when the
carriages returning from the ball rumbled past, Basset
lurked in the next room and listened to the whole conversation, which struck him all the more as Francoeur came
from his own region and served in the same regiment as
himself, though Basset was much older than Francoeur.
And now he thought of a monk of his acquaintance, a
specialist in casting out devils. Basset proposed soon to introduce Francoeur to him; he had a great affection for
quacks, and was delighted at the prospect of seeing a devil
expelled.

Rosalie, well satisfied with the outcome of her visit, slept
well. In the morning she bought a new apron, and arrayed
in this she went to meet her husband, who was marching
his tired veterans into the city to the accompaniment of
ghastly singing. He kissed her, hoisted her up in the air,
and said: "You smell of the burning of Troy! I have you

again, fair Helen!" Rosalie blushed; she thought it necessary to respond fully to his questions, and told him that she
had gone to see the colonel about their quarters, that his
leg had actually caught fire, and that her apron had been
burnt. He was annoyed that she had not waited for his
arrival, but he forgot all that in a thousand jokes about the
burning apron. Thereupon he presented his men to the
commandant, and praised all their physical shortcomings
and spiritual virtues so astutely that he quite gained the
good will of the old gentleman, who thought to himself:
"The woman loves him, but she is German and doesn't
understand any Frenchman; a Frenchman always has the
devil in him!" He had Francoeur admitted to his room, to
make his better acquaintance, and found him well informed
about fortification; but what specially pleased the commandant was his discovery in the soldier of an enthusiast for
fireworks, who had organized all sorts of pyrotechnical
displays for his regiment. The commandant revealed to him
his new invention for a fireworks show on the king's birthday. Francoeur entered into the project, interrupted by
the leg-burning of the previous day, with rousing enthusiasm. Now the old man revealed to him that with two other
veterans he should relieve the garrison of Fort Ratonneau,
where was a great powder magazine, and that there with
his soldiers he should busy himself stuffing rockets, twisting pin-wheels, and tieing firecrackers. But while handing
him the inventory and the key of the powder tower, the
commandant recalled the wife's words, and held the key,
saying: "But the devil has stopped plaguing you, I hope;
you aren't going to get me into trouble?" "Don't paint the
devil on the wall or he'll be your reflection!" answered
Francoeur with an air of assurance. This gave the com-

mandant confidence; he handed over the key, the inventory, and an order to the small occupying garrison to retire. Francoeur was dismissed; on the ground floor Basset fell upon his neck. The two immediately recognized each other; each told the other briefly his news. But since Francoeur was accustomed to obey strictly all military orders, he extricated himself and invited Basset to come next Sunday, his free day, as his guest to Fort Ratonneau, of which he had the honor to be the commandant.

The entry to the fort was cheery for all concerned. The relieved veterans had had more than enough of gazing on the beautiful view over Marseilles, and their replacements were delighted with the prospect, with the elegant structure, and with the comfortable rooms and beds. They bought from the outgoing garrison a couple of goats, a pair of pigeons, a dozen hens, and some devices for capturing game in the neighborhood; for idle soldiers are hunters by nature. When Francoeur assumed his command, he immediately ordered his two soldiers, Brunet and Tessier, to open the powder magazine with him and check the inventory, and then to carry a certain supply to the workshop for firework construction. The inventory was correct; he set one of his men to the task of firework making, and with the other he reviewed all his cannons and mortars, to polish up the brass ones and paint the iron ones black. He loaded a sufficient number of shells and bombs, and disposed all his armament to command the single entry to the fort. "Our fort will never be taken!" he kept crying excitedly. "I will hold the fort, even though a hundred thousand Englishmen land and attack it! But the place has been sloppily kept up."

"Things look the same in all the forts and batteries,"

said Tessier. "The old commandant with his peg leg can't climb up so far; and thank God, the English haven't yet taken it into their heads to make a landing."

"That must all be changed," said Francoeur. "I will burn my tongue out before I surrender, to let our enemies lay Marseilles in ashes, or before I'll show we're afraid of them!"

His wife was obliged to clean grass and moss from the stonework, to whitewash it, and to air the food supplies in the casemates. In the first days there was hardly time for sleep, so hard did the tireless Francoeur drive. In that time his skill accomplished what would have taken anyone else a good month. In this occupation his fantasies left him in peace. He was hasty and touchy, but always for a fixed purpose; and Rosalie blessed the day that had brought him into this higher atmosphere, where the devil seemed to have no power over him. The weather also had turned warm and bright, through a shift of wind, so that a second summer seemed to have greeted them. Every day ships slipped in and out of the harbor, saluting the harbor forts and receiving their salutes. Rosalie, who had never seen the sea, thought she was transported to another world; and her small boy was in bliss, after his long confinement in carts and inns. He enjoyed complete freedom in the small enclosed garden, which the previous occupants had adorned, in the manner of soldiers, especially artillerymen, with artistic geometrical designs in boxwood. Above fluttered the fleur-de-lys flag, Francoeur's pride, a significant symbol to his wife, whose first name was Lilie, and the special joy of the child.

Thus came their first Sunday, blessed by all. Francoeur ordered his wife to prepare something out of the ordinary for the midday meal, as he was expecting his friend Basset.

In particular, he stipulated a good omelette, for the fort's hens were busily laying; and he also deposited in the kitchen a number of wild birds that Brunet had shot. In the midst of these preparations Basset arrived, out of breath. He was delighted with the transformation of the fort. As commissioned by the commandant, he inquired about the fireworks; he was amazed at the great number of prepared rockets and star-shells. The wife went about her kitchen tasks; the two soldiers went out to pick some fruit for the dessert. All were determined to make a day of it, and to read aloud the newspaper that Basset had brought with him. Now Basset seated himself in the garden opposite Francoeur and stared at him silently. Francoeur asked his reason. "I was just thinking," said Basset, "that you look as well as ever, and that everything you do is so reasonable."

"Who doubts that, I'd like to know," said Francoeur, angrily. Basset tried to dodge the question, but there was something terrifying in Francoeur's manner; his dark eyes flashed, his head straightened up, his lips protruded. Poor Basset's heart sank at his own blabbing; he spoke in a thin voice like a muted fiddle of rumors in the commandant's quarters that Francoeur was plagued by the devil, and of his own good intention to have Francoeur exorcised by a monk, Father Philip, whom he had bidden to come before dinner under the pretext of saying mass in the little chapel for the garrison, deprived of sacred services. Francoeur was enraged at this report; he swore that he would take a bloody revenge on anyone who had told such lies about him; he knew nothing about the devil, and had no reason to suppose there was any such person, for he had never had the honor of making his acquaintance. Basset said that he was not guilty; he had learned of the matter when the commandant was talking to himself, and apparently this devil was the cause of Francoeur's dismissal from his regiment. "And who brought this news to the commandant?" asked Francoeur, shaking with rage. "Your wife," answered Basset. "But with the best of intentions, in order to excuse you, if you should play any of your wild tricks here."

"I'm done with her!" shouted Francoeur, smiting himself on the head. "She has betrayed me, destroyed me! She tells secrets to the commandant! She has done a lot for me and suffered much, but she has brought me endless trouble! I owe her nothing further! Now we part!"

Gradually he grew outwardly more calm, as his inward fury increased. He brooded on the image of the black-clad cleric, as a man bitten by a mad dog sees forever the dog in his mind's eye. Then Father Philip entered the garden; Francoeur stepped impetuously forward to ask his business. The monk thought best to bring his exorcising powers into play, and sharply accosted the devil, while his hands traced in air the lines of the cross above Francoeur's head. All this infuriated Francoeur, who, as commandant of the fort, ordered him to begone immediately. But Philip, undismayed, confronted all the more boldly the devil in Francoeur. When he went so far as to raise his staff, Francoeur's military pride could not endure the threat. With the strength of rage he seized Philip by his gown and threw him over the grilled entrance gate, and had the good man's robe not caught on the spikes and left him dangling, he would have got a bad fall down the stone steps.

Near this gate the table had been set out, and this reminded Francoeur of dinner. He called for food, and Rosalie brought it. She was somewhat flushed with her cooking, but she was in very high spirits, for she did not notice the monk outside the gate. He had hardly recovered from his first shock and was praying silently, to avert new perils. Nor did she notice that her husband and Basset were staring at the table, the one moodily, the other in confusion. She asked about the two soldiers, but Francoeur said: "They can eat afterward. I am so hungry I could tear the world to pieces." She then dished out the soup, giving Basset, out of politeness, the larger portion. Then she went back to her kitchen to cook the omelette.

"How did the commandant like my wife?" asked Francoeur.

"Very well," answered Basset. "He wished he had been as lucky in his captivity as you were."

"He shall have her! She asked about the two soldiers who are absent; she didn't even ask what I wanted. She tried to win you over, as the commandant's servant; that's why she filled your plate to overflowing. She offered you the biggest glass of wine; and take notice, she'll bring you the biggest piece of omelette. If that happens, I'll take my stand; out she goes, to leave me here alone."

Basset tried to answer, but at that moment the wife entered with the omelette. She had already cut it into three pieces. She went to Basset and put a piece on his plate, saying: "You won't get a better omelette than that at the commandant's! You must give me credit!" Francoeur looked sourly at the serving dish. The empty gap was almost as big as the two remaining pieces. He stood up and said: "There's nothing else for it; we have parted!" With these words he went to the powder magazine, opened the iron doors, entered, and shut them behind him. The wife stared after him in distress and dropped the dish. "Dear God, the devil is plaguing him! If only he doesn't contrive some mischief in the powder magazine!"

"Is that the powder magazine?" cried Basset. "He'll

blow himself up! Save yourself and your child!" With
these words he ran out. The monk likewise did not dare to
venture in again, but ran after him. Rosalie hurried into the
dwelling for her child and snatched him from sleep in his
cradle. She knew not what she was doing; instinctively, as
she had once followed Francoeur, now she fled from him
with her child, saying to herself: "My child, I'm doing this
only for your sake; for me, it would be better to die with
him. Hagar, you did not suffer as I do, for now I am casting out myself!" A prey to such thoughts, she took the
wrong path down the hill, and stopped at the marshy bank
of the river. Out of weariness she could go no farther, and
so she seated herself in a small boat drawn part way up the
bank. In this, easily dislodged, she let herself drift downstream. Hearing a shot in the harbor, she did not dare look
around, but thought that the fort was blown up, and half
of her life destroyed. And so she lapsed gradually into a
feverish, semi-conscious state.

Meanwhile the two soldiers, loaded with apples and
grapes, had approached the fort. But "Back!" shouted
Francoeur in his loud voice, and a bullet from a flint-lock
whistled over their heads. He announced through a speaking-trumpet: "I will talk to you from the high wall; but I
am in command here alone, and I plan to live here alone,
as long as it pleases the devil!" They did not know what
that might mean, but there was nothing to do but yield to
the sergeant's orders. They went down to the steep slope
of the fort, called the high wall. Hardly had they arrived
there when they saw Rosalie's bed and the child's cradle
descending by a rope. Their own beds and equipment followed. Francoeur shouted through the speaking-trumpet:
"Take your own things: and bring the bed, cradle, and
clothes of my runaway wife to the commandant. You'll

find her there. Tell her: 'Satan sends you all this, and this old flag, to cover your shame and that of the commandant!' " Thereupon he threw down the great French flag that had waved over the fort; and he continued: "I hereby declare war on the commandant. He may prepare his weapons until evening; then I shall open fire. He need not spare me, for by the devil I shall not spare him. He may use all his means, but he won't take me. He has given me the key to the powder magazine, and I'll use it. If he tries to capture me, I'll fly with it to heaven, and from heaven to hell. That will raise a dust!" At length Brunet ventured to speak; he shouted up: "Think of our gracious king, your master. Surely you won't rebel against him!" Francoeur answered: "In me resides the king of all the kings of this world! In me is the devil! And in the devil's name I command you not to say a word, or I'll smash you to pieces!" After this threat the two packed up their belongings and left the rest; they knew well that great stones were piled up above, which could shatter everything at the foot of the steep slope.

When the pair arrived at the commandant's quarters in Marseilles, they found him already taking measures, as Basset had given him a full report. He sent the two soldiers to the fort with a cart, to save the wife's goods from the threatening rain, and he sent others to find the woman and her child. Meanwhile he summoned his officers, to discuss with them a course of action. This council of war was chiefly concerned about the possible destruction of the beautiful fort, if it should be blown up. Soon appeared an envoy from the city, where rumors were rife, pointing out that the destruction of the city's finest quarter would be quite unavoidable. It was generally agreed that they should not attempt a full-scale assault, for there was no honor to be gained by subduing one man alone, while enormous losses might be avoided by making concessions. Sleep would finally allay Francoeur's rage, and then a determined band could scale the fort and tie up the defender. Hardly had this decision been reached when the two soldiers who had brought back Rosalie's bed and possessions were admitted. They had a message from Francoeur to deliver: the devil had informed him that they wanted to take him in his sleep; but he warned them, out of love for certain devil's darlings who would be employed on that mission, that he would sleep peacefully in his locked powder magazine with weapons loaded; and before they could break down the doors he would blow up the tower with a shot into the powder kegs. "He is right," said the commandant. "He can't do otherwise; we'll have to starve him out."

"He has got together our stock of supplies for the whole winter," remarked Brunet. "We'll have to wait half a year at least. Besides, he said that the ships bringing in supplies for the city must pay a handsome toll, otherwise he'll sink them to the bottom; and as a token that no one is to slip in by night without his consent, this evening he will send a few shells over the river."

"In fact, he's shooting now!" cried one of the officers. All ran to a window on an upper floor. What a show! At every corner of the fort the cannons opened their fiery jaws, shells whizzed through the air, and in the city yelling mobs rushed for cover. Only a few chose to show their courage by braving the danger. But these were well rewarded, for in brilliant light Francoeur sent up a bundle of rockets from a howitzer and a cluster of star-shells from a mortar, and followed these by countless others fired from muskets. The commandant admitted that the device was excellent; he had never dared to send up rockets from artil-

lery! The effect was unquestionably meteoric, and Francoeur almost deserved a pardon for it.

This nocturnal illumination had another effect that certainly no one could have foreseen—it saved the lives of
Rosalie and her child. Both had fallen asleep in the peaceful
rocking of the boat; and Rosalie dreamed that she saw her
mother lit up and consumed by inward flames. She asked
her mother why she was so tortured; she seemed to hear a
loud voice in answer: "My curse burns me as it does you,
and if you can't release me from it, I remain the victim of
all evil!" The voice tried to continue, but Rosalie was already awakened. She saw above her a cluster of brilliant
bursting star-shells, and she heard close by a sailor's voice
call out: "Hard a-port, or we'll run down a boat with a
woman and child in it." The prow of a big ship rose up
behind her like the gaping jaw of a whale. It swung away,
but her little craft was stove in at the side. "Help my poor
child!" she shouted. A sailor caught her skiff with a boat-
hook and held it fast until, soon after, the ship came to
anchor. "If it hadn't been for the fireworks on Fort Ratonneau," said the sailor, "I wouldn't have seen you and we
would have sunk you without meaning to. What are you
doing so late and alone on the river? And why didn't you
yell at us?" Rosalie promptly answered his questions and
asked urgently to be taken to the commandant's house. Out
of pity the sailor lent her his boy to show her the way.

She found a great commotion at the commandant's. She
begged him to remember his promise, that he would forgive her husband for three offenses. He denied that their
talk had dealt with such offenses as this, but only with his
tricks and pranks, whereas this misdeed was diabolically
serious. "So you are to blame!" said the wife steadfastly,
for she felt herself no longer abandoned by fate. "I made

clear to you my poor man's condition, and yet you trusted
him with such a dangerous post! You promised me secrecy,
and yet you told everything to your servant Basset. With
his foolish craftiness and smartness he has got us into all
this trouble, not my poor husband. You are responsible for
everything; you will have to make your accounting to the
king for it!" The commandant denied that he had said a
word to Basset; the latter admitted that he had listened to
his master's soliloquy, and so all the guilt was deposited on
the commandant's soul. The old man said that he would
have himself shot dead next day in front of the fort, in
order to expiate with his life his guilt before his king. But
Rosalie begged him not to be in too much of a hurry; he
should reflect that she had once rescued him from the fire.

She was assigned a room in the commandant's house; she
put her child to sleep while she meditated and begged God
to reveal how she might save her mother from hell's flames
and her husband from the curse. But she sank, on her
knees, into a deep sleep; and in the morning she was aware
of no dream or inspiration. The commandant, who had
made an early-morning attempt upon the fort, returned
disheartened. To be sure he had lost none of his men, but
Francoeur had sent so many balls whizzing to right and left
and overhead with such accuracy that they owed their
lives only to his forbearance. He had shut off the river with
warning shots, and no one could use the main highway.
In short, all communication with the city was cut off for
the day; and the city threatened that if the commandant did
not proceed circumspectly, and if he should make a full-
scale assault as if in enemy country, the city would call out
its citizens and annihilate the veterans.

Thus for three days the commandant held his hand.
Every evening was enlivened by fireworks; and every

evening Rosalie reminded him of his promises. On the third evening he told her that the assault would take place on the following noon; the city had given in, as its communications were broken and a famine might ensue. He would storm the entrance, while a detachment would try to climb unnoticed up the opposite side, in order to take her husband in the rear, before he could dash into the magazine. The action would cause losses, the outcome was far from sure, but he wished to avert the reproach that, through weakness, he had allowed a madman to succeed in defying a whole city. Rather any disaster than such a suspicion. He had tried to settle his affairs with God and the world; Rosalie and her child would not be overlooked in his will. Rosalie fell at his feet and asked him what would be her husband's fate if he should be taken in the assault. The commandant averted his head and said softly: "Death, unquestionably. No court-martial would accept a plea of insanity; there is too much penetration, foresight, and shrewdness in all his behavior. The devil cannot be summoned before the court; Francoeur must suffer for him." Rosalie burst into tears, then collected herself and inquired whether, if she should return the fort into the commandant's control, without bloodshed or danger, his offense might be pardoned on the ground of insanity. "Yes, I swear it!" cried the commandant. "But there's no use; he hates you more than anybody; yesterday he called to one of our outposts that he would surrender the fort if we would send him his wife's head."

"I know him," said the wife. "I will cast out the devil in him, I will bring him peace, even though I should die with him. It would be so much gained for me if I should die by his hand, for I am bound to him by the holiest of vows." The commandant begged her to think it over well and sought to learn what she had in mind; however, he did not resist her prayers or renounce the hope that by this course he might escape a general holocaust.

Father Philip had slipped into the house. He reported that crazy Francoeur had now hung out a great white flag on which the devil's likeness was painted. But the commandant was not interested in his news; he ordered him to go to Rosalie, who wished to confess to him. After Rosalie had made her confession in divine peace of mind, she begged Father Philip to accompany her to a certain stone rampart, where no cannon-ball could reach him. There she would hand over the child with money for his rearing, as she could not yet part from her darling. He promised her, reluctantly, after informing himself whether he would actually be secure against artillery fire, for his confidence in his power to exorcise devils had totally deserted him. He concluded that the demons he had previously cast out might not have been the devil in person, but only some sort of minor imps.

Rosalie, weeping, dressed her child once more in white with red ribbons, then took him on her arm and went silently down the steps. Below stood the old commandant; he could do no more than press her hand, turning aside out of shame in showing his tears to the spectators. She went down the street, no one knowing her purpose. Father Philip hung a little behind, since he would gladly have been dispensed of his mission. A number of idlers followed down the street, asking him what was up. Many cursed Rosalie, as Francoeur's wife, but the curses did not disturb her.

Meanwhile the commandant led his men by sheltered ways to the places from which the attack would be delivered, if the woman could not conjure away her husband's madness. At the gate the crowd promptly abandoned Rosalie, for Francoeur was firing from time to time over this open space. Father Philip complained that he was feeling faint and would have to lie down Rosalie said she was sorry, and pointed to the rampart, where she planned to nurse her child a final time and lay him in her cloak. He could be fetched back from there, and would lie there in security, if she should not be able to return to him. Father Philip crouched behind the stone wall, and Rosalie walked determinedly to the rampart, where she suckled her child, blessed him, wrapped him in her cloak, and lulled him asleep. Then she left him with a sob that seemed to break up the clouds within her and permit the blue sky and strength-bringing sun to beam upon her. Now she was visible to her cruel husband; as she stepped out on the rampart, a light flashed from the tower; a shock which almost felled her, a roar combined with a screaming whistle indicated that death had passed her very near. But she was no longer afraid; an inner voice assured her that nothing could die that had survived that day. Her love for her husband and child ruled in her heart, as she saw her husband stand, loading his weapons, on the battlements, and heard her child crying behind her. She was more sorry for them than for her own distresses; the hard course before her was not the most grievous thought in her heart. A second shot deafened her ears and splattered stone fragments in her face; but she prayed and looked up to heaven. She entered on a narrow approach, a lengthened causeway, designed to concentrate evilly on any attacker the annihilating firepower of two cannons loaded with grape-shot.

"What are you looking at, woman?" roared Francoeur. "Don't look up into the sky; your angels won't come; here is your devil and your death!"

"Neither death nor the devil will keep me any longer from you!" she said confidently, and walked further up the high steps.

"Woman," he cried, "you are braver than the devil, but that won't help you any." He blew on his slow-match, which was on the point of going out. Sweat glistened on his brow and cheeks; it seemed that two natures were warring within him. Rosalie did not wish to check this struggle and to anticipate the moment on which she was beginning to count. She did not advance, but knelt down on the stair, only three steps from the cannons, at the point where their fire crossed. He tore open his coat and waistcoat, the better to breathe, he clutched at his black hair, hanging in disordered locks, and tore at it in a frenzy. As he beat wildly on his brow, his head-wound opened. Tears and blood extinguished the burning match; a sharp gust of wind blew the powder from the touch-holes of the cannon and dislodged the devil-flag from the tower. "The chimney-sweeper is retreating! He wants to get out of the chimney!" he cried, and covered his eyes. Then he reflected a moment, opened the grilled gate, tottered to his wife's side, raised her up and kissed her. Finally he said: "The black miner has worked his way through. Light is shining in my brain again, air is blowing through; love shall light a fire again, so that we shan't freeze any more. Dear God, what crimes I have committed in these last few days! But let's not waste time; they will give me only a few hours of freedom. Where is my child? I must kiss him, while I am still free. And what is death? Didn't I die once already, when you left me? And now you have come back; and your return gives me more than your parting from me could take away, an unending consciousness of my existence. A few moments would be enough. Now I would gladly live with you, even if your faults outweighed my despair. But I know military law; and thank God I can now die with my eyes open, as a penitent Christian."

Rosalie, enraptured and almost choked by her tears, could hardly stammer that he was pardoned, that she had done nothing wrong, and that their child was near by. Hastily she bound up his wounds, then she helped him down the steps to the rampart where she had left the child. She found him there with good Father Philip, who had crept stealthily up behind protecting walls. As the boy held out his hands to his father, he let something fly out. While the three embraced, Father Philip told how a pair of doves had fluttered down from the fort and played sweetly with the boy, let him caress them, and had, as it were, comforted him in his abandonment. On seeing this, the holy father had ventured to approach the child. Said Francoeur: "Like good angels, they had been my boy's playmates in the fort; faithfully they sought him out. Surely they will return and will never leave him." And in fact the doves hovered about amicably, bearing green leaves in their beaks. "Our sin is remitted!" said Francoeur. "Never again will I grumble about peace; peace is so beautiful!"

Meanwhile the commandant approached with his staff. He had seen the happy outcome through his spyglass. Francoeur handed over his sword; the commandant assured him of pardon, as his wound had robbed him of his reason, and he ordered a surgeon to examine the wound and dress it better. Francoeur sat down and calmly submitted; he had eyes only for his wife and child. The surgeon, surprised that he gave no evidence of pain, removed from the wound a splinter of bone, which had provoked infection. It seemed that Francoeur's powerful constitution had gradually and constantly labored to expel this, until finally an external force, his own hands, had in desperation broken through the outer crust. The surgeon insisted that had it not been for this happy conjuncture incurable madness would have consumed the unhappy Francoeur. To avoid any ill effects from over-exertion, he was transported on a cart. His entry into Marseilles resembled a triumphal procession, amid a population always inclined to prize bravery above virtue. Women threw laurel wreaths into the vehicle, all crowded round to have a look at the proud rascal who had held at bay so many thousand men for three whole days. But the men presented their floral offerings to Rosalie and her child, and applauded her as their deliverer; they swore that they would richly reward her and her child, since she had saved their city from destruction.

It is unlikely that such a day could be matched, in one person's life, by anything else worth the telling, although it was in the peaceful years to follow that the personages, again favored by fortune and freed from the curse, experienced happiness. The good old commandant adopted Francoeur as his son, and though he could not confer his name upon him, left him his blessing and a share of his property. But what stirred Rosalie more intimately was news from Prague, years later. A friend of her mother's reported that in the grip of suffering she had for a full year repented of the curse she had laid upon her daughter, and in her ardent longing for release of body and soul, weary of the world and of herself, she had lingered on until a day when Rosalie's fidelity and submission operated divinely on her spirit; and on that day, soothed by an inward gleam, she had fallen asleep in trustful faith in her Redeemer.

> Grace remits the curse of sin;
> Love can cast the devil out.

✤ Adventure of the German Student

by WASHINGTON IRVING

Washington Irving (1783–1859) was America's first pure man of letters. Modern critics have reproached him for not being more ruggedly American, something he did not want to be and could not have been. Yet he wished to enrich his own country with "the color of romance and tradition," and he wrote (in a single night) one of the most celebrated stories in world literature, *Rip Van Winkle*. He was a lover of Europe's romantic past, and spent much of his life abroad. In Germany he fell under the spell of the German Romantics, such as Tieck and Hoffmann, specialists in the supernatural and in horror. Under their influence he wrote his *Tales of a Traveller* (1824), from which the present story is taken. It is presumed to be told at a hunting-dinner by "an old gentleman with a haunted head."

ON A STORMY NIGHT, in the tempestuous times of the French revolution, a young German was returning to his lodgings, at a late hour, across the old part of Paris. The lightning gleamed, and the loud claps of thunder rattled through the lofty narrow streets but I should first tell you something about this young German.

Gottfried Wolfgang was a young man of good family. He had studied for some time at Göttingen, but being of a visionary and enthusiastic character, he had wandered into those wild and speculative doctrines which have so often bewildered German students. His secluded life, his intense application, and the singular nature of his studies, had an effect on both mind and body. His health was impaired; his imagination diseased. He had been indulging in fanciful speculations on spiritual essences, until, like Swedenborg,* he had an ideal world of his own around him. He took up a notion, I do not know from what cause, that there was an evil influence hanging over him; an evil genius or spirit seeking to ensnare him and ensure his perdition. Such an idea working on his melancholy temperament, produced the most gloomy effects. He became haggard and desponding. His friends discovered the mental malady preying upon him, and determined that the best cure was a change of scene; he was sent, therefore, to finish his studies amidst the splendors and gayeties of Paris.

Wolfgang arrived at Paris at the breaking out of the revolution. The popular delirium at first caught his enthusiastic mind, and he was captivated by the political and philosophical theories of the day: but the scenes of blood which followed shocked his sensitive nature, disgusted him with society and the world, and made him more than ever a recluse. He shut himself up in a solitary apartment in the *Pays Latin,* the quarter of students. There, in a gloomy street not far from the monastic walls of the Sorbonne, he pursued his favorite speculations. Sometimes he spent hours together in the great libraries of Paris, those catacombs of departed authors, rummaging among their hordes of dusty and obsolete works in quest of food for his unhealthy appetite. He was, in a manner, a literary ghoul, feeding in the charnel-house of decayed literature.

Wolfgang, though solitary and recluse, was of an ardent temperament, but for a time it operated merely upon his imagination. He was too shy and ignorant of the world to make any advances to the fair, but he was a passionate admirer of female beauty, and in his lonely chamber would

* Emanuel Swedenborg, Swedish scientist, philosopher, and religious mystic.—Ed.

often lose himself in reveries on forms and faces which he had seen, and his fancy would deck out images of loveliness far surpassing the reality.

While his mind was in this excited and sublimated state, a dream produced an extraordinary effect upon him. It was of a female face of transcendent beauty. So strong was the impression made, that he dreamt of it again and again. It haunted his thoughts by day, his slumbers by night; in fine, he became passionately enamored of this shadow of a dream. This lasted so long that it became one of those fixed ideas which haunt the minds of melancholy men, and are at times mistaken for madness.

Such was Gottfried Wolfgang, and such his situation at the time I mentioned. He was returning home late one stormy night, through some of the old and gloomy streets of the *Marais*, the ancient part of Paris. The loud claps of thunder rattled among the high houses of the narrow streets. He came to the Place de Grève, the square where public executions are performed. The lightning quivered about the pinnacles of the ancient Hôtel de Ville, and shed flickering gleams over the open space in front. As Wolfgang was crossing the square, he shrank back with horror at finding himself close by the guillotine. It was the height of the reign of terror, when this dreadful instrument of death stood ever ready, and its scaffold was continually running with the blood of the virtuous and the brave. It had that very day been actively employed in the work of carnage, and there it stood in grim array, amidst a silent and sleeping city, waiting for fresh victims.

Wolfgang's heart sickened within him, and he was turning shuddering from the horrible engine, when he beheld a shadowy form, cowering as it were at the foot of the steps which led up to the scaffold. A succession of vivid flashes of lightning revealed it more distinctly. It was a female figure, dressed in black. She was seated on one of the lower steps of the scaffold, leaning forward, her face hid in her lap; and her long dishevelled tresses hanging to the ground, streaming with the rain which fell in torrents. Wolfgang paused. There was something awful in this solitary monument of woe. The female had the appearance of being above the common order. He knew the times to be full of vicissitude, and that many a fair head, which had once been pillowed on down, now wandered houseless. Perhaps this was some poor mourner whom the dreadful axe had rendered desolate, and who sat here heartbroken on the strand of existence, from which all that was dear to her had been launched into eternity.

He approached, and addressed her in the accents of sympathy. She raised her head and gazed wildly at him. What was his astonishment at beholding, by the bright glare of the lightning, the very face which had haunted him in his dreams. It was pale and disconsolate, but ravishingly beautiful.

Trembling with violent and conflicting emotions, Wolfgang again accosted her. He spoke something of her being exposed at such an hour of the night, and to the fury of such a storm, and offered to conduct her to her friends. She pointed to the guillotine with a gesture of dreadful signification.

"I have no friend on earth!" said she.

"But you have a home," said Wolfgang.

"Yes—in the grave!"

The heart of the student melted at the words.

"If a stranger dare make an offer," said he, "without danger of being misunderstood, I would offer my humble dwelling as a shelter; myself as a devoted friend. I am friendless myself in Paris, and a stranger in the land; but if my life could be of service, it is at your disposal, and should be sacrificed before harm or indignity should come to you."

There was an honest earnestness in the young man's manner that had its effect. His foreign accent, too, was in his favor; it showed him not to be a hackneyed inhabitant of Paris. Indeed, there is an eloquence in true enthusiasm that is not to be doubted. The homeless stranger confided herself implicitly to the protection of the student.

He supported her faltering steps across the Pont-Neuf, and by the place where the statue of Henry the Fourth had been overthrown by the populace. The storm had abated, and the thunder rumbled at a distance. All Paris was quiet; that great volcano of human passion slumbered for a while, to gather fresh strength for the next day's eruption. The student conducted his charge through the ancient streets of the *Pays Latin,* and by the dusky walls of the Sorbonne, to the great dingy hotel which he inhabited. The old portress who admitted them stared with surprise at the unusual sight of the melancholy Wolfgang with a female companion.

On entering his apartment, the student, for the first time, blushed at the scantiness and indifference of his dwelling. He had but one chamber—an old-fashioned saloon—heavily carved, and fantastically furnished with the remains of former magnificence, for it was one of those hotels in the quarter of the Luxembourg palace, which had once belonged to nobility. It was lumbered with books and papers, and all the usual apparatus of a student, and his bed stood in a recess at one end.

When lights were brought, and Wolfgang had a better opportunity of contemplating the stranger, he was more than ever intoxicated by her beauty. Her face was pale, but of a dazzling fairness, set off by a profusion of raven hair that hung clustering about it. Her eyes were large and brilliant, with a singular expression approaching almost to wildness. As far as her black dress permitted her shape to be seen, it was of perfect symmetry. Her whole appearance was highly striking, though she was dressed in the simplest style. The only thing approaching to an ornament which she wore, was a broad black band round her neck, clasped by diamonds.

The perplexity now commenced with the student how to dispose of the helpless being thus thrown upon his protection. He thought of abandoning his chamber to her, and seeking shelter for himself elsewhere. Still he was so fascinated by her charms, there seemed to be such a spell upon his thoughts and senses, that he could not tear himself from her presence. Her manner, too, was singular and unaccountable. She spoke no more of the guillotine. Her grief had abated. The attentions of the student had first won her confidence, and then, apparently, her heart. She was evidently an enthusiast like himself, and enthusiasts soon understand each other.

In the infatuation of the moment, Wolfgang avowed his passion for her. He told her the story of his mysterious dream, and how she had possessed his heart before he had even seen her. She was strangely affected by his recital, and acknowledged to have felt an impulse towards him equally unaccountable. It was the time for wild theory and wild actions. Old prejudices and superstitions were done away; everything was under the sway of the "Goddess of Reason." Among other rubbish of the old times, the forms and ceremonies of marriage began to be considered superfluous bonds for honorable minds. Social compacts were the vogue. Wolfgang was too much of a theorist not to be tainted by the liberal doctrines of the day.

"Why should we separate?" said he; "our hearts are

united; in the eye of reason and honor we are as one. What need is there of sordid forms to bind high souls together?"

The stranger listened with emotion: she had evidently received illumination at the same school.

"You have no home or family," continued he, "let me be everything to you, or rather let us be everything to one another. If form is necessary, form shall be observed—there is my hand. I pledge myself to you forever."

"Forever?" said the stranger, solemnly.

"Forever!" repeated Wolfgang.

The stranger clasped the hand extended to her: "Then I am yours," murmured she, and sank upon his bosom.

The next morning the student left his bride sleeping, and sallied forth at an early hour to seek more spacious apartments suitable to the change in his situation. When he returned, he found the stranger lying with her head hanging over the bed, and one arm thrown over it. He spoke to her, but received no reply. He advanced to awaken her from her uneasy posture. On taking her hand, it was cold—there was no pulsation—her face was pallid and ghastly. In a word, she was a corpse.

Horrified and frantic, he alarmed the house. A scene of confusion ensued. The police was summoned. As the officer of police entered the room, he started back on beholding the corpse.

"Great heaven!" cried he, "how did this woman come here?"

"Do you know anything about her?" said Wolfgang eagerly.

"Do I?" exclaimed the officer: "she was guillotined yesterday."

He stepped forward; undid the black collar round the neck of the corpse, and the head rolled on the floor!

The student burst into a frenzy. "The fiend! the fiend

has gained possession of me!" shrieked he; "I am lost forever."

They tried to soothe him, but in vain. He was possessed with the frightful belief that an evil spirit had reanimated the dead body to ensnare him. He went distracted, and died in a mad-house.

Here the old gentleman with the haunted head finished his narrative.

"And is this really a fact?" said the inquisitive gentleman.

"A fact not to be doubted," replied the other. "I had it from the best authority. The student told it me himself. I saw him in a mad-house in Paris."

My Aunt Margaret's Mirror

by SIR WALTER SCOTT

Sir Walter Scott (1771–1832) was a very nice man, perhaps the nicest great man in literary history. He had every virtue, and only the most trifling of faults. For a dozen years or so he was the most popular poet writing in English; his *Waverley Novels* had an immense effect on literature, life, and manners, helping to inspire even backwoods America with Gothic medievalism. As a silent partner in a publishing house which went bankrupt in 1826, he assumed, needlessly, the firm's enormous obligations, and spent his last years writing desperately to pay off what he regarded as a debt of honor. *My Aunt Margaret's Mirror* (1828) was a product of this necessity.

I

YOU ARE FOND (said my aunt) of sketches of the society which has passed away. I wish I could describe to you Sir Philip Forester, the "chartered libertine" of Scottish good company, about the end of the last century. I never saw him indeed; but my mother's traditions were full of his wit, gallantry, and dissipation. This gay knight flourished about the end of the seventeenth and beginning of the eighteenth century. He was the Sir Charles Easy and the Lovelace * of his day and country, renowned for the number of duels he had fought and the successful intrigues which he had carried on. The supremacy which he had attained in the fashionable world was absolute; and when we combine it with one or two anecdotes, for which,

* Sir Charles Easy, the "careless husband" in Colley Cibber's comedy of the same name; Lovelace, a conscienceless charmer in Samuel Richardson's *Clarissa Harlow.*—Ed.

"if laws were made for every degree," he ought certainly to have been hanged, the popularity of such a person really serves to show, either that the present times are much more decent, if not more virtuous, than they formerly were, or that high-breeding then was of more difficult attainment than that which is now so called, and, consequently, entitled the successful professor to a proportional degree of plenary indulgences and privileges. No beau of this day could have borne out so ugly a story as that of Pretty Peggy Grindstone, the miller's daughter at Sillermills; it had well-nigh made work for the Lord Advocate. But it hurt Sir Philip Forester no more than the hail hurts the hearthstone. He was as well received in society as ever, and dined with the Duke of A——the day the poor girl was buried. She died of heartbreak. But that has nothing to do with my story.

Now, you must listen to a single word upon kith, kin, and ally; I promise you I will not be prolix. But it is necessary to the authenticity of my legend that you should know that Sir Philip Forester, with his handsome person, elegant accomplishments, and fashionable manners, married the younger Miss Falconer of King's-Copland. The elder sister of this lady had previously become the wife of my grandfather, Sir Geoffrey Bothwell, and brought into our family a good fortune. Miss Jemima, or Miss Jemmie, Falconer, as she was usually called, had also about ten thousand pounds sterling, then thought a very handsome portion indeed.

The two sisters were extremely different, though each had their admirers while they remained single. Lady Bothwell had some touch of the old King's-Copland blood about her. She was bold, though not to the degree of audacity; ambitious, and desirous to raise her house and family; and was, as has been said, a considerable spur to my grandfather, who was otherwise an indolent man, but whom, unless he has been slandered, his lady's influence involved in some political matters which had been more wisely let alone. She was a woman of high principle, however, and masculine good sense, as some of her letters testify, which are still in my wainscot cabinet.

Jemmie Falconer was the reverse of her sister in every respect. Her understanding did not reach above the ordinary pitch, if, indeed, she could be said to have attained it. Her beauty, while it lasted, consisted, in a great measure, of delicacy of complexion and regularity of features, without any peculiar force of expression. Even these charms faded under the sufferings attendant on an ill-sorted match. She was passionately attached to her husband, by whom she was treated with a callous, yet polite, indifference, which, to one whose heart was as tender as her judgment was weak, was more painful perhaps than absolute ill-usage. Sir Philip was a voluptuary, that is, a completely selfish egotist, whose disposition and character resembled the rapier he wore— polished, keen, and brilliant, but inflexible and unpitying. As he observed carefully all the usual forms towards his lady, he had the art to deprive her even of the compassion of the world; and useless and unavailing as that may be while actually possessed by the sufferer, it is, to a mind like Lady Forester's, most painful to know she has it not.

The tattle of society did its best to place the peccant husband above the suffering wife. Some called her a poor spiritless thing, and declared that, with a little of her sister's spirit, she might have brought to reason any Sir Philip what- soever, were it the termagant Falconbridge himself. But the greater part of their acquaintance affected candour, and saw faults on both sides; though, in fact, there only existed the oppressor and the oppressed. The tone of such critics was—"To be sure, no one will justify Sir Philip Forester, but then we all know Sir Philip, and Jemmie Falconer might have known what she had to expect from the beginning. What made her set her cap at Sir Philip? He would never have looked at her if she had not thrown herself at his head, with her poor ten thousand pounds. I am sure, if it is money he wanted, she spoiled his market. I know where Sir Philip could have done much better. And then, if she *would* have the man, could she not try to make him more comfortable at home, and have his friends oftener, and not plague him with the squalling children, and take care all was handsome and in good style about the house? I declare I think Sir Philip would have made a very domestic man, with a woman who knew how to manage him."

Now these fair critics, in raising their profound edifice of domestic felicity, did not recollect that the cornerstone was wanting, and that, to receive good company with good cheer, the means of the banquet ought to have been furnished by Sir Philip, whose income, dilapidated as it was, was not equal to the display of the hospitality required, and at the same time to the supply of the good knight's *menus plaisirs*. So, in spite of all that was so sagely suggested by female friends, Sir Philip carried his good-humour everywhere abroad, and left at home a solitary mansion and a pining spouse.

At length, inconvenienced in his money affairs, and tired even of the short time which he spent in his own dull house, Sir Philip Forester determined to take a trip to the continent, in the capacity of a volunteer. It was then common for men of fashion to do so; and our knight perhaps was of opinion that a touch of the military character, just enough to exalt, but not render pedantic, his qualities as a *beau garçon*, was necessary to maintain possession of the elevated situation which he held in the ranks of fashion.

Sir Philip's resolution threw his wife into agonies of terror; by which the worthy baronet was so much annoyed that, contrary to his wont, he took some trouble to soothe her apprehensions, and once more brought her to shed tears in which sorrow was not altogether unmingled with pleasure. Lady Bothwell asked, as a favour, Sir Philip's permission to receive her sister and her family into her own house during his absence on the continent. Sir Philip readily consented to a proposition which saved expense, silenced the foolish people who might have talked of a deserted wife and family, and gratified Lady Bothwell; for whom he felt some respect, as for one who often spoke to him, always with freedom, and sometimes with severity, without being deterred either by his raillery or the prestige of his reputation.

A day or two before Sir Philip's departure, Lady Bothwell took the liberty of asking him, in her sister's presence, the direct question which his timid wife had often desired, but never ventured, to put to him.

"Pray, Sir Philip, what route do you take when you reach the continent?"

"I go from Leith to Helvoet by a packet with advices."

"That I comprehend perfectly," said Lady Bothwell, drily; "but you do not mean to remain long at Helvoet, I presume, and I should like to know what is your next object?"

"You ask me, my dear lady," answered Sir Philip, "a question which I have not dared to ask myself. The answer depends on the fate of war. I shall, of course, go to headquarters, wherever they may happen to be for the time, deliver my letters of introduction, learn as much of the noble art of war as may suffice a poor interloping amateur, and then take a glance at the sort of thing of which we read so much in the 'Gazette.' "

"And I trust, Sir Philip," said Lady Bothwell, "that you will remember that you are a husband and a father; and that, though you think fit to indulge this military fancy, you will not let it hurry you into dangers which it is certainly unnecessary for any save professional persons to encounter?"

"Lady Bothwell does me too much honour," replied the adventurous knight, "in regarding such a circumstance with the slightest interest. But to soothe your flattering anxiety, I trust your ladyship will recollect, that I cannot expose to hazard the venerable and paternal character which you so obligingly recommend to my protection, without putting in some peril an honest fellow, called Philip Forester, with whom I have kept company for thirty years, and with whom, though some folks consider him a coxcomb, I have not the least desire to part."

"Well, Sir Philip, you are the best judge of your own affairs; I have little right to interfere—you are not my husband."

"God forbid!" said Sir Philip, hastily; instantly adding, however, "God forbid that I should deprive my friend Sir Geoffrey of so inestimable a treasure."

"But you are my sister's husband," replied the lady; "and I suppose you are aware of her present distress of mind——"

"If hearing of nothing else from morning to night can make me aware of it," said Sir Philip, "I should know something of the matter."

"I do not pretend to reply to your wit, Sir Philip,"

answered Lady Bothwell; "but you must be sensible that all this distress is on account of apprehensions for your personal safety."

"In that case, I am surprised that Lady Bothwell, at least, should give herself so much trouble upon so insignificant a subject."

"My sister's interest may account for my being anxious to learn something of Sir Philip Forester's motions; about which, otherwise, I know, he would not wish me to concern myself. I have a brother's safety too to be anxious for."

"You mean Major Falconer, your brother by the mother's side. What can he possibly have to do with our present agreeable conversation?"

"You have had words together, Sir Philip," said Lady Bothwell.

"Naturally; we are connexions," replied Sir Philip, "and as such have always had the usual intercourse."

"That is an evasion of the subject," answered the lady. "By words, I mean angry words, on the subject of your usage of your wife."

"If," replied Sir Philip Forester, "you suppose Major Falconer simple enough to intrude his advice upon me, Lady Bothwell, in my domestic matters, you are indeed warranted in believing that I might possibly be so far displeased with the interference as to request him to reserve his advice till it was asked."

"And being on these terms, you are going to join the very army in which my brother Falconer is now serving?"

"No man knows the path of honour better then Major Falconer," said Sir Philip. "An aspirant after fame, like me, cannot choose a better guide than his footsteps."

Lady Bothwell rose and went to the window, the tears gushing from her eyes.

"And this heartless raillery," she said, "is all the consideration that is to be given to our apprehensions of a quarrel which may bring on the most terrible consequences? Good God, of what can men's hearts be made, who can thus dally with the agony of others?"

Sir Philip Forester was moved; he laid aside the mocking tone in which he had hitherto spoken.

"Dear Lady Bothwell," he said, taking her reluctant hand, "we are both wrong: you are too deeply serious; I, perhaps, too little so. The dispute I had with Major Falconer was of no earthly consequence. Had anything occurred betwixt us that ought to have been settled *par voie du fait*, as we say in France, neither of us are persons that are likely to postpone such a meeting. Permit me to say, that were it generally known that you or my Lady Forester are apprehensive of such a catastrophe, it might be the very means of bringing about what would not otherwise be likely to happen. I know your good sense, Lady Bothwell, and that you will understand me when I say that really my affairs require my absence for some months. This Jemima cannot understand; it is a perpetual recurrence of questions, why can you not do this, or that, or the third thing; and, when you have proved to her that her expedients are totally ineffectual, you have just to begin the whole round again. Now, do you tell her, dear Lady Bothwell, that *you* are satisfied. She is, you must confess, one of those persons with whom authority goes farther than reasoning. Do but repose a little confidence in me, and you shall see how amply I will repay it."

Lady Bothwell shook her head, as one but half satisfied. "How difficult it is to extend confidence when the basis on which it ought to rest has been so much shaken! But I will do my best to make Jemima easy; and further, I can only say that, for keeping your present purpose I hold you responsible both to God and man."

"Do not fear that I will deceive you," said Sir Philip; "the safest conveyance to me will be through the general post-office, Helvoetsluys, where I will take care to leave orders for forwarding my letters. As for Falconer, our only encounter will be over a bottle of Burgundy; so make yourself perfectly easy on his score."

Lady Bothwell could *not* make herself easy; yet she was sensible that her sister hurt her own cause by "taking on," as the maid-servants call it, too vehemently; and by showing before every stranger, by manner, and sometimes by words also, a dissatisfaction with her husband's journey that was sure to come to his ears, and equally certain to displease him. But there was no help for this domestic dissension, which ended only with the day of separation.

I am sorry I cannot tell, with precision, the year in which Sir Philip Forester went over to Flanders; but it was one of those in which the campaign opened with extraordinary fury; and many bloody, though indecisive, skirmishes were fought between the French on the one side and the Allies on the other. In all our modern improvements, there are none, perhaps, greater than the accuracy and speed with which intelligence is transmitted from any scene of action to those in this country whom it may concern. During Marlborough's campaigns the sufferings of the many who had relations in, or along with, the army were greatly augmented by the suspense in which they were detained for weeks, after they had heard of bloody battles in which, in all probability, those for whom their bosoms throbbed with anxiety had been personally engaged. Amongst those who were most agonized by this state of uncertainty was the —I had almost said deserted—wife of the gay Sir Philip

Forester. A single letter had informed her of his arrival on the continent; no others were received. One notice occurred in the newspapers, in which Volunteer Sir Philip Forester was mentioned as having been entrusted with a dangerous reconnaissance, which he had executed with the greatest courage, dexterity, and intelligence, and received the thanks of the commanding-officer. The sense of his having acquired distinction brought a momentary glow into the lady's pale cheek; but it was instantly lost in ashen whiteness at the recollection of his danger. After this they had no news whatever, neither from Sir Philip nor even from their brother Falconer. The case of Lady Forester was not indeed different from that of hundreds in the same situation; but a feeble mind is necessarily an irritable one, and the suspense which some bear with constitutional indifference or philosophical resignation, and some with a disposition to believe and hope the best, was intolerable to Lady Forester, at once solitary and sensitive, low-spirited, and devoid of strength of mind, whether natural or acquired.

II

As she received no further news of Sir Philip, whether directly or indirectly, his unfortunate lady began now to feel a sort of consolation even in those careless habits which had so often given her pain. "He is so thoughtless," she repeated a hundred times a day to her sister, "he never writes when things are going on smoothly—it is his way; had anything happened he would have informed us."

Lady Bothwell listened to her sister without attempting to console her. Probably she might be of opinion, that even the worst intelligence which could be received from Flanders might not be without some touch of consolation; and that the Dowager Lady Forester, if so she was doomed to be called, might have a source of happiness unknown to the wife of the gayest and finest gentleman in Scotland. This conviction became stronger as they learned from inquiries made at headquarters that Sir Philip was no longer with the army; though whether he had been taken or slain in some of those skirmishes which were perpetually occurring, and in which he loved to distinguish himself, or whether he had, for some unknown reason or capricious change of mind, voluntarily left the service, none of his country-men in the camp of the Allies could form even a conjecture. Meantime his creditors at home became clamorous, entered into possession of his property, and threatened his person, should he be rash enough to return to Scotland. These ad-ditional disadvantages aggravated Lady Bothwell's dis-pleasure against the fugitive husband; while her sister saw nothing in any of them save what tended to increase her grief for the absence of him whom her imagination now represented, as it had before marriage, gallant, gay, and affectionate.

About this period there appeared in Edinburgh a man of singular appearance and pretensions. He was commonly called the Paduan Doctor, from having received his educa-tion at that famous university. He was supposed to possess some rare receipts in medicine, with which, it was affirmed, he had wrought remarkable cures. But though, on the one hand, the physicians of Edinburgh termed him an empiric, there were many persons, and among them some of the clergy, who, while they admitted the truth of the cures and the force of his remedies, alleged that Doctor Baptista Damiotti made use of charms and unlawful arts in order to obtain success in his practice. The resorting to him was even solemnly preached against, as a seeking of health from idols, and a trusting to the help which was to come from Egypt. But the protection which the Paduan Doctor received from some friends of interest and consequence enabled him to set these imputations at defiance, and to assume, even in the city of Edinburgh, famed as it was for abhorrence of witches and necromancers, the dangerous character of an expounder of futurity. It was at length rumoured that, for a certain gratification, which of course was not an inconsiderable one, Doctor Baptista Damiotti could tell the fate of the absent, and even show his visitors the personal form of their absent friends, and the action in which they were engaged at the moment. This rumour came to the ears of Lady Forester, who had reached that pitch of mental agony in which the sufferer will do anything, or endure anything, that suspense may be converted into certainty.

Gentle and timid in most cases, her state of mind made her equally obstinate and reckless, and it was with no small surprise and alarm that her sister, Lady Bothwell, heard her express a resolution to visit this man of art and learn from him the fate of her husband. Lady Bothwell remonstrated on the improbability that such pretensions as those of this foreigner could be founded in anything but imposture.

"I care not," said the deserted wife, "what degree of ridicule I may incur; if there be any one chance out of a hundred that I may obtain some certainty of my husband's fate, I would not miss that chance for whatever else the world can offer me."

Lady Bothwell next urged the unlawfulness of resorting to such sources of forbidden knowledge.

"Sister," replied the sufferer, "he who is dying of thirst cannot refrain from drinking even poisoned water. She who suffers under suspense must seek information, even were the powers which offer it unhallowed and infernal. I go to learn my fate alone, and this very evening will I know it: the sun that rises to-morrow shall find me, if not more happy, at least more resigned."

"Sister," said Lady Bothwell, "if you are determined upon this wild step, you shall not go alone. If this man be an impostor, you may be too much agitated by your feelings to detect his villainy. If, which I cannot believe, there be any truth in what he pretends, you shall not be exposed alone to a communication of so extraordinary a nature. I will go with you, if indeed you determine to go. But yet reconsider your project, and renounce inquiries which cannot be prosecuted without guilt, and perhaps without danger."

Lady Forester threw herself into her sister's arms, and, clasping her to her bosom, thanked her a hundred times for the offer of her company; while she declined with a melancholy gesture the friendly advice with which it was accompanied.

When the hour of twilight arrived, which was the period when the Paduan Doctor was understood to receive the visits of those who came to consult with him, the two ladies left their apartments in the Canongate of Edinburgh, having their dress arranged like that of women of an inferior description, and their plaids disposed around their faces as they were worn by the same class; for, in those days of aristocracy, the quality of the wearer was generally indicated by the manner in which her plaid was disposed, as well as by the fineness of its texture. It was Lady Bothwell who had suggested this species of disguise, partly to avoid observation as they should go to the conjurer's house, and partly in order to make trial of his penetration, by appear-

ing before him in a feigned character. Lady Forester's
servant, of tried fidelity, had been employed by her to
propitiate the Doctor by a suitable fee, and a story intimat-
ing that a soldier's wife desired to know the fate of her
husband—a subject upon which, in all probability, the
sage was very frequently consulted.

To the last moment, when the palace clock struck eight,
Lady Bothwell earnestly watched her sister, in hopes that
she might retreat from her rash undertaking; but as mild-
ness, and even timidity, is capable at times of vehement and
fixed purposes, she found Lady Forester resolutely unmoved and determined when the moment of departure arrived. Ill satisfied with the expedition, but determined not
to leave her sister at such a crisis, Lady Bothwell accompanied Lady Forester through more than one obscure street
and lane, the servant walking before and acting as their
guide. At length he suddenly turned into a narrow court,
and knocked at an arched door, which seemed to belong to
a building of some antiquity. It opened, though no one appeared to act as porter; and the servant, stepping aside from
the entrance, motioned the ladies to enter. They had no
sooner done so than it shut, and excluded their guide. The
two ladies found themselves in a small vestibule, illuminated
by a dim lamp, and having, when the door was closed, no
communciation with the external light or air. The door of
an inner apartment, partly open, was at the farther side of
the vestibule.

"We must not hesitate now, Jemima," said Lady Bothwell, and walked forwards into the inner room, where, surrounded by books, maps, philosophical utensils, and other
implements of peculiar shape and appearance, they found
the man of art.

There was nothing very peculiar in the Italian's appearance. He had the dark complexion and marked features of his country, seemed about fifty years old, and was handsomely, but plainly, dressed in a full suit of black clothes, which was then the universal costume of the medical profession. Large wax-lights, in silver sconces, illuminated the apartment, which was reasonably furnished. He rose as the ladies entered; and, notwithstanding the inferiority of their dress, received them with the marked respect due to their quality, and which foreigners are usually punctilious in rendering to those to whom such honours are due.

Lady Bothwell endeavoured to maintain her proposed incognito; and, as the Doctor ushered them to the upper end of the room, made a motion declining his courtesy, as unfitted for their condition. "We are poor people, sir," she said; "only my sister's distress has brought us to consult your worship whether——"

He smiled as he interrupted her—"I am aware, madam, of your sister's distress, and its cause; I am aware, also, that I am honoured with a visit from two ladies of the highest consideration—Lady Bothwell and Lady Forester. If I could not distinguish them from the class of society which their present dress would indicate, there would be small possibility of my being able to gratify them by giving the information which they come to seek."

"I can easily understand——" said Lady Bothwell.

"Pardon my boldness to interrupt you, milady," cried the Italian; "your ladyship was about to say, that you could easily understand that I had got possession of your names by means of your domestic. But in thinking so, you do injustice to the fidelity of your servant, and, I may add, to the skill of one who is also not less your humble servant—Baptista Damiotti."

"I have no intention to do either, sir," said Lady Bothwell, maintaining a tone of composure, though somewhat surprised, "but the situation is something new to me. If you know who we are, you also know, sir, what brought us here."

"Curiosity to know the fate of a Scottish gentleman of rank, now, or lately, upon the continent," answered the seer; "his name is Il Cavaliere Philippo Forester—a gentleman who has the honour to be husband to this lady, and, with your ladyship's permission for using plain language, the misfortune not to value as it deserves that inestimable advantage."

Lady Forester sighed deeply, and Lady Bothwell replied—

"Since you know our object without our telling it, the only question that remains is, whether you have the power to relieve my sister's anxiety?"

"I have, madam," answered the Paduan scholar; "but there is still a previous inquiry. Have you the courage to behold with your own eyes what the Cavaliere Philippo Forester is now doing, or will you take it on my report?"

"That question my sister must answer for herself," said Lady Bothwell.

"With my own eyes will I endure to see whatever you have power to show me," said Lady Forester, with the same determined spirit which had stimulated her since her resolution was taken upon this subject.

"There may be danger in it."

"If gold can compensate the risk——" said Lady Forester, taking out her purse.

"I do not such things for the purpose of gain," answered the foreigner. "I dare not turn my art to such a purpose. If I take the gold of the wealthy, it is but to bestow it on the poor; nor do I ever accept more than the sum I have already received from your servant. Put up your purse, madam: an adept needs not your gold."

Lady Bothwell, considering this rejection of her sister's offer as a mere trick of an empiric, to induce her to press a larger sum upon him, and willing that the scene should be commenced and ended, offered some gold in turn, observing, that it was only to enlarge the sphere of his charity.

"Let Lady Bothwell enlarge the sphere of her own charity," said the Paduan, "not merely in giving of alms, in which I know she is not deficient, but in judging the character of others; and let her oblige Baptista Damiotti by believing him honest, till she shall discover him to be a knave. Do not be surprised, madam, if I speak in answer to your thoughts rather than your expressions, and tell me once more whether you have courage to look on what I am prepared to show?"

"I own, sir," said Lady Bothwell, "that your words strike me with some sense of fear; but whatever my sister desires to witness, I will not shrink from witnessing along with her."

"Nay, the danger only consists in the risk of your resolution failing you. The sight can only last for the space of seven minutes; and should you interrupt the vision by speaking a single word, not only would the charm be broken, but some danger might result to the spectators. But if you can remain steadily silent for the seven minutes, your curiosity will be gratified without the slightest risk; and for this I will engage my honour."

Internally Lady Bothwell thought the security was but an indifferent one; but she suppressed the suspicion, as if she had believed that the adept, whose dark features wore a half-formed smile, could in reality read even her most secret reflections. A solemn pause then ensued, until Lady Forester gathered courage enough to reply to the physician, as he termed himself, that she would abide with firmness and silence the sight which he had promised to exhibit to them. Upon this, he made them a low obeisance, and saying he went to prepare matters to meet their wish, left the apartment. The two sisters, hand in hand, as if seeking by that close union to divert any danger which might threaten them, sat down on two seats in immediate contact with each other—Jemima seeking support in the manly and habitual courage of Lady Bothwell; and she, on the other hand, more agitated than she had expected, endeavouring to fortify herself by the desperate resolution which circumstances had forced her sister to assume. The one perhaps said to herself, that her sister never feared anything; and the other might reflect, that what so feeble-minded a woman as Jemima did not fear, could not properly be a subject of apprehension to a person of firmness and resolution like her own.

In a few moments the thoughts of both were diverted from their own situation by a strain of music so singularly sweet and solemn that, while it seemed calculated to avert or dispel any feeling unconnected with its harmony, increased, at the same time, the solemn excitation which the preceding interview was calculated to produce. The music was that of some instrument with which they were unacquainted; but circumstances afterwards led my ancestress to believe that it was that of the harmonica,* which she heard at a much later period in life.

When these heaven-born sounds had ceased, a door opened in the upper end of the apartment, and they saw

* Harmonica: a set of glass or metal pieces, played by striking with a mallet.—Ed.

Damiotti, standing at the head of two or three steps, sign to them to advance. His dress was so different from that which he had worn a few minutes before, that they could hardly recognise him; and the deadly paleness of his countenance, and a certain stern rigidity of muscles, like that of one whose mind is made up to some strange and daring action, had totally changed the somewhat sarcastic expression with which he had previously regarded them both, and particularly Lady Bothwell. He was barefooted, excepting a species of sandals in the antique fashion; his legs were naked beneath the knees; above them he wore hose, and a doublet of dark crimson silk close to his body; and over that a flowing loose robe, something resembling a surplice, of snow-white linen; his throat and neck were uncovered; and his long, straight, black hair was carefully combed down at full length.

As the ladies approached at his bidding, he showed no gesture of that ceremonious courtesy of which he had been formerly lavish. On the contrary, he made the signal of advance with an air of command; and when, arm in arm, and with insecure steps, the sisters approached the spot where he stood, it was with a warning frown that he pressed his finger to his lips, as if reiterating his condition of absolute silence, while, stalking before them, he led the way into the next apartment.

This was a large room, hung with black, as if for a funeral. At the upper end was a table, or rather a species of altar, covered with the same lugubrious colour, on which lay divers objects resembling the usual implements of sorcery. These objects were not indeed visible as they advanced into the apartment; for the light which displayed them, being only that of two expiring lamps, was extremely faint. The master—to use the Italian phrase for persons of this description—approached the upper end of the room, with a genuflexion like that of a Catholic to the crucifix, and at the same time crossed himself. The ladies followed in silence, and arm in arm. Two or three low broad steps led to a platform in front of the altar, or what resembled such. Here the sage took his stand, and placed the ladies beside him, once more earnestly repeating by signs his injunctions of silence. The Italian then, extending his bare arm from under his linen vestment, pointed with his forefinger to five large flambeaux, or torches, placed on each side of the altar. They took fire successively at the approach of his hand, or rather of his finger, and spread a strong light through the room. By this the visitors could discern that, on the seeming altar, were disposed two naked swords laid crosswise; a large open book, which they conceived to be a copy of the Holy Scriptures, but in a language to them unknown; and beside this mysterious volume was placed a human skull. But what struck the sisters most was a very tall and broad mirror, which occupied all the space behind the altar, and, illumined by the lighted torches, reflected the mysterious articles which were laid upon it.

The master then placed himself between the two ladies, and, pointing to the mirror, took each by the hand, but without speaking a syllable. They gazed intently on the polished and sable space to which he had directed their attention. Suddenly the surface assumed a new and singular appearance. It no longer simply reflected the objects placed before it, but, as if it had self-contained scenery of its own, objects began to appear within it, at first in a disorderly, in-distinct, and miscellaneous manner, like form arranging itself out of chaos, at length in distinct and defined shape and symmetry. It was thus that, after some shifting of light and darkness over the face of the wonderful glass, a long perspective of arches and columns began to arrange itself on its sides, and a vaulted roof on the upper part of it; till, after many oscillations, the whole vision gained a fixed and stationary appearance, representing the interior of a foreign church. The pillars were stately, and hung with scutcheons; the arches were lofty and magnificent; the floor was lettered with funeral inscriptions. But there were no separate shrines, no images, no display of chalice or crucifix on the altar. It was, therefore, a Protestant church upon the continent. A clergyman dressed in the Geneva gown and band stood by the communion-table, and, with the Bible opened before him, and his clerk awaiting in the background, seemed prepared to perform some service of the church to which he belonged.

At length there entered the middle aisle of the building a numerous party, which appeared to be a bridal one, as a lady and gentleman walked first, hand in hand, followed by a large concourse of persons of both sexes, gaily, nay richly, attired. The bride, whose features they could distinctly see, seemed not more than sixteen years old, and extremely beautiful. The bridegroom, for some seconds, moved rather with his shoulder towards them and his face averted; but his elegance of form and step struck the sisters at once with the same apprehension. As he turned his face suddenly, it was frightfully realised, and they saw, in the gay bridegroom before them, Sir Philip Forester. His wife uttered an imperfect exclamation, at the sound of which the whole scene stirred and seemed to separate.

"I could compare it to nothing," said Lady Bothwell, while recounting the wonderful tale, "but to the dispersion of the reflection offered by a deep and calm pool when a stone is suddenly cast into it, and the shadows become dissipated and broken."

The master pressed both the ladies' hands severely, as if to remind them of their promise, and of the danger which they incurred. The exclamation died away on Lady Forester's tongue without attaining perfect utterance, and the scene in the glass, after the fluctuation of a minute, again resumed to the eye its former appearance of a real scene, existing within the mirror, as if represented in a picture, save that the figures were movable instead of being stationary.

The representation of Sir Philip Forester, now distinctly visible in form and feature, was seen to lead on towards the clergyman that beautiful girl, who advanced at once with diffidence and with a species of affectionate pride. In the meantime, and just as the clergyman had arranged the bridal company before him, and seemed about to commence the service, another group of persons, of whom two or three were officers, entered the church. They moved, at first, forward, as though they came to witness the bridal ceremony, but suddenly one of the officers, whose back was towards the spectators, detached himself from his companions, and rushed hastily towards the marriage party, when the whole of them turned towards him, as if attracted by some exclamation which had accompanied his advance. Suddenly the intruder drew his sword; the bridegroom unsheathed his own and made towards him; swords were also drawn by other individuals, both of the marriage party and of those who had last entered. They fell into a sort of confusion, the clergyman and some elder and graver persons labouring apparently to keep the peace, while the hotter spirits on both sides brandished their weapons. But now the period of the brief space during which the soothsayer, as he pretended, was permitted to exhibit his art was arrived. The fumes again mixed together, and dissolved gradually from observation; the vaults and columns of the church rolled asunder and disappeared; and the front of the mirror reflected nothing save the blazing torches and the melancholy apparatus placed on the altar or table before it.

The Doctor led the ladies, who greatly required his support, into the apartment from whence they came; where wine, essences, and other means of restoring suspended animation had been provided during their absence. He motioned them to chairs, which they occupied in silence; Lady Forester, in particular, wringing her hands and casting her eyes up to heaven, but without speaking a word, as if the spell had been still before her eyes.

"And what we have seen is even now acting?" said Lady Bothwell, collecting herself with difficulty.

"That," answered Baptista Damiotti, "I cannot justly, or with certainty, say. But it is either now acting or has been acted during a short space before this. It is the last remarkable transaction in which the Cavaliere Forester has been engaged."

Lady Bothwell then expressed anxiety concerning her sister, whose altered countenance and apparent unconsciousness of what passed around her excited her apprehensions how it might be possible to convey her home.

"I have prepared for that," answered the adept: "I have directed the servant to bring your equipage as near to this place as the narrowness of the street will permit. Fear not for your sister; but give her, when you return home, this composing-draught, and she will be better to-morrow morning. Few," he added, in a melancholy tone, "leave this house as well in health as they entered it. Such being the consequence of seeking knowledge by mysterious means, I leave you to judge the condition of those who have the power of gratifying such irregular curiosity. Farewell, and forget not the potion."

"I will give her nothing that comes from you," said Lady Bothwell: "I have seen enough of your art already. Perhaps you would poison us both to conceal your own necromancy. But we are persons who want neither the means of making our wrongs known nor the assistance of friends to right them."

"You have had no wrongs from me, madam," said the adept. "You sought one who is little grateful for such honour. He seeks no one, and only gives responses to those who invite and call upon him. After all, you have but learned a little sooner the evil which you must still be doomed to endure. I hear your servant's step at the door, and will detain your ladyship and Lady Forester no longer. The next packet from the continent will explain what you have already partly witnessed. Let it not, if I may advise, pass too suddenly into your sister's hands."

So saying, he bid Lady Bothwell good-night. She went, lighted by the adept, to the vestibule, where he hastily threw a black cloak over his singular dress, and opening the door, entrusted his visitors to the care of the servant. It was with difficulty that Lady Bothwell sustained her sister to the carriage, though it was only twenty steps distant.

When they arrived at home, Lady Forester required medical assistance. The physician of the family attended, and shook his head on feeling her pulse.

"Here has been," he said, "a violent and sudden shock on the nerves. I must know how it has happened."

Lady Bothwell admitted they had visited the conjurer, and that Lady Forester had received some bad news respecting her husband, Sir Philip.

"That rascally quack would make my fortune were he

to stay in Edinburgh," said the graduate: "this is the seventh nervous case I have heard of his making for me, and all by effect of terror." He next examined the composing-draught which Lady Bothwell had unconsciously brought in her hand, tasted it, and pronounced it very germane to the matter, and what would save an application to the apothecary. He then paused, and looking at Lady Bothwell very significantly, at length added, "I suppose I must not ask your ladyship anything about this Italian warlock's proceedings?"

"Indeed, Doctor," answered Lady Bothwell, "I consider what passed as confidential; and though the man may be a rogue, yet, as we were fools enough to consult him, we should, I think, be honest enough to keep his counsel."

"*May* be a knave; come," said the Doctor, "I am glad to hear your ladyship allows such a possibility in anything that comes from Italy."

"What comes from Italy may be as good as what comes from Hanover, Doctor.* But you and I will remain good friends, and that it may be so, we will say nothing of Whig and Tory."

"Not I," said the Doctor, receiving his fee, and taking his hat; "a Carolus serves my purpose as well as a Willielmus.† But I should like to know why old Lady St. Ringan's, and all that set, go about wasting their decayed lungs in puffing this foreign fellow."

"Ay, you had best 'set him down a Jesuit,' as Scrub ‡ says." On these terms they parted.

* George I, the first Hanoverian king of England, acceded to the throne in 1714. The Stuart pretender resided in Italy.—Ed.

† Carolus, a coin issued by Charles II of England (ruled 1660–1685); Willielmus, a coin issued by William III (ruled 1689–1702). —Ed.

‡ Scrub: a comic valet in Farquhar's *Beaux' Stratagem.*—Ed.

The poor patient, whose nerves, from an extraordinary state of tension, had at length become relaxed in as extraordinary a degree, continued to struggle with a sort of imbecility, the growth of superstitious terror, when the shocking tidings were brought from Holland which fulfilled even her worst expectations.

They were sent by the celebrated Earl of Stair, and contained the melancholy event of a duel betwixt Sir Philip Forester and his wife's half-brother, Captain Falconer, of the Scotch Dutch, as they were then called, in which the latter had been killed. The cause of quarrel rendered the incident still more shocking. It seemed that Sir Philip had left the army suddenly, in consequence of being unable to pay a very considerable sum, which he had lost to another volunteer at play. He had changed his name, and taken up his residence at Rotterdam, where he had insinuated himself into the good graces of an ancient and rich burgomaster, and, by his handsome person and graceful manners, captivated the affections of his only child, a very young person, of great beauty, and the heiress of much wealth. Delighted with the specious attractions of his proposed son-in-law, the wealthy merchant, whose idea of the British character was too high to admit of his taking any precaution to acquire evidence of his condition and circumstances, gave his consent to the marriage. It was about to be celebrated in the principal church of the city, when it was interrupted by a singular occurrence.

Captain Falconer having been detached to Rotterdam to bring up a part of the brigade of Scottish auxiliaries, who were in quarters there, a person of consideration in the town, to whom he had been formerly known, proposed to him for amusement to go the high church to see a countryman of his own married to the daughter of a wealthy burgomaster. Captain Falconer went accordingly, accompanied by his Dutch acquaintance, with a party of his friends, and two or three officers of the Scotch brigade. His astonishment may be conceived when he saw his own brother-in-law, a married man, on the point of leading to the altar the innocent and beautiful creature, upon whom he was about to practise a base and unmanly deceit. He proclaimed his villainy on the spot, and the marriage was interrupted of course. But against the opinion of more thinking men, who considered Sir Philip Forester as having thrown himself out of the rank of men of honour, Captain Falconer admitted him to the privilege of such, accepted a challenge from him, and in the rencounter received a mortal wound. Such are the ways of Heaven, mysterious in our eyes.

Lady Forester never recovered the shock of this dismal intelligence.

"And did this tragedy," said I, "take place exactly at the time when the scene in the mirror was exhibited?"

"It is hard to be obliged to maim one's story," answered my aunt; "but to speak the truth, it happened some days sooner than the apparition was exhibited."

"And so there remained a possibility," said I, "that by some secret and speedy communication the artist might have received early intelligence of that incident."

"The incredulous pretended so," replied my aunt.

"What became of the adept?" demanded I.

"Why, a warrant came down shortly afterwards to arrest him for high treason, as an agent of the Chevalier St. George; * and Lady Bothwell, recollecting the hints which had escaped the Doctor, an ardent friend of the

* Chevalier St. George: the exiled Stuart pretender to the British throne.—Ed.

Protestant succession, did then call to remembrance that this man was chiefly *prôné* * among the ancient matrons of her own political persuasion. It certainly seemed probable that intelligence from the continent, which could easily have been transmitted by an active and powerful agent, might have enabled him to prepare such a scene of phantasmagoria as she had herself witnessed. Yet there were so many difficulties in assigning a natural explanation, that, to the day of her death, she remained in great doubt on the subject, and much disposed to cut the Gordian knot by admitting the existence of supernatural agency."

"But, my dear aunt," said I, "what became of the man of skill?"

"Oh, he was too good a fortune-teller not to be able to foresee that his own destiny would be tragical if he waited the arrival of the man with the silver greyhound upon his sleeve.† He made, as we say, a moonlight flitting, and was nowhere to be seen or heard of. Some noise there was about papers or letters found in the house, but it died away, and Doctor Baptista Damiotti was soon as little talked of as Galen or Hippocrates."

"And Sir Philip Forester," said I, "did he too vanish for ever from the public scene?"

"No," replied my kind informer. "He was heard of once more, and it was upon a remarkable occasion. It is said that we Scots, when there was such a nation in existence, have, among our full peck of virtues, one or two little barleycorns of vice. In particular, it is alleged that we rarely forgive, and never forget, any injuries received; that we used to make an idol of our resentment, as poor Lady Con-

* *Prôné:* cried up, patronized.—Ed.

† Man with the silver greyhound: king's messenger, warrant server.—Ed.

stance * did of her grief; and are addicted, as Burns says, to 'Nursing our wrath to keep it warm.' Lady Bothwell was not without this feeling; and, I believe, nothing whatever, scarce the restoration of the Stuart line, could have happened so delicious to her feelings as an opportunity of being revenged on Sir Philip Forester for the deep and double injury which had deprived her of a sister and of a brother. But nothing of him was heard or known till many a year had passed away.

"At length—it was on a Fastern's E'en (Shrovetide) assembly, at which the whole fashion of Edinburgh attended, full and frequent, and when Lady Bothwell had a seat amongst the lady patronesses, that one of the attendants on the company whispered into her ear that a gentleman wished to speak with her in private.

" 'In private, and in an assembly room! he must be mad; tell him to call upon me to-morrow morning.'

" 'I said so, my lady,' answered the man, 'but he desired me to give you this paper.'

"She undid the billet, which was curiously folded and sealed. It only bore the words, 'On business of life and death,' written in a hand which she had never seen before. Suddenly it occurred to her that it might concern the safety of some of her political friends; she therefore followed the messenger to a small apartment where the refreshments were prepared, and from which the general company was excluded. She found an old man, who at her approach rose up and bowed profoundly. His appearance indicated a broken constitution, and his dress, though sedulously rendered conforming to the etiquette of a ball-room, was worn and tarnished, and hung in folds about his emaci-

---

* Lady Constance: unidentified.—Ed.

ated person. Lady Bothwell was about to feel for her purse, expecting to get rid of the supplicant at the expense of a little money, but some fear of a mistake arrested her purpose. She therefore gave the man leisure to explain himself.

" 'I have the honour to speak with the Lady Bothwell?'

" 'I am Lady Bothwell; allow me to say that this is no time or place for long explanations. What are your commands with me?'

" 'Your ladyship,' said the old man, 'had once a sister.'

" 'True; whom I loved as my own soul.'

" 'And a brother.'

" 'The bravest, the kindest, the most affectionate," said Lady Bothwell.

" 'Both these beloved relatives you lost by the fault of an unfortunate man,' continued the stranger.

" 'By the crime of an unnatural, bloody-minded murderer,' said the lady.

" 'I am answered,' replied the old man, bowing, as if to withdraw.

" 'Stop, sir, I command you,' said Lady Bothwell. 'Who are you, that, at such a place and time, come to recall these horrible recollections? I insist upon knowing.'

" 'I am one who intends Lady Bothwell no injury; but, on the contrary, to offer her the means of doing a deed of Christian charity, which the world would wonder at, and which Heaven would reward; but I find her in no temper for such a sacrifice as I was prepared to ask.'

" 'Speak out, sir; what is your meaning?' said Lady Bothwell.

" 'The wretch that has wronged you so deeply,' rejoined the stranger, 'is now on his death-bed. His days have been days of misery, his nights have been sleepless hours of anguish; yet he cannot die without your forgiveness. His life has been an unremitting penance; yet he dares not part from his burden while your curses load his soul.'

" 'Tell him,' said Lady Bothwell, sternly, 'to ask pardon of that Being whom he has so greatly offended, not of an erring mortal like himself. What could my forgiveness avail him?'

" 'Much,' answered the old man. 'It will be an earnest of that which he may then venture to ask from his Creator, lady, and from yours. Remember, Lady Bothwell, you too have a death-bed to look forward to; your soul may—all human souls must—feel the awe of facing the judgment-seat, with the wounds of an untented conscience, raw and rankling—what thought would it be then that should whisper, "I have given no mercy, how then shall I ask it?" '

" 'Man, whosoever thou mayst be,' replied Lady Bothwell, 'urge me not so cruelly. It would be but blasphemous hypocrisy to utter with my lips the words which every throb of my heart protests against. They would open the earth and give to light the wasted form of my sister, the bloody form of my murdered brother. Forgive him! Never —never.'

" 'Great God!' cried the old man, holding up his hands, 'is it thus the worms which thou hast called out of dust obey the commands of their Maker? Farewell, proud and unforgiving woman. Exult that thou hast added to a death in want and pain the agonies of religious despair; but never again mock Heaven by petitioning for the pardon which thou hast refused to grant.'

"He was turning from her.

" 'Stop,' she exclaimed; 'I will try—yes, I will try to pardon him.'

" 'Gracious lady,' said the old man, 'you will relieve the overburdened soul which dare not sever itself from its sinful companion of earth without being at peace with you. What do I know—your forgiveness may perhaps preserve for penitence the dregs of a wretched life.'

" 'Ha!' said the lady, as a sudden light broke on her, 'it is the villain himself.' And grasping Sir Philip Forester, for it was he, and no other, by the collar, she raised a cry of 'Murder—murder! seize the murderer!'

"At an exclamation so singular, in such a place, the company thronged into the apartment; but Sir Philip Forester was no longer there. He had forcibly extricated himself from Lady Bothwell's hold, and had run out of the apartment, which opened on the landing-place of the stair. There seemed no escape in that direction, for there were several persons coming up the steps, and others descending. But the unfortunate man was desperate. He threw himself over the balustrade, and alighted safely in the lobby, though a leap of fifteen feet at least, then dashed into the street, and was lost in darkness. Some of the Bothwell family made pursuit, and had they come up with the fugitive they might have perhaps slain him; for in those days men's blood ran warm in their veins. But the police did not interfere, the matter most criminal having happened long since, and in a foreign land. Indeed, it was always thought that this extraordinary scene originated in a hypocritical experiment, by which Sir Philip desired to ascertain whether he might return to his native country in safety from the resentment of a family which he had injured so deeply. As the result fell out so contrary to his wishes, he is believed to have returned to the continent, and there died in exile."

So closed the tale of the MYSTERIOUS MIRROR.

❧ El Verdugo

by HONORÉ DE BALZAC

Honoré de Balzac (1799–1850) "is the master of us all," said
Henry James. He creates, by observation and intuition, a fic-
tional world which for modern readers takes the place of the
real world of early nineteenth-century France.

Literary historians label him a Romantic Realist. He was
Romantic in his liking for excessive characters, driven by excessive emotions—love, greed, or even duty. He was Romantic
also in his exuberant imagination and in his taste for violence
and melodrama. His realism appears, in our selection, only in
the backgrounds and supporting details of his work.

El Verdugo was written in 1830. It relates an episode (surely
imaginary) of Napoleon's occupation of Spain (1808–1813).
The translation is by Ellen Marriage. It is taken from *The
Works of Balzac* (New York, 1901).

MIDNIGHT had just sounded from the belfry tower of
the little town of Menda.* A young French officer,
leaning over the parapet of the long terrace at the further
end of the castle gardens, seemed to be unusually absorbed
in deep thought for one who led the reckless life of a
soldier; but it must be admitted that never was the hour,
the scene, and the night more favorable to meditation.

The blue dome of the cloudless sky of Spain was overhead; he was looking out over the coy windings of a lovely
valley lit by the uncertain starlight and the soft radiance of
the moon. The officer, leaning against an orange-tree in
blossom, could also see, a hundred feet below him, the town
of Menda, which seemed to nestle for shelter from the

---

* Menda: an invented name.—Ed.

north wind at the foot of the crags on which the castle itself was built. He turned his head and caught sight of the sea; the moonlit waves made a broad frame of silver for the landscape.

There were lights in the castle windows. The mirth and movement of a ball, the sounds of the violins, the laughter of the officers and their partners in the dance was borne towards him, and blended with the far-off murmur of the waves. The cool night had a certain bracing effect upon his frame, wearied as he had been by the heat of the day. He seemed to bathe in the air, made fragrant by the strong, sweet scent of flowers and of aromatic trees in the gardens.

The castle of Menda belonged to a Spanish grandee, who was living in it at that time with his family. All through the evening the oldest daughter of the house had watched the officer with such a wistful interest that the Spanish lady's compassionate eyes might well have set the young Frenchman dreaming. Clara was beautiful; and although she had three brothers and a sister, the broad lands of the Marqués de Legañes appeared to be sufficient warrant for Victor Marchand's belief that the young lady would have a splendid dowry. But how could he dare to imagine that the most fanatical believer in blue blood in all Spain would give his daughter to the son of a grocer in Paris? Moreover, the French were hated. It was because the Marquis had been suspected of an attempt to raise the country in favor of Ferdinand VII that General G——, who governed the province, had stationed Victor Marchand's battalion in the little town of Menda to overawe the neighboring districts which received the Marqués de Legañes' word as law. A recent despatch from Marshal Ney had given ground for fear that the English might ere long effect a landing on the coast, and had indicated the Marquis as being in correspondence with the Cabinet in London.

In spite, therefore, of the welcome with which the Spaniards had received Victor Marchand and his soldiers, that officer was always on his guard. As he went towards the terrace, where he had just surveyed the town and the districts confided to his charge, he had been asking himself what construction he ought to put upon the friendliness which the Marquis had invariably shown him, and how to reconcile the apparent tranquillity of the country with his General's uneasiness. But a moment later these thoughts were driven from his mind by the instinct of caution and very legitimate curiosity. It had just struck him that there was a very fair number of lights in the town below. Although it was the Feast of St. James, he himself had issued orders that very morning that all lights must be put out in the town at the hour prescribed by military regulations. The castle alone had been excepted in this order. Plainly here and there he saw the gleam of bayonets, where his own men were at their accustomed posts; but in the town there was a solemn silence, and not a sign that the Spaniards had given themselves up to the intoxication of a festival. He tried vainly for awhile to explain this breach of the regulations on the part of the inhabitants; the mystery seemed but so much the more obscure because he had left instructions with some of his officers to do police duty that night, and make the rounds of the town.

With the impetuosity of youth, he was about to spring through a gap in the wall preparatory to a rapid scramble down the rocks, thinking to reach a small guard-house at the nearest entrance into the town more quickly than by the beaten track, when a faint sound stopped him. He fancied that he could hear the light footstep of a woman along the graveled garden walk. He turned his head and saw no one; for one moment his eyes were dazzled by the wonderful brightness of the sea, the next he saw a sight so ominous that he stood stock-still with amazement, thinking that his senses must be deceiving him. The white moonbeams lighted the horizon, so that he could distinguish the sails of ships still a considerable distance out at sea. A shudder ran through him; he tried to persuade himself that this was some optical illusion brought about by chance effects of moonlight on the waves; and even as he made the attempt, a hoarse voice called to him by name. The officer glanced at the gap in the wall; saw a soldier's head slowly emerge from it, and knew the grenadier whom he had ordered to accompany him to the castle.

"Is that you, Commandant?"

"Yes. What is it?" returned the young officer in a low voice. A kind of presentiment warned him to act cautiously.

"Those beggars down there are creeping about like worms; and, by your leave, I came as quickly as I could to report my little reconnoitering expedition."

"Go on," answered Victor Marchand.

"I have just been following a man from the castle who came round this way with a lantern in his hand. A lantern is a suspicious matter with a vengeance! I don't imagine that there was any need for that good Christian to be lighting tapers at this time of night. Says I to myself, 'They mean to gobble us up!' and I set myself to dogging his heels; and that is how I found out that there is a pile of faggots, sir, two or three steps away from here."

Suddenly a dreadful shriek rang through the town below, and cut the man short. A light flashed in the Commandant's face, and the poor grenadier dropped down with a bullet through his head. Ten paces away a bonfire flared up like a conflagration. The sounds of music and laughter ceased all at once in the ballroom; the silence of death, broken only by groans, succeeded to the rhythmical murmur of the festival. Then the roar of cannon sounded from across the white plain of the sea.

A cold sweat broke out on the young officer's forehead. He had left his sword behind. He knew that his men had been murdered, and that the English were about to land. He knew that if he lived he would be dishonored; he saw himself summoned before a court-martial. For a moment his eyes measured the depth of the valley; the next, just as he was about to spring down, Clara's hand caught his.

"Fly!" she cried. "My brothers are coming after me to kill you. Down yonder at the foot of the cliff you will find Juanito's Andalusian. Go!"

She thrust him away. The young man gazed at her in dull bewilderment; but obeying the instinct of self-preservation, which never deserts even the bravest, he rushed across the park in the direction pointed out to him, springing from rock to rock in places unknown to any save the goats. He heard Clara calling to her brothers to pursue him; he heard their balls whistling about his ears; but he reached the foot of the cliff, found the horse, mounted, and fled with lightning speed.

A few hours later the young officer reached General G——'s quarters, and found him at dinner with the staff.

"I put my life in your hands!" cried the haggard and exhausted Commandant of Menda.

He sank into a seat, and told his horrible story. It was received with an appalling silence.

"It seems to me that you are more to be pitied than to blame," the terrible General said at last. "You are not answerable for the Spaniard's crimes, and unless the Marshal decides otherwise, I acquit you."

These words brought but cold comfort to the unfortunate officer.

"When the Emperor comes to hear about it!" he cried.

"Oh, he will be for having you shot," said the General, "but we shall see. Now we will say no more about this," he added severely, "except to plan a revenge that shall strike a salutary terror into this country, where they carry on war like savages."

An hour later a whole regiment, a detachment of cavalry, and a convoy of artillery were upon the road. The General and Victor marched at the head of the column. The soldiers had been told of the fate of their comrades, and their rage knew no bounds. The distance between headquarters and the town of Menda was crossed at a wellnigh miraculous speed. Whole villages by the way were found to be under arms; every one of the wretched hamlets was surrounded, and their inhabitants decimated.

It so chanced that the English vessels still lay out at sea, and were no nearer the shore, a fact inexplicable until it was known afterwards that they were artillery transports which had outsailed the rest of the fleet. So the townsmen of Menda, left without the assistance on which they had reckoned when the sails of the English appeared, were surrounded by French troops almost before they had had time to strike a blow. This struck such terror into them that they offered to surrender at discretion. An impulse of devotion, no isolated instance in the history of the Peninsula, led the actual slayers of the French to offer to give themselves up; seeking in this way to save the town, for from the General's reputation for cruelty it was feared that he would give Menda over to the flames, and put the whole population to the sword. General G—— took their offer, stipulating that every soul in the castle, from the lowest servant to the Marquis, should likewise be given up to him. These terms being accepted, the General promised to spare the lives of the rest of the townsmen, and to prohibit his soldiers from pillaging or setting fire to the town. A heavy contribution was levied, and the wealthiest inhabitants were taken as hostages to guarantee payment within twenty-four hours.

The General took every necessary precaution for the safety of his troops, provided for the defence of the place, and refused to billet his men in the houses of the town. After they had bivouacked, he went up to the castle and entered it as a conqueror. The whole family of the Legañes and their household were gagged, shut up in the great ball-room, and closely watched. From the windows it was easy to see the whole length of the terrace above the town.

The staff was established in an adjoining gallery, where the General forthwith held a council as to the best means of preventing the landing of the English. An aide-de-camp was despatched to Marshal Ney, orders were issued to plant batteries along the coast, and then the General and his staff turned their attention to their prisoners. The two hundred Spaniards given up by the townsfolk were shot down then and there upon the terrace. And after this military execution, the General gave orders to erect gibbets to the number of the prisoners in the ballroom in the same place, and to send for the hangman out of the town. Victor took advantage of the interval before dinner to pay a visit to the prisoners. He soon came back to the general.

"I am come in haste," he faltered out, "to ask a favor."

"*You!*" exclaimed the General, with bitter irony in his tones.

"Alas!" answered Victor, "it is a sorry favor. The Marquis has seen them erecting the gallows, and hopes that you will commute the punishment for his family; he entreats you to have the nobles beheaded."

"Granted," said the General.

"He further asks that they may be allowed the consolations of religion, and that they may be unbound; they give you their word that they will not attempt to escape."

"That I permit," said the General, "but you are answerable for them."

"The old noble offers you all that he has if you will pardon his youngest son."

"Really!" cried the Commander. "His property is forfeit already to King Joseph." * He paused; a contemptuous thought set wrinkles in his forehead, as he added, "I will do better than they ask. I understand what he means by that last request of his. Very good. Let him hand down his name to posterity; but whenever it is mentioned, all Spain shall remember his treason and its punishment! I will give the fortune and his life to any one of the sons who will do the executioner's office. . . . There, don't talk any more about them to me."

Dinner was ready. The officers sat down to satisfy an appetite whetted by hunger. Only one among them was absent from the table—that one was Victor Marchand. After long hesitation, he went to the ballroom, and heard the last sighs of the proud house of Leganés. He looked sadly at the scene before him. Only last night, in this very

* King Joseph: Joseph Bonaparte, brother of Napoleon.—Ed.

room, he had seen their faces whirled past him in the waltz, and he shuddered to think that those girlish heads with those of the three young brothers must fall in a brief space by the executioner's sword. There sat the father and mother, their three sons and two daughters, perfectly motionless, bound to their gilded chairs. Eight serving men stood with their hands tied behind them. These fifteen prisoners, under sentence of death, exchanged grave glances; it was difficult to read the thoughts that filled them from their eyes, but profound resignation and regret that their enterprise should have failed so completely was written on more than one brow.

The impassive soldiers who guarded them respected the grief of their bitter enemies. A gleam of curiosity lighted up all faces when Victor came in. He gave orders that the condemned prisoners should be unbound, and himself unfastened the cords that held Clara a prisoner. She smiled mournfully at him. The officer could not refrain from lightly touching the young girl's arm; he could not help admiring her dark hair, her slender waist. She was a true daughter of Spain, with a Spanish complexion, a Spaniard's eyes, blacker than the raven's wing beneath their long curving lashes.

"Did you succeed?" she asked, with a mournful smile, in which a certain girlish charm still lingered.

Victor could not repress a groan. He looked from the faces of the three brothers to Clara, and again at the three young Spaniards. The first, the oldest of the family, was a man of thirty. He was short, and somewhat ill-made; he looked haughty and proud, but a certain distinction was not lacking in his bearing, and he was apparently no stranger to the delicacy of feeling for which in olden times the chivalry of Spain was famous. His name was Juanito.

The second son, Felipe, was about twenty years of age; he was like his sister Clara; and the youngest was a child of eight. In the features of the little Manuel a painter would have discerned something of that Roman steadfastness which David has given to the children's faces in his Republican *genre* pictures. The old Marquis, with his white hair, might have come down from some canvas of Murillo's. Victor threw back his head in despair after this survey; how should one of these accept the General's offer! Nevertheless he ventured to intrust it to Clara. A shudder ran through the Spanish girl, but she recovered herself almost instantly, and knelt before her father.

"Father," she said, "bid Juanito swear to obey the commands that you shall give him, and we shall be content."

The Marquesa trembled with hope, but as she leant towards her husband and learned Clara's hideous secret, the mother fainted away. Juanito understood it all, and leapt up like a caged lion. Victor took it upon himself to dismiss the soldiers, after receiving an assurance of entire submission from the Marquis. The servants were led away and given over to the hangman and their fate. When only Victor remained on guard in the room, the old Marqués de Legañes rose to his feet.

"Juanito," he said. For all answer Juanito bowed his head in a way that meant refusal; he sank down into his chair, and fixed tearless eyes upon his father and mother in an intolerable gaze. Clara went over to him and sat on his knee; she put her arms about him, and pressed kisses on his eyelids, saying gaily:

"Dear Juanito, if you but knew how sweet death at your hands will be to me! I shall not be compelled to submit to the hateful touch of the hangman's fingers. You will snatch me away from the evils to come and . . . Dear,

kind Juanito, you could not bear the thought of my belonging to any one—well, then?"

The velvet eyes gave Victor a burning glance; she seemed
to try to awaken in Juanito's heart his hatred for the
French.

"Take courage," said his brother Felipe, "or our well-
nigh royal line will be extinct."

Suddenly Clara sprang to her feet. The group round
Juanito fell back, and the son who had rebelled with such
good reason was confronted with his aged father.

"Juanito, I command you!" said the Marquis solemnly.

The young Count gave no sign, and his father fell on his
knees; Clara, Manuel, and Felipe unconsciously followed
his example, stretching out suppliant hands to him who
must save their family from oblivion, and seeming to echo
their father's words.

"Can it be that you lack the fortitude of a Spaniard and
true sensibility, my son? Do you mean to keep me on my
knees? What right have you to think of your own life and
of your own sufferings?—Is this my son, madame?" the
old Marquis added, turning to his wife.

"He will consent to it," cried the mother in agony of
soul. She had seen a slight contraction of Juanito's brows
which she, his mother, alone understood.

Mariquita, the second daughter, knelt, with her slender
clinging arms about her mother; the hot tears fell from her
eyes, and her little brother Manuel upbraided her for weeping. Just at that moment the castle chaplain came in; the
whole family surrounded him and led him up to Juanito.
Victor felt that he could endure the sight no longer, and
with a sign to Clara he hurried from the room to make one
last effort for them. He found the General in boisterous

spirits; the officers were still sitting over their dinner and drinking together; the wine had loosened their tongues.

An hour later, a hundred of the principal citizens of Menda were summoned to the terrace by the General's orders to witness the execution of the family of Legañes. A detachment had been told off to keep order among the Spanish townsfolk, who were marshaled beneath the gallows whereon the Marquis' servants hung; the feet of those martyrs of their cause all but touched the citizens' heads. Thirty paces away stood the block; the blade of a scimitar glittered upon it, and the executioner stood by in case Juanito should refuse at the last.

The deepest silence prevailed, but before long it was broken by the sound of many footsteps, the measured tramp of a picket of soldiers, and the jingling of their weapons. Mingled with these came other noises—loud talk and laughter from the dinner-table where the officers were sitting; just as the music and the sound of the dancers' feet had drowned the preparations for last night's treacherous butchery.

All eyes turned to the castle, and beheld the family of nobles coming forth with incredible composure to their death. Every brow was serene and calm. One alone among them, haggard and overcome, leant on the arm of the priest, who poured forth all the consolations of religion for the one man who was condemned to live. Then the executioner, like the spectators, knew that Juanito had consented to perform his office for a day. The old Marquis and his wife, Clara and Mariquita, and their two brothers knelt a few paces from the fatal spot. Juanito reached it, guided by the priest. As he stood at the block the executioner plucked him by the sleeve and took him aside, probably to give him certain instructions. The confessor so placed the victims that they could not witness the executions, but one and all stood upright and fearless, like Spaniards, as they were.

Clara sprang to her brother's side before the others.

"Juanito," she said to him, "be merciful to my lack of courage. Take me first!"

As she spoke, the footsteps of a man running at full speed echoed from the walls, and Victor appeared upon the scene. Clara was kneeling before the block; her white neck seemed to appeal to the blade to fall. The officer turned faint, but he found strength to rush to her side.

"The General grants you your life if you will consent to marry me," he murmured.

The Spanish girl gave the officer a glance full of proud disdain.

"Now, Juanito!" she said in her deep-toned voice.

Her head fell at Victor's feet. A shudder ran through the Marquesa de Leganés, a convulsive tremor that she could not control, but she gave no other sign of her anguish.

"Is this where I ought to be, dear Juanito? Is it all right?" little Manuel asked his brother.

"Oh, Mariquita, you are weeping!" Juanito said when his sister came.

"Yes," said the girl; "I am thinking of you, poor Juanito; how unhappy you will be when we are gone."

Then the Marquis' tall figure approached. He looked at the block where his children's blood had been shed, turned to the mute and motionless crowd, and said in a loud voice as he stretched out his hands to Juanito:

"Spaniards! I give my son a father's blessing.—Now, *Marquis*, strike 'without fear'; thou art 'without reproach.' "

But when his mother came near, leaning on the confessor's arm—"She fed me from her breast!" Juanito cried, in tones that drew a cry of horror from the crowd. The uproarious mirth of the officers over their wine died away before that terrible cry. The Marquesa knew that Juanito's courage was exhausted; at one bound she sprang to the balustrade, leapt forth, and was dashed to pieces on the rocks below. A cry of admiration broke from the spectators. Juanito swooned.

"General" said an officer, half drunk by this time, "Marchand has just been telling me something about this execution; I will wager that it was not by your orders——"

"Are you forgetting, gentlemen, that in a month's time five hundred families in France will be in mourning, and that we are still in Spain?" cried General G——. "Do you want us to leave our bones here?"

But not a man at the table, not even a subaltern, dared to empty his glass after that speech.

In spite of the respect in which all men hold the Marqués de Legañes, in spite of the title of *El Verdugo* (the executioner) conferred upon him as a patent of nobility by the King of Spain, the great noble is consumed by a gnawing grief. He lives a retired life, and seldom appears in public. The burden of his heroic crime weighs heavily upon him, and he seems to wait impatiently till the birth of a second son shall release him, and he may go to join the Shades that never cease to haunt him.

❧ The Shot

by ALEXANDER SERGEYEVITCH PUSHKIN

Alexander Sergeyevitch Pushkin is regarded as the creator of modern Russian nationalist literature. He was born in Moscow in 1799. His father came of the old Russian gentry; his mother's grandfather was an Abyssinian prince, brought to the court of Peter the Great. Pushkin early displayed his poetic genius, writing in French and Russian celebrations of love, adventure, and vengeance, influenced by Byron and the western Romantics. His tragedy *Boris Godunov* and his verse-novel, *Eugene Onegin*, rank among the masterpieces of Russian literature. He died, in 1837, in a pistol duel provoked by some light words which he took to reflect on his wife's honor.

The Shot was written in 1830. The translation, by T. Keane, appeared in a collection of Pushkin's stories published in London in 1896.

I

WE WERE STATIONED in the little town of N——. The life of an officer in the army is well known. In the morning, drill and the riding-school; dinner with the Colonel or at a Jewish restaurant; in the evening, punch and cards. In N—— there was not one open house, not a single marriageable girl. We used to meet in each other's rooms, where, except our uniforms, we never saw anything.

One civilian only was admitted into our society. He was about thirty-five years of age, and therefore we looked upon him as an old fellow. His experience gave him great advantage over us, and his habitual taciturnity, stern disposition, and caustic tongue produced a deep impression upon our young minds. Some mystery surrounded his existence; he had the appearance of a Russian, although his name was a foreign one. He had formerly served in the Hussars, and with distinction. Nobody knew the cause that had induced him to retire from the service and settle in a wretched little village, where he lived poorly and, at the same time, extravagantly. He always went on foot, and constantly wore a shabby black overcoat, but the officers of our regiment were ever welcome at his table. His dinners, it is true, never consisted of more than two or three dishes, prepared by a retired soldier, but the champagne flowed like water. Nobody knew what his circumstances were, or what his income was, and nobody dared to question him about them. He had a collection of books, consisting chiefly of works on military matters and a few novels. He willingly lent them to us to read, and never asked for them back; on the other hand, he never returned to the owner the books that were lent to him. His principal amusement was shooting with a pistol. The walls of his room were riddled with bullets, and were as full of holes as a honeycomb. A rich collection of pistols was the only luxury in the humble cottage where he lived. The skill which he had acquired with his favorite weapon was simply incredible; and if he had offered to shoot a pear off somebody's forage-cap, not a man in our regiment would have hesitated to place the object upon his head.

Our conversation often turned upon duels. Silvio—so I will call him—never joined in it. When asked if he had ever fought, he dryly replied that he had; but he entered into no particulars, and it was evident that such questions were not to his liking. We came to the conclusion that he had upon his conscience the memory of some unhappy victim of his terrible skill. Moreover, it never entered into the head of any of us to suspect him of anything like cowardice. There are persons whose mere look is sufficient to repel such a suspicion. But an unexpected incident occurred which astounded us all.

One day, about ten of our officers dined with Silvio. They drank as usual, that is to say, a great deal. After dinner we asked our host to hold the bank for a game at faro. For a long time he refused, for he hardly ever played, but at last he ordered cards to be brought, placed half a hundred ducats upon the table, and sat down to deal. We took our places round him, and the play began. It was Silvio's custom to preserve a complete silence when playing. He never disputed, and never entered into explanations. If the punter made a mistake in calculating, he immediately paid him the difference or noted down the surplus. We were acquainted with this habit of his, and we always allowed him to have his own way; but among us on this occasion was an officer who had only recently been transferred to our regiment. During the course of the game, this officer absently scored one point too many. Silvio took the chalk and noted down the correct account according to his usual custom. The officer, thinking that he had made a mistake, began to enter into explanations. Silvio continued dealing in silence. The officer, losing patience, took the brush and rubbed out what he considered was wrong. Silvio took the chalk and corrected the score again. The officer, heated with wine, play, and the laughter of his comrades, considered himself grossly insulted, and in his rage he seized a brass candlestick from the table, and hurled it at Silvio, who barely succeeded in avoiding the missile. We were filled with consternation. Silvio rose, white with rage, and with gleaming eyes, said:

"My dear sir, have the goodness to withdraw, and thank God that this has happened in my house."

None of us entertained the slightest doubt as to what

the result would be, and we already looked upon our new comrade as a dead man. The officer withdrew, saying that he was ready to answer for his offence in whatever way the banker liked. The play went on for a few minutes longer, but feeling that our host was no longer interested in the game, we withdrew one after the other, and repaired to our respective quarters, after having exchanged a few words upon the probability of there soon being a vacancy in the regiment.

The next day, at the riding-school, we were already asking each other if the poor lieutenant was still alive, when he himself appeared among us. We put the same question to him, and he replied that he had not yet heard from Silvio. This astonished us. We went to Silvio's house and found him in the courtyard shooting bullet after bullet into an ace pasted upon the gate. He received us as usual, but did not utter a word about the event of the previous evening. Three days passed, and the lieutenant was still alive. We asked each other in astonishment: "Can it be possible that Silvio is not going to fight?"

Silvio did not fight. He was satisfied with a very lame explanation, and became reconciled to his assailant.

This lowered him very much in the opinion of all our young fellows. Want of courage is the last thing to be pardoned by young men, who usually look upon bravery as the chief of all human virtues, and the excuse for every possible fault. But, by degrees, everything became forgotten, and Silvio regained his former influence.

I alone could not approach him on the old footing. Being endowed by nature with a romantic imagination, I had become attached more than all the others to the man whose life was an enigma, and who seemed to me the hero of some mysterious drama. He was fond of me; at least, with me alone did he drop his customary sarcastic tone, and converse on different subjects in a simple and unusually agreeable manner. But after this unlucky evening, the thought that his honor had been tarnished, and that the stain had been allowed to remain upon it in accordance with his own wish, was ever present in my mind, and prevented me treating him as before. I was ashamed to look at him. Silvio was too intelligent and experienced not to observe this and guess the cause of it. This seemed to vex him; at least I observed once or twice a desire on his part to enter into an explanation with me, but I avoided such opportunities, and Silvio gave up the attempt. From that time forward I saw him only in the presence of my comrades, and our confidential conversations came to an end.

The inhabitants of the capital, with minds occupied by so many matters of business and pleasure, have no idea of the many sensations so familiar to the inhabitants of villages and small towns, as, for instance, the awaiting the arrival of the post. On Tuesdays and Fridays our regimental bureau used to be filled with officers: some expecting money, some letters, and others newspapers. The packets were usually opened on the spot, items of news were communicated from one to another, and the bureau used to present a very animated picture. Silvio used to have his letters addressed to our regiment, and he was generally there to receive them.

One day he received a letter, the seal of which he broke with a look of great impatience. As he read the contents, his eyes sparkled. The officers, each occupied with his own letters, did not observe anything.

"Gentlemen," said Silvio, "circumstances demand my immediate departure; I leave to-night. I hope that you will not refuse to dine with me for the last time. I shall expect you, too," he added, turning towards me. "I shall expect you without fail."

With these words he hastily departed, and we, after agreeing to meet at Silvio's, dispersed to our various quarters.

I arrived at Silvio's house at the appointed time, and found nearly the whole regiment there. All his things were already packed; nothing remained but the bare, bullet-riddled walls. We sat down to table. Our host was in an excellent humor, and his gayety was quickly communicated to the rest. Corks popped every moment, glasses foamed incessantly, and, with the utmost warmth, we wished our departing friend a pleasant journey and every happiness. When we rose from the table it was already late in the evening. After having wished everybody good-bye, Silvio took me by the hand and detained me just at the moment when I was preparing to depart.

"I want to speak to you," he said in a low voice.

I stopped behind.

The guests had departed, and we two were left alone. Sitting down opposite each other, we silently lit our pipes. Silvio seemed greatly troubled; not a trace remained of his former convulsive gayety. The intense pallor of his face, his sparkling eyes, and the thick smoke issuing from his mouth, gave him a truly diabolical appearance. Several minutes elapsed, and then Silvio broke the silence.

"Perhaps we shall never see each other again," said he; "before we part, I should like to have an explanation with you. You may have observed that I care very little for the opinion of other people, but I like you, and I feel that it would be painful to me to leave you with a wrong impression upon your mind."

He paused, and began to knock the ashes out of his pipe. I sat gazing silently at the ground.

"You thought it strange," he continued, "that I did not demand satisfaction from that drunken idiot R——. You will admit, however, that having the choice of weapons, his life was in my hands, while my own was in no great danger. I could ascribe my forbearance to generosity alone, but I will not tell a lie. If I could have chastised R—— without the least risk to my own life, I should never have pardoned him."

I looked at Silvio with astonishment. Such a confession completely astounded me. Silvio continued:

"Exactly so: I have no right to expose myself to death. Six years ago I received a slap in the face, and my enemy still lives."

My curiosity was greatly excited.

"Did you not fight with him?" I asked. "Circumstances probably separated you."

"I did fight with him," replied Silvio; "and here is a souvenir of our duel."

Silvio rose and took from a cardboard box a red cap with a gold tassel and embroidery (what the French call a *bonnet de police*); he put it on—a bullet had passed through it about an inch above the forehead.

"You know," continued Silvio, "that I served in one of the Hussar regiments. My character is well known to you: I am accustomed to taking the lead. From my youth this has been my passion. In our time dissoluteness was the fashion, and I was the most outrageous man in the army. We used to boast of our drunkenness; I beat in a drinking bout the famous Bourtsoff,* of whom Denis Davidoff has sung. Duels in our regiment were constantly taking place, and in all of them I was either second or principal. My

* A cavalry officer, notorious for his drunken escapades. Davidoff was a military poet who flourished in the reign of Alexander I

comrades adored me, while the regimental commanders, who were constantly being changed, looked upon me as a necessary evil.

"I was calmly enjoying my reputation, when a young man belonging to a wealthy and distinguished family—I will not mention his name—joined our regiment. Never in my life have I met with such a fortunate fellow! Imagine to yourself youth, wit, beauty, unbounded gayety, the most reckless bravery, a famous name, untold wealth—imagine all these, and you can form some idea of the effect that he would be sure to produce among us. My supremacy was shaken. Dazzled by my reputation, he began to seek my friendship, but I received him coldly, and without the least regret he held aloof from me. I took a hatred to him. His success in the regiment and in the society of ladies brought me to the verge of despair. I began to seek a quarrel with him; to my epigrams he replied with epigrams which always seemed to me more spontaneous and more cutting than mine, and which were decidedly more amusing, for he joked while I fumed. At last, at a ball given by a Polish landed proprietor, seeing him the object of the attention of all the ladies, and especially of the mistress of the house, with whom I was upon very good terms, I whispered some grossly insulting remark in his ear. He flamed up and gave me a slap in the face. We grasped our swords; the ladies fainted; we were separated; and that same night we set out to fight.

"The dawn was just breaking. I was standing at the appointed place with my three seconds. With inexplicable impatience I awaited my opponent. The spring sun rose, and it was already growing hot. I saw him coming in the distance. He was walking on foot, accompanied by one second. We advanced to meet him. He approached, holding his cap filled with black cherries. The seconds measured twelve paces for us. I had to fire first, but my agitation was so great, that I could not depend upon the steadiness of my hand; and in order to give myself time to become calm, I ceded to him the first shot. My adversary would not agree to this. It was decided that we should cast lots. The first number fell to him, the constant favorite of fortune. He took aim, and his bullet went through my cap. It was now my turn. His life at last was in my hands; I looked at him eagerly, endeavoring to detect if only the faintest shadow of uneasiness. But he stood in front of my pistol, picking out the ripest cherries from his cap and spitting out the stones, which flew almost as far as my feet. His indifference annoyed me beyond measure. 'What is the use,' thought I, 'of depriving him of life, when he attaches no value whatever to it?' A malicious thought flashed through my mind. I lowered my pistol.

" 'You don't seem to be ready for death just at present,' I said to him: 'you wish to have your breakfast; I do not wish to hinder you.'

" 'You are not hindering me in the least,' replied he. 'Have the goodness to fire, or just as you please—the shot remains yours; I shall always be ready at your service.'

"I turned to the seconds, informing them that I had no intention of firing that day, and with that the duel came to an end.

"I resigned my commission and retired to this little place. Since then not a day has passed that I have not thought of revenge. And now my hour has arrived."

Silvio took from his pocket the letter that he had received that morning, and gave it to me to read. Some one (it seemed to be his business agent) wrote to him from Moscow, that a *certain person* was going to be married to a young and beautiful girl.

"You can guess," said Silvio, "who the certain person is.

I am going to Moscow. We shall see if he will look death in the face with as much indifference now, when he is on the eve of being married, as he did once with his cherries!"

With these words, Silvio rose, threw his cap upon the floor, and began pacing up and down the room like a tiger in his cage. I had listened to him in silence; strange conflicting feelings agitated me.

The servant entered and announced that the horses were ready. Silvio grasped my hand tightly, and we embraced each other. He seated himself in his *telega,** in which lay two trunks, one containing his pistols, the other his effects. We said good-bye once more, and the horses galloped off.

II

Several years passed, and family circumstances compelled me to settle in the poor little village of M——. Occupied with agricultural pursuits, I ceased not to sigh in secret for my former noisy and careless life. The most difficult thing of all was having to accustom myself to passing the spring and winter evenings in perfect solitude. Until the hour for dinner I managed to pass away the time somehow or other, talking with the bailiff, riding about to inspect the work, or going round to look at the new buildings; but as soon as it began to get dark, I positively did not know what to do with myself. The few books that I had found in the cupboards and storerooms I already knew by heart. All the stories that my housekeeper Kirilovna could remember I had heard over and over again. The songs of the peasant women made me feel depressed. I tried drinking spirits, but it made my head ache; and moreover, I confess I was afraid of becoming a drunkard from mere chagrin, that is to say,

* *Telega:* a rude springless wagon.—Ed.

the saddest kind of drunkard, of which I had seen many examples in our district.

I had no near neighbors, except two or three topers, whose conversation consisted for the most part of hiccups and sighs. Solitude was preferable to their society. At last I decided to go to bed as early as possible, and to dine as late as possible; in this way I shortened the evening and lengthened out the day, and I found that the plan answered very well.

Four versts from my house was a rich estate belonging to the Countess B——; but nobody lived there except the steward. The Countess had only visited her estate once, in the first year of her married life, and then she had remained there no longer than a month. But in the second spring of my hermitical life a report was circulated that the Countess, with her husband, was coming to spend the summer on her estate. The report turned out to be true, for they arrived at the beginning of June.

The arrival of a rich neighbor is an important event in the lives of country people. The landed proprietors and the people of their households talk about it for two months beforehand and for three years afterwards. As for me, I must confess that the news of the arrival of a young and beautiful neighbor affected me strongly. I burned with impatience to see her, and the first Sunday after her arrival I set out after dinner for the village of A——, to pay my respects to the Countess and her husband, as their nearest neighbor and most humble servant.

A lackey conducted me into the Count's study, and then went on to announce me. The spacious apartment was furnished with every possible luxury. Around the walls were cases filled with books and surmounted by bronze busts; over the marble mantelpiece was a large mirror; on the floor was a green cloth covered with carpets. Unaccustomed to luxury in my own poor corner, and not having seen the wealth of other people for a long time, I awaited the appearance of the Count with some little trepidation, as a suppliant from the provinces awaits the arrival of the minister. The door opened, and a handsome-looking man, of about thirty-two years of age, entered the room. The Count approached me with a frank and friendly air; I endeavored to be self-possessed and began to introduce myself, but he anticipated me. We sat down. His conversation, which was easy and agreeable, soon dissipated my awkward bashfulness; and I was already beginning to recover my usual composure, when the Countess suddenly entered, and I became more confused than ever. She was indeed beautiful. The Count presented me. I wished to appear at ease, but the more I tried to assume an air of unconstraint, the more awkward I felt. They, in order to give me time to recover myself and to become accustomed to my new acquaintances, began to talk to each other, treating me as a good neighbor, and without ceremony. Meanwhile, I walked about the room, examining the books and pictures. I am no judge of pictures, but one of them attracted my attention. It represented some view in Switzerland, but it was not the painting that struck me, but the circumstance that the canvas was shot through by two bullets, one planted just above the other.

"A good shot that!" said I, turning to the Count.

"Yes," replied he, "a very remarkable shot. . . . Do you shoot well?" he continued.

"Tolerably," replied I, rejoicing that the conversation had turned at last upon a subject that was familiar to me. "At thirty paces I can manage to hit a card without fail,— I mean, of course, with a pistol that I am used to."

"Really?" said the Countess, with a look of the greatest interest. "And you, my dear, could you hit a card at thirty paces?"

"Some day," replied the Count, "we will try. In my time I did not shoot badly, but it is now four years since I touched a pistol."

"Oh!" I observed, "in that case, I don't mind laying a wager that Your Excellency will not hit the card at twenty paces; the pistol demands practice every day. I know that from experience. In our regiment I was reckoned one of the best shots. It once happened that I did not touch a pistol for a whole month, as I had sent mine to be mended; and would you believe it, Your Excellency, the first time I began to shoot again, I missed a bottle four times in succession at twenty paces. Our captain, a witty and amusing fellow, happened to be standing by, and he said to me: 'It is evident, my friend, that your hand will not lift itself against the bottle.' No, Your Excellency, you must not neglect to practise, or your hand will soon lose its cunning. The best shot that I ever met used to shoot at least three times every day before dinner. It was as much his custom to do this as it was to drink his daily glass of brandy."

The Count and Countess seemed pleased that I had begun to talk.

"And what sort of a shot was he?" asked the Count.

"Well, it was this way with him, Your Excellency: if he saw a fly settle on the wall—you smile, Countess, but, before Heaven, it is the truth—if he saw a fly, he would call out: 'Kouzka, my pistol!' Kouzka would bring him a loaded pistol—bang! and the fly would be crushed against the wall."

"Wonderful!" said the Count. "And what was his name?"

"Silvio, Your Excellency."

"Silvio!" exclaimed the Count, starting up. "Did you know Silvio?"

"How could I help knowing him, Your Excellency: we were intimate friends; he was received in our regiment like a brother officer, but it is now five years since I had any tidings of him. Then Your Excellency also knew him?"

"Oh, yes, I knew him very well. Did he ever tell you of one very strange incident in his life?"

"Does Your Excellency refer to the slap in the face that he received from some blackguard at a ball?"

"Did he tell you the name of this blackguard?"

"No, Your Excellency, he never mentioned his name. . . . Ah! Your Excellency!" I continued, guessing the the truth: "pardon me . . . I did not know . . . could it really have been you?"

"Yes, I myself," replied the Count, with a look of extraordinary agitation; "and that bullet-pierced picture is a memento of our last meeting."

"Ah, my dear," said the Countess, "for Heaven's sake, do not speak about that; it would be too terrible for me to listen to."

"No," replied the Count: "I will relate everything. He knows how I insulted his friend, and it is only right that he should know how Silvio revenged himself."

The Count pushed a chair towards me, and with the liveliest interest I listened to the following story:

"Five years ago I got married. The first month—the honeymoon—I spent here, in this village. To this house I am indebted for the happiest moments of my life, as well as for one of its most painful recollections.

"One evening we went out together for a ride on horseback. My wife's horse became restive; she grew frightened, gave the reins to me, and returned home on foot. I rode on before. In the courtyard I saw a travelling carriage, and I was told that in my study sat waiting for me a man, who would not give his name, but who merely said that he had business with me. I entered the room and saw in the darkness a man, covered with dust and wearing a beard of several days' growth. He was standing there, near the fireplace. I approached him, trying to remember his features.

" 'You do not recognize me, Count?' said he, in a quivering voice.

" 'Silvio!' I cried, and I confess that I felt as if my hair had suddenly stood on end.

" 'Exactly,' continued he. 'There is a shot due to me, and I have come to discharge my pistol. Are you ready?'

"His pistol protruded from a side pocket. I measured twelve paces and took my stand there in that corner, begging him to fire quickly, before my wife arrived. He hesitated, and asked for a light. Candles were brought in. I closed the doors, gave orders that nobody was to enter, and again begged him to fire. He drew out his pistol and took aim. . . . I counted the seconds. . . . I thought of her. . . . A terrible minute passed! Silvio lowered his hand.

" 'I regret,' said he, 'that the pistol is not loaded with cherry-stones . . . the bullet is heavy. It seems to me that this is not a duel, but a murder. I am not accustomed to taking aim at unarmed men. Let us begin all over again; we will cast lots as to who shall fire first.'

"My head went round . . . I think I raised some objection. . . . At last we loaded another pistol, and rolled up two pieces of paper. He placed these latter in his cap—the same through which I had once sent a bullet—and again I drew the first number.

" 'You are devilish lucky, Count,' said he, with a smile that I shall never forget.

"I don't know what was the matter with me, or how it was that he managed to make me do it . . . but I fired and hit that picture."

The Count pointed with his finger to the perforated picture; his face glowed like fire; the Countess was whiter than her own handkerchief; and I could not restrain an exclamation.

"I fired," continued the Count, "and, thank Heaven, missed my aim. Then Silvio . . . at that moment he was really terrible . . . Silvio raised his hand to take aim at me. Suddenly the door opens, Marsha rushes into the room, and with a loud shriek throws herself upon my neck. Her presence restored to me all my courage.

" 'My dear,' said I to her, 'don't you see that we are joking? How frightened you are! Go and drink a glass of water and then come back to us; I will introduce you to an old friend and comrade.'

"Marsha still doubted.

" 'Tell me, is my husband speaking the truth?' said she, turning to the terrible Silvio: 'is it true that you are only joking?'

" 'He is always joking, Countess,' replied Silvio: 'once he gave me a slap in the face in a joke; on another occasion he sent a bullet through my cap in a joke; and just now, when he fired at me and missed me, it was all in a joke. And now I feel inclined for a joke.'

"With these words he raised his pistol to take aim at me —right before her! Marsha threw herself at his feet.

" 'Rise, Marsha; are you not ashamed!' I cried in a rage: 'and you, sir, will you cease to make fun of a poor woman? Will you fire or not?'

" 'I will not,' replied Silvio: 'I am satisfied. I have seen your confusion, your alarm. I forced you to fire at me.

That is sufficient. You will remember me. I leave you to your conscience.'

"Then he turned to go, but pausing in the doorway, and looking at the picture that my shot had passed through, he fired at it almost without taking aim, and disappeared. My wife had fainted away; the servants did not venture to stop him, the mere look of him filled them with terror. He went out upon the steps, called his coachman, and drove off before I could recover myself."

The Count was silent. In this way I learned the end of the story, whose beginning had once made such a deep impression upon me. The hero of it I never saw again. It is said that Silvio commanded a detachment of Hetairists * during the revolt under Alexander Ypsilanti, and that he was killed in the battle of Skoulana.

* Hetairists: Greek rebels against Turkish rule, led by Prince Ypsilanti (1792–1828).—Ed.

❧ Jean-François Bluestockings

by CHARLES NODIER

Charles Nodier (1780–1814) was born in Besançon, a small city in the Franche-Comté, a province of eastern France. During a part of the Revolution his father was mayor of the city and chief prosecutor. The young man, hostile to Napoleon, spent a number of years abroad; he supported the royalist Restoration in 1814. He was appointed Librarian of the Paris Bibliothèque de l'Arsénal in 1824. There he assembled, for famous *soirées de l'Arsénal,* a group of young Romantics, including Hugo, Musset, and Sainte-Beuve.

The story of Jean-François Bluestockings (1832) records a memory of his school days under the Revolution. It is hard, or impossible, to distinguish therein the share of fact and that of fancy. The translation is by Morris Bishop.

IN 1793 there lived in Besançon an idiot, a monomaniac, a madman, whom all my companions who have had the fortune, good or ill, to live as long as I will remember as I do. His name was Jean-François Touvet, but he was much more commonly called, in the disrespectful language of street-people and students, Jean-François Bluestockings, since he never wore hose of another color. He was a young man of twenty-four or twenty-five, I should think, tall and well-knit, and with the most noble countenance one can imagine. His black, unruly, unpowdered hair, brushed back from his forehead, his heavy, ample, mobile eyebrows, his great eyes, exhibiting a tender expression tempered by a certain habit of gravity, the regularity of his fine features, the almost celestial benevolence of his smile,

made a total effect capable of imposing affection and respect even on the vulgar who pursue with their stupid
jokes the most touching of human infirmities. "It's Jean-
François Bluestockings," they would say with a nudge of
the elbow. "He comes of a decent family of the Franche-
Comté; he's never done anyone any harm. They say he's
gone mad from booklearning. Let him go along, or you'll
just make him worse."

And Jean-François Bluestockings in fact would go along,
paying no attention to anything; for that eye which I can't
properly describe was nexer fixed on the horizon, but incessantly looked up at the sky, with which the person in
question, a visionary, seemed to be carrying on a secret
colloquy, evident only in the perpetual movement of his
lips.

The poor fellow's costume was, however, of a sort to
rouse the laughter of passers-by and especially of visitors
to the town. Jean-François was the son of a worthy tailor
in the rue d'Anvers, who had spared nothing to educate his
son, because of his exceptional promise, which inspired
hopes that he would enter the priesthood and that his brilliant sermons would bring him eventually to the episcopate.
He had in fact been the prize-winner in all his classes, and
the learned Abbé Barbélenet, the sage Quintilian of our
fathers, often inquired, during his emigration,* what had
happened to his favorite pupil; but he got no satisfactory
answer, for there was no hint of the man of genius in the
state of deterioration and disrepute into which Jean-
François Bluestockings had fallen. The old tailor, who had
many other children, economized of necessity on his ex-

* Emigration: i.e., escape abroad, after the French Revolution,
of priests who refused the oath of allegiance to the Republic.—Ed.

penses for Jean-François, and though he kept his son always clean enough, he dressed him only in odds and ends that his trade enabled him to acquire cheap, and in cast-offs of his younger brothers, made over for his use. This sort of ac-coutrement, so ill suited to his tall figure, confined him in a sort of bulging sheath, allowing more than half of his fore-arm to emerge from his green cutaway coat, and giving him a sadly comic appearance. His breeches, tight upon his thighs, and pulled down carefully but vainly, barely reached at his knees the blue stockings that conferred upon him his popular name. As for his three-cornered hat, a ri-diculous form of headgear for anyone, the shape contrived by its maker and Jean-François' manner of wearing it made his face, poetic and majestic, an absurdity. If I should live a thousand years I should never forget Jean-François Blue-stockings' grotesque outfit or his little three-cornered hat.

One of the most remarkable aspects of this good young man's madness is that it was noticeable only in unimportant conversations, in which the mind deals with familiar mat-ters. If one accosted him to talk of rain and fine weather, of the play, of the newspaper, of town gossip, of national concerns, he would listen with attention and reply politely; but the words pouring from his lips crowded so tumultu-ously that before he finished his first sentence they fell into a tangled rigmarole, from which he could not extricate his thought. He would continue nonetheless, more and more unintelligibly, and more and more substituting for an ordinary man's natural, logical phrase the babble of a child who does not know the value of words, or the rambling drivel of an old man who has forgotten that value. Then people would laugh; and Jean-François would fall silent, without anger, perhaps without notice, raising his fine, great black eyes to heaven, as if to seek inspirations more worthy of him in the region where he had fixed all his ideas and feelings.

But it was quite different when the conversation dealt with precision on an intellectual or scientific question of some interest. Then the divergent, scattering rays of that sick mind assembled suddenly in a sheaf, as do those of the sun in Archimedes' lens, and conferred so much brilliancy on his speech that one may well doubt whether Jean-François, in the full possession of his reason, would ever have been more learned, clear, and persuasive. The most difficult problems of the exact sciences, of which he had made a special study, were just a game for him; and the solution would pass so readily from his mind to his lips that one would regard it less as the result of reflection and calculation than as that of a mechanical operation subject to the actuation of a key or spring. It seemed to those who then listened to him—and who were worthy to hear him—that so lofty a faculty was not bought too dear at the cost of the common advantage of easily enunciating vulgar ideas in vulgar language. But the vulgar are the judges; and for them the man in question was only an idiot in blue stockings, incapable of carrying on even the conversation of ordinary men. And that was quite true.

As the rue d'Anvers comes almost to the high school, I would pass there four times a day on my way to and fro. But it was only at the mid-day hours, and on warm, sunny days, that I was sure to find Jean-François there, on a little stool, before his father's shop. Usually he was surrounded by a circle of stupid students, who were amused by the extravagance of his bizarre phrases. When still far off I was made aware of this occurrence by the shouts of laughter of his auditors; and when I arrived, with my strapped dictionaries under my arm, I sometimes had trouble in making my way to him. But I felt constantly a fresh pleasure in our meetings, for, boy though I was, I thought that I had penetrated the secret of his double life, and I felt that I was confirming my theory at each encounter.

One evening at the beginning of autumn, a dark day with a storm threatening, the rue d'Anvers, not a busy street, incidentally, seemed totally deserted except for one man. This was Jean-François, sitting motionless with his eyes uplifted, as usual. He had not yet been brought in, with his stool. Not to distract him, I approached quietly; and when he seemed to be conscious of me, I leaned over to speak in his ear.

"What, you are all alone!" I said to him without thinking—for ordinarily I would approach him with some question about the aorist or logarithms, about the hypotenuse or the trope, or with some other difficulties in my literary-scientific studies. Then I bit my lips, thinking that my stupid remark, which would bring him down to earth from the empyrean, would plunge him into his customary balderdash, which I could never hear without a violent pang in my heart.

"Alone!" Jean-François replied, seizing me by the arm. "Only an idiot is alone; only a blind man cannot see, it is only a paralytic whose feeble legs cannot support themselves and stand firm on the earth. . . ."

"Well, here we go again," I said to myself, while he continued to talk in obscure phrases—which I wish I could recall, for perhaps they contained more sense than I then imagined. "Poor Jean-François is off again; but I will check him. I know the magic wand which will free him from his enchantments. . . . In fact it is possible," I exclaimed, "that the planets are inhabited, as Monsieur de Fontenelle supposed,* and that you have secret dealings with their inhabitants, like Monsieur le comte de Gabalis." † I stopped, proud of having displayed such magnificent erudition.

Jean-François smiled, cast his gentle glance upon me, and said: "Do you know what a planet is?"

"I suppose that it is a world that more or less resembles ours."

"And what is a world? Do you know that?"

"A large body which regularly performs certain revolutions in space."

"And space—have you realized what that may be?"

"Now wait a minute," said I. "I have to recall our definitions. Space? It's a subtle, infinite medium, in which move stars and worlds."

"I'll accept that. And what are stars and worlds relatively to space?"

"Probably wretched atoms, lost therein like dust in the air."

"And the matter forming stars and worlds, what do you think that is in comparison with the subtle matter that fills space?"

"How can I answer that? There is no possible expression to compare such gross bodies with so pure an element."

"Excellent! And could you understand, my boy, how a God, creator of everything, who has given to those gross bodies inhabitants, no doubt imperfect but yet, like us two, animated with the need of a better life, would have left space uninhabited?"

"No, I couldn't understand it!" I answered in an outburst. "I even think that just as we are much superior in refinement of organization to the matter in which we are

* In his *Entretiens sur la pluralité des mondes* (1686).—Ed.
† In the *Entretiens* of Montfaucon de Villars (1670).—Ed.

bound, the inhabitants of space must likewise be much superior to the subtle matter that envelops them. But how could I come to know them?"

"By learning to see them," replied Jean-François, very gently thrusting me away. At the same time his head subsided against the back of his tripartite stool. His glance resumed its fixity, his lips their movement.

I went on my way, discreetly. Hardly had I taken a few steps before I heard behind me his father and mother urging him to come in, since the weather was threatening. He submitted as usual to their slightest persuasions; but his return to the real world was always accompanied by that flux of incoherent words which furnished to the yokels of the quarter their customary amusement.

I continued on my course, wondering whether it might not be possible that Jean-François had two souls, one belonging to the gross world in which we live, the other purified in the subtle space into which he imagined he could penetrate by means of thought. I became rather entangled in this theory, and I would still be entangled by it.

Thus I arrived at home, more preoccupied, and especially otherwise preoccupied than if my kite-string had broken in my hands or if my ball, violently flung, had fallen from the rue des Cordeliers into the garden of Monsieur de Grobois. My father questioned me about my upset state; and I have never lied to him. I reported to him, without forgetting a word, my conversation with Jean-François Bluestockings. Said he: "I thought that all these fantasies were buried forever, with the books of Swedenborg and Saint-Martin, in the grave of my old friend Cazotte; * but it appears that this young man, who has passed a few days

* Jacques Cazotte, French poet and fiction-writer; Emanuel Swedenborg, Swedish scientist, philosopher, and religious mystic; Louis Claude de Saint-Martin, French mystical philosopher.—Ed.

in Paris, has been infected by the same follies. Incidentally, there is a certain finesse of observation in the ideas that his double-talk suggested to you, and your own explanation requires only that it be reduced to its exact expression. The faculties of intelligence are not so indivisible that they may not be afflicted separately by an infirmity of body and mind. Thus the mental deterioration that poor Jean-François displays in the commoner activities of his judgment may well not have attacked the properties of his memory; that is why he replies sensibly when he is questioned about things that he has learned slowly and retained with difficulty, whereas he talks nonsense about things that present themselves unexpectedly to his senses, concerning which he has never needed to erect an exact formula. I should be much surprised if that were not to be observed in the case of most madmen. But I don't know if you have understood me."

"I think I have understood you, father; and forty years from now I should be able to write down your exact words."

"That is more than I would ask of you," he replied, embracing me. "Within a few years you will be well enough fortified by more serious studies against illusions which impose themselves only on weak spirits or sick minds. Remember this only—since you are so sure of your future recollections—that there is nothing simpler than the notions that approach the truth, and nothing more specious than the notions that depart from it."

"It is true," I thought on my way to bed, "that *The Arabian Nights* are incomparably more pleasant to read than the first volume of Bezout; * and who has ever believed for a moment in *The Arabian Nights*?"

* Bezout: mathematician, author of *A General Theory of Algebraic Equations.*—Ed.

The storm was still rumbling on. It was so beautiful that I could not help opening my pretty casement window on the rue Neuve, opposite that charming fountain which my grandfather the architect presented to the city. It is adorned with a bronze siren, who often, at the bidding of my charmed imagination, mingled her poetic chants with the murmur of the water. I gazed attentively at the fiery meteors descending from the clouds, clashing and crashing, as if ready to shatter all the worlds together. And sometimes, when the flaming curtain was ripped apart in thunder, my eye, quicker than the lightning, darted into the infinite heaven opening above; it seemed to me more pure and tranquil than a lovely springtime sky. "Oh!" I then said to myself, "if the vast plains of space should after all contain inhabitants, how pleasant it would be to repose with them from all the tempests of earth! What unalloyed peace is to be enjoyed in that limpid region which is never agitated, never deprived of the sun's beams, and which laughs, luminous and placid, above our hurricanes as above our miseries! O delicious vales of heaven," I cried, weeping profusely, "God has not created you to be deserts; some day I shall visit you, my arm linked to that of my father!"

My conversation with Jean-François had left upon me an impression which sometimes frightened me. Nature came to life about me, as if my feeling for it had made some spark of divinity flash forth from the most insensible objects. If I had been better informed, I should have understood pantheism. As it was, I invented it.

However, I took my father's advice to heart. I avoided even conversation with Jean-François Bluestockings, or I approached him only when he was involved in one of those eternal tangled sentences that seemed to have no other purpose than to terrify logic and to exhaust the dictionary. As for Jean-François Bluestockings, he did not recognize me, or he did not give any evidence that he distinguished me from the other schoolboys of my age, although I had been the only one who had guided him, when I was so inclined, to consecutive conversations and sensible definitions.

Scarcely a month passed after my interview with the visionary; and for this episode I am perfectly sure of the date. It was the very day when the school year opened, after six weeks of vacation which began on September 1; consequently it was October 16, 1793. It was nearly noon; I was returning from the school more gayly than I had entered it, with two of my comrades who followed the same route to their homes and who were taking the same courses as I was—but they have left me far behind. They are both living; I could designate them without fear of their protesting my statements, if their names, justly famous, could decently be divulged in an account in which, no doubt, one expects no more than the verisimilitude required in a fantasy—and after all I don't offer it myself as anything else.

Arriving at a certain street-corner where we commonly separated to take different courses, we were all struck by the contemplative attitude of Jean-François Bluestockings. He was standing like a statue in the exact middle of the street-junction, motionless, his arms crossed, his air sadly pensive, his eyes imperturbably fixed on some point high above the western horizon. Some passers-by had gathered about him, and were looking vainly for whatever extraordinary object seemed to absorb all his attention.

"What's he looking at up there?" they were inquiring among themselves. "A flight of strange birds? Or has a balloon gone up?"

"I'll tell you!" said I, pushing through the crowd, plying

my elbows to right and left. "Tell us, Jean-François; what new thing have you noticed this morning in the subtle matter of space, where all the worlds are in motion?"

"Don't you know it as well as I do?" he answered me with a wave of his arm, describing with a pointed finger a long arc from the horizon to the zenith. "Follow with your eyes those traces of blood, and you will see Marie-Antoinette, Queen of France, on her way to heaven!"

Then the bystanders dispersed, shrugging their shoulders; they had concluded from his reply that he was crazy. I also went my way, merely surprised that Jean-François Bluestockings had landed so exactly on the name of the last of our queens, as this positive detail fell into the category of true facts of which he had lost his knowledge.

My father was in a habit of assembling two or three friends for dinner on the first day of each fortnight. One of his guests, a stranger to the city, came in rather late. "Excuse me," said he, taking his seat. "The story was going around, according to some private letters, that unfortunate Marie-Antoinette was to be put on trial. I delayed a little to get the mail leaving Paris on October 13. But the newspapers say nothing of it."

"Marie-Antoinette, Queen of France," said I with assurance, "died on the scaffold this morning a few minutes before noon, as I was coming back from school."

"Ah! mon Dieu!" cried my father. "Who could have told you that?"

I was abashed, and blushed. But I had said too much to keep silence. I replied, trembling: "It was Jean-François Bluestockings."

I ventured to raise my eyes toward my father. His extreme indulgence for me did not reassure me about the displeasure that my indiscretion must have inspired in him.

"Jean-François Bluestockings!" he said with a laugh. "Fortunately we can be calm about news reaching us from that source. That cruel, needless, dastardly act will not be committed."

Said my father's friend: "Who is this Jean-François Bluestockings who announces events a hundred leagues distant, at the moment when he presumes they are taking place? Is he a somnambulist, a convulsionary, a pupil of Mesmer or Cagliostro?"

"Something like it," replied my father, "but more worthy of interest. He's an honest visionary, an inoffensive maniac, a poor madman who is to be pitied, as he deserved to be loved. He comes from an honorable family of worthy artisans, not well off. He was their hope and pride, a lad of great promise. The first year of a minor magistracy that I exercised here * was the last year of his studies. He quite wore out my arm in crowning him, and the variety of his achievements added to their value; you would have said that it was easy for him to open all the doors of human intelligence. The hall almost cracked open with the noise of applause when he came up to receive a prize without which all the others are worthless, that is, the prize for good conduct and the virtues of an exemplary youth. There was not a father present who wouldn't have been glad to number him among his sons, and apparently not a rich man who wouldn't have been delighted to have him for a son-in-law. I don't mention the girls, who must naturally have been captivated by his angelic beauty and his fortunate age, between eighteen and twenty. And that is what destroyed him—not that his modesty was overcome by the seductions of his triumph, but he was undone by the proper

* Antoine-Melchior Nodier was elected mayor and magistrate of Besançon in 1790.—Ed.

results of the impression he had made. You have heard of the lovely Madame de Sainte-A——. She was then in Franche-Comté, where her family is so well remembered, and where her sisters have established themselves. She was looking for a tutor for her son, who was not over twelve; and the glory which had just attached itself to the humble name of Jean-François determined her choice in his favor. Four or five years ago that was the way to begin an honorable career for a young man who had profited by his studies and who was not led astray by mad ambitions. From now on I can tell you only what I had from imperfect reports. Unfortunately the lovely lady who had thus rewarded the youthful talent of Jean-François was mother also of a daughter, and this daughter was charming. Jean-François could not see her without loving her; however, well recognizing the impossibility of rising to her level, he seems to have sought to distract himself from an invincible passion, which came to light only in the first periods of his illness, by devoting himself to studies dangerous to his reason, to the delusions of occult sciences and the visions of an exalted spiritualism. He went totally mad; he was dismissed from Corbeil, the home of his protectors, with all the attentions that his condition demanded. But no gleam has lightened the darkness of his mind since his return to his family. You see that there is little basis for his assertions, and that we have no reason to be alarmed by them."

Nevertheless, it was learned on the following day that the Queen had been brought to trial, and two days afterward that she was dead.

My father feared the impression I was bound to receive from the extraordinary coincidence of this catastrophe and the prediction. He spared no pains to convince me that chance is fertile in providing such concurrences. He cited

a dozen examples, which serve as arguments only for ignorant credulity, but are scouted by both philosophy and
religion.

A few weeks later I left for Strasbourg, where I was
about to undertake some new studies. The times were not
favorable to spiritualist doctrines, and I easily forgot Jean-
François in the midst of the emotions that daily tormented
society.

Circumstances brought me back in the following spring.
One morning (I think it was the third of Messidor *) I
entered my father's bedroom to give him my customary
morning kiss before beginning my daily excursion in search
of plants and butterflies. "We need no longer pity poor
Jean-François for having lost his reason," he said, pointing
to the newspaper. "It is better for him to be mad than to
learn of the tragic death of his benefactress, his pupil, and
the young lady who is supposed to have been the first cause
of his mental derangement. These innocent creatures have
also fallen victims to the executioner."

"Is it possible!" I exclaimed. "Alas, I had told you nothing of Jean-François, because I know that you fear the
influence on me of certain mysterious ideas he communicated to me. But he is dead!"

"Dead!" said my father sharply. "And since when?"

"Since three days ago, the twenty-ninth of Prairial.† He
had been standing motionless since early morning in the
midst of the little square, on the very spot where I found
him at the time of the Queen's death. A good many people
gathered around him, although he kept perfect silence, for
his preoccupation was so deep that it could not be distracted

* Third of Messidor: June 21, in the revolutionary calendar.—Ed.
† Twenty-ninth of Prairial: June 17, in the revolutionary calendar.—Ed.

by any question. Finally, at four o'clock, his attention seemed to become even more fixed. A few minutes later he raised his arms toward heaven with a strange expression of exaltation or pain, took a few steps, speaking the names of the persons you have just mentioned, uttered a cry, and fell. People rushed toward him and hastily lifted him up, but all in vain. He was dead."

"The twenty-ninth of Prairial, at a few minutes after four——" said my father, consulting his newspaper. "That is exactly the day and the hour! . . . Listen——" he continued after a moment's reflection, fixing his eyes on mine. "Don't refuse me the request I am going to make of you. If ever you tell this story when you are a grown man, don't give it out as true, because it would expose you to ridicule."

"Are there reasons which can exempt a man from proclaiming publicly what he recognizes as the truth?" I rejoined respectfully.

"There is one that outweighs all the others," said my father, shaking his head. "Truth? Truth is useless."

❦ Chairolas

by EDWARD BULWER-LYTTON

Edward George Earle Lytton Bulwer-Lytton (1803–1873) became the first Baron Bulwer-Lytton, and as such is commonly known. He was dedicated to authorship from his early youth, and produced an impressive mass of prose and verse, at the same time engaging in an active political career. Few no doubt today read his novels, such as *Pelham, Rienzi,* and *The Last Days of Pompeii.* But he was a sharp observer of human behavior, and possessed a very pretty wit.

Chairolas first appeared in 1834. Though it stems from the eighteenth-century *conte philosophique,* it is Romantic in its bold, melodramatic imaginations and in its play of whimsical fancy.

I

ONCE UPON A TIME there existed a kingdom called Paida,* stretching to the west of that wide tract of land known to certain ancient travellers by the name of Callipaga.† The heirs apparent to the throne of this kingdom were submitted to a very singular ordeal. At the extremity of the empire was a chain of mountains, separating Paida from an immense region, the chart of which no geographer had ever drawn. Various and contradictory were all the accounts of this region, from the eldest to the latest time. According to some it was the haunt of robbers and demons; every valley was beset with danger; the fruits of every tree were poisonous; and evil spirits lurked in every path, sometimes to fascinate, and sometimes to terrify, the

* Paida: suggesting the Greek *paideia,* "education" or "youth."—Ed.

† Callipaga: suggesting the Greek *cali pagi,* "beautiful snare."—Ed.

inexperienced traveller to his destruction. Others, on the contrary, asserted that no land on earth equalled the beauty and the treasures of this mystic region. The purest air circulated over the divinest landscapes; the inhabitants were beneficent genii; and the life they led was that of happiness without alloy, and excitement without satiety. At the age of twenty the heir to the throne was ordained, by immemorial custom, to penetrate alone into this debated and enigmatical realm. It was supposed to require three years to traverse the whole of it, nor was it until this grand tour for the royalty of Paida was completed, that the adventurer was permitted to return home and aspire to the heritage of the crown. It happened, however, that a considerable proportion of these travellers never again re-entered their native land—detained, according to some, by the beautiful fairies of the unknown region; or, according to others, sacrificed by its fiends. One might imagine that those princes who were fortunate enough to return, travellers too respectable to be addicted to gratuitous invention, would have been enabled by their testimony to reconcile the various reports of the country into which they had penetrated. But after their return the austere habits of royalty compelled them to discretion and reserve; and the hints which had escaped them from time to time, when conversing with their more confidential courtiers, so far from elucidating, confirmed the mystery; for each of the princes had evidently met with a different fortune: with one the reminiscences bequeathed by his journey seemed brilliant and delightful; while, perhaps, with his successor, the unknown region was never alluded to without a shudder or a sigh. Thus the only persons who could have reconciled conflicting rumours were exactly those who the most kept alive the debate; and the empire was still divided into two

parties, who, according to the bias of their several dispositions, represented the neighbouring territory as an Elysium
or a Tartarus.

The present monarch had of course undergone the customary ordeal. Naturally bold and cheerful, he had commenced his eventful journey with eagerness and hope, and
had returned to Paida an altered and melancholy man. He
swayed his people with great ability and success, he entered
into all the occupations of his rank, and did not reject its
pleasures and its pomps; but it was evident that his heart
was not with his pursuits. He was a prey to some secret
regret; but, whether he sighed to regain the land he had
left, or was saddened by the adventures he had known in
it, was a matter of doubt and curiosity even to his queen.
Several years of his wedded life were passed without
promise of an heir, and the eyes of the people were already
turned to the eldest nephew of the sovereign, when it was
formally announced to the court that the queen had been
graciously pleased to become in the family way.

In due process of time a son made his appearance. He
was declared a prodigy of beauty, and there was something
remarkably regal in the impatience of his cries. Nothing
could exceed the joy of the court, unless it was the grief
of the king's eldest nephew. The king himself, indeed, was
perhaps also an exception to the general rapture; he looked
wistfully on the crimson cheeks of his first-born son, and
muttered to himself, "These boys are a great subject of
anxiety."

"And of pride," said a small sweet voice that came from
the cradle.

The king was startled—for even in Paida a king's son
does not speak as soon as he is born: he looked again at the
little prince's face—it was not from him that the voice
came; his royal highness had just fallen asleep.

"Dost thou not behold me, O king?" said the voice again.

And now the monarch beheld upon the pillow a small creature scarcely taller than a needle, but whose shape was modelled in the most beautiful proportions of manhood.

"Know," continued the apparition, while the king remained silent with consternation, "that I am the good Genius of the new-born; each mortal hath at his birth his guardian spirit, though the Genius be rarely visible. I bring to thy son the three richest gifts that can be bestowed upon man; but, alas! they are difficult to preserve—teach him to guard them as his most precious treasure."

The Genius vanished. The king recovered from his amaze, and, expecting to find some jewels of enormous value, hastily removed the coverlid, and saw by the side of his child an eagle's feather, a pigeon's feather, and a little tuft of the down of a swan.

II

The prince grew up strong, handsome, and graceful; he evinced the most amiable dispositions; he had much of that tender and romantic enthusiasm which we call Sentiment, and which serves to render the virtues so lovely; he had an intuitive admiration for all that is daring and noble; and his ambition would, perhaps, have led him into dangerous excesses were it not curbed, or purified, by a singular disinterestedness and benevolence of disposition, which rendered him fearful to injure and anxious to serve those with whom he came into contact. The union of such qualities was calculated to conduct him to glory, but to render him scrupulous as to its means; his desire to elevate himself was strong, but it was blended with a stronger wish to promote the welfare of others. Princes of this nature were not common in Paida, and the people looked with the most sanguine hopes to the prospect of his reign. He had, however, some little drawbacks to the effect of his good qualities. His susceptibilities made him too easy with his friends, and somewhat too bashful with strangers; with the one he found it difficult to refuse anything, with the other he was too keenly alive to ridicule and the fear of shame. But the first was a failing very easily forgiven at a court, and the second was one that a court would, in all probability, correct. The king took considerable pains with the prince's education. His talents were great, and he easily mastered whatever he undertook; but at each proof of the sweetness of his disposition, or the keenness of his abilities, the good king seemed to feel rather alarm than gratification. "Alas!" he would mutter to himself, "that fatal region—that perilous ordeal!" and then turn hastily away.

These words fed the prince's curiosity without much exciting his fear. The journey presented nothing terrible to his mind, for the courtiers, according to their wont, deemed it disloyal to report to him any but the most flattering accounts of the land he was to visit; and he attributed the broken expressions of his father partly to the melancholy of his constitution, and partly to the over-acuteness of paternal anxiety. For the rest, it was a pleasant thing to get rid of his tutors and the formalities of a court; and with him, as with all the young, hope was an element in which fear could not breathe. He longed for his twentieth year, and forgot to enjoy the pleasures of boyhood in his anticipation of the excitement of youth.

III

The fatal time arrived; the Prince Chairolas had taken leave of his weeping mother, embraced his friends, and was receiving the last injunctions of his father, while his horses impatiently snorted at the gates of the palace.

"My son," said the king, with more than his usual gravity, "from the journey you are about to make you are nearly sure of returning a wiser man, but you may not return a better one. The three charms which you have always worn about your person you must be careful to preserve." Here the king for the first time acquainted the wondering prince with the visit to his infant pillow, and repeated the words of the guardian spirit. Chairolas had always felt a lively curiosity to know why, from his infancy, he had been compelled to wear about his royal person three things so apparently worthless as an eagle's feather, a pigeon's feather, and the tuft of a swan's down, and still more why such seeming trifles had been gorgeously set in jewels. The secret now made known to him elevated his self-esteem; he was evidently, then, a favourite with the superior powers, and marked from his birth for no ordinary destinies.

"Alas!" concluded the king, "had I received such talismans, perhaps——"; he broke off abruptly, once more embraced his son, and hastened to shroud his meditations in the interior of his palace.

Meanwhile the prince set out upon his journey. The sound of the wind-instruments upon which his guards played cheerily, the caracoles of his favourite charger, the excitement of the fresh air, the sense of liberty, and the hope of adventure—all conspired to elevate his spirits. He forgot father, mother, and home. Never was journey undertaken under gayer presentiments, or by a more joyous mind.

IV

At length the prince arrived at the spot where his attendants were to quit him. It was the entrance of a narrow defile through precipitous and lofty mountains. Wild trees of luxuriant foliage grew thickly along the path. It seemed a primeval vale, desolate even in its beauty, as though man had never trodden it before. The prince paused for a moment, his friends and followers gathered round him with their adieus, and tears, and wishes, but still Hope animated and inspired him; he waved his hand gaily, spurred his steed, and the trees soon concealed his form from the gaze of his retinue.

He proceeded for some time with slowness and difficulty, so entangled was the soil by its matted herbage, so obstructed was the path by the interlaced and sweeping boughs. At length, towards evening, the ground became more open; and, descending a gentle hill, a green and lovely plain spread itself before him. It was intersected by rivulets, and variegated with every species of plant and tree; it was a garden in which Nature seemed to have shown how well she can dispense with Art. The prince would have been very much enchanted if he had not begun to be very hungry; and, for the first time, he recollected that it was possible to be starved. He looked round anxiously, but vainly, for some sign of habitation, and then he regarded the trees to see if they bore fruit; but, alas! it was the spring of the year, and he could only console himself with observing that the abundance of the blossoms promised plenty of fruit for the autumn,—a long time for a prince to wait for his dinner!

He still, however, continued to proceed, when suddenly he came upon a beaten track, evidently made by art. His horse neighed as its hoofs rang upon the hardened soil, and, breaking of itself into a quicker pace, soon came to a wide arcade overhung with roses. "This must conduct to some mansion," thought Chairolas.

But the night came on, and still the prince was in the arcade; the stars, peeping through, here and there served to guide his course, until at length lights, more earthly and more brilliant, broke upon him. The arcade ceased, and Chairolas found himself at the gates of a mighty city, over whose terraces, rising one above the other, the moon shone bright and still.

"Who is there?" asked a voice at the gate.

"Chairolas, Prince of Paida!" answered the traveller.

The gates opened instantly. "Princes are ever welcome at the city of Chrysaor," * said the same voice.

And as Chairolas entered, he saw himself instantly surrounded by a group of both sexes richly attired, and bending to the earth with Eastern adoration, while, as with a single voice, they shouted out, "Welcome to the Prince of Paida!"

A few minutes more, and Chairolas was in the magnificent chamber of a magnificent house, seated before a board replete with the rarest viands and the choicest wines.

"All this is delightful," thought the prince, as he finished his supper; "but I see nothing of either fairies or fiends."

His soliloquy was interrupted by the master of the mansion, who came to conduct the prince to his couch. Scarcely was his head upon his pillow ere he fell asleep,— a sure sign that he was a stranger at Chrysaor, where the prevalent disease was the want of rest.

The next day, almost before Chairolas was dressed, his lodging was besieged by all the courtiers of the city. He found that, though his dialect was a little different from theirs, the language itself was much the same; for, perhaps, there is no court in the universe where a prince is not toler-

---

* Chrysaor: Greek, "gold-sworded." The significance is not clear.—Ed.

ably well understood. The servile adulation which Chairolas had experienced in Paida was not nearly so delightful
as the polished admiration he received from the courtiers
of Chrysaor. While they preserved that tone of equality
without which all society is but the interchange of ceremonies, they evinced, by a thousand nameless attentions,
their respect for his good qualities, which they seemed to
penetrate as by an instinct. The gaiety, the animation, the
grace of those he saw, perfectly intoxicated the prince. He
was immediately involved in a round of engagements. It
was impossible that he should ever be alone.

v

As the confusion of first impressions wore off, Chairolas
remarked a singular peculiarity in the manners of his new
friends. They were the greatest laughers he had ever met.
Not that they laughed loudly, but that they laughed constantly. This habit was not attended with any real merri-
ment or happiness. Many of the saddest persons laughed
the most. It was also remarkable that the principal objects
of the cachinnatory ebullitions were precisely such as
Chairolas had been taught to consider the most serious, and
the farthest removed from ludicrous associations. They
never laughed at anything witty or humorous, at a comedy
or a joke. But if one of their friends became poor, then
how they laughed at his poverty! If a child broke the heart
of a father, or a wife ran away from her husband, or a great
lord cheated at play, or ruined his tradesmen, then they had
no command over their muscles. In a word, misfortune or
vice made a principal object of this epidemical affection.
But not the only object, they laughed at anything that
differed from their general habits. If a virgin blushed—if a
sage talked wisdom—if a man did anything uncommon,

no matter what, they were instantly seized with this jovial convulsion. They laughed at generosity—they laughed at sentiment—they laughed at patriotism—and, though affecting to be exceedingly pious, they laughed with particular pleasure at any extraordinary show of religion.

Chairolas was extremely puzzled; for he saw that, if they laughed at what was bad, they laughed also at what was good: it seemed as if they had no other mode of condemning or applauding. But what perplexed him yet more was a strange transformation to which this people were subject. Their faces were apt to turn, even in a single night, into enormous rhododendrons; * and it was very common to see a human figure walking about as gaily as possible with a flower upon his shoulders instead of a face.

Resolved to enlighten himself as to this peculiarity of custom, Chairolas one day took aside a courtier who appeared to him the most intelligent of his friends. Grinaldibus Hassan Sneeraskin (so was the courtier termed) laughed longer than ever when he heard the perplexity of the prince.

"Know," said he, as soon as he had composed himself, "that there are two penal codes in this city. For one set of persons, whom you and I never see except in the streets,—persons who hew the wood and draw the water—persons who work for the other classes,—we have punishments, such as hanging, and flogging, and shutting up in prisons, and Heaven knows what;—punishments, in short, that are contained in the ninety-nine volumes of the Hatchet and Rope Pandects. But, for the other set, with whom you mix every day,—the very best society, in short,—we have an-

---

* It is not to be presumed that Chrysaor was the original nursery of the rhododendron; though, in Fairyland, any flower is privileged to grow, without permission from the naturalist (author's note).

other code, which punishes only by laughter. And you have no notion how severe the punishment is considered. It is thus that we keep our social system in order, and laugh folly and error out of countenance."

"An admirable—a most gentle code!" cried the prince. "But," he added, after a moment's reflection, "I see you sometimes laughing at that which to me seems entitled to reverence, while you show the most courteous respect to things which seem to me the fit objects of ridicule."

"Prince, you do not yet understand us: we never laugh at people who do exactly like the rest of us. We only laugh at singularity; because with us singularity is crime."

"Singularity—even in wisdom or virtue?"

"In wisdom or virtue? of course. Nothing so singular as such singularity; therefore nothing so criminal."

"But those persons with rhododendrons instead of faces?"

"Are the worst of our criminals. If we continue to laugh at persons for a certain time, and the laughter fail to correct their vicious propensities, their faces undergo the transformation you have witnessed, no matter how handsome they were before."

"This is indeed laughing people out of countenance," said Chairolas, amazed. "What an affliction!"

"Indeed it is. Take care," added Grinaldibus Hassan Sneeraskin, with paternal unction,—"take care that you never do anything to deserve a laugh—the torture is inexpressible—the transformation is awful!"

VI

This conversation threw Chairolas into a profound reverie. The charm of the society was invaded; it now admitted restraint and fear. If ever he should be laughed at!

if ever he should become a rhododendron!—terrible
thought! He remembered various instances he had hitherto
but little observed, in which he more than suspected that
he had already been unconsciously afflicted with symptoms
of this greatest of all calamities. His reason allowed the
justice of his apprehension; for he could not flatter himself
that in all respects he was exactly like the courtiers of
Chrysaor.

That night he went to a splendid entertainment given
by the prime minister. Conscious of great personal attractions, and magnificently attired, he felt, at his first entrance
into the gorgeous halls, the flush of youthful and elated
vanity. It was his custom to wear upon his breast one of the
most splendid ornaments. It was the tuft of the fairy swan's
down set in brilliants of great price. Something there was
in this ornament which shed a kind of charm over his whole
person. It gave a more interesting dignity to his mien, a
loftier aspect to his brow, a deeper and a softer expression
to his eyes. So potent is the gift of a good Genius, as all our
science upon such subjects assures us.

Still, as Chairolas passed through the rooms, he perceived, with a thrill of terror, that a smile ill suppressed met
him at every side; and when he turned his head to look
back, he perceived that the fatal smile had expanded into a
laugh. All his complacency vanished; terror and shame possessed him. Yes, he was certainly laughed at! He felt his
face itching already—certainly the leaves were sprouting!

He hastened to escape from the crowded rooms—passed
into the lighted and voluptuous gardens—and seated himself in a retired and sequestered alcove. Here he was surprised by the beautiful Mikra,* a lady to whom he had

* Mikra: Greek, "small."—Ed.

been paying assiduous court, and who appeared to take a lively interest in his affairs.

"Prince Chairolas here!" cried the lady, seating herself by his side; "alone too, and sad! How is this?"

"Alas!" answered the prince, despondingly, "I feel that I am regarded as a criminal: how can I hope for your love! In a word—dreadful confession!—I am certainly laughed at. I shall assuredly blossom in a week or two. Light of my eyes! design to compassionate my affliction, and instruct my ignorance. Acquaint me with the crime I have committed."

"Prince," said the gentle Mikra, much moved by her lover's dejection, "do not speak thus. Perhaps I ought to have spared you this pain. But delicacy restrained me——"

"Speak!—speak in mercy!"

"Well then—but pardon me—that swan's down tuft, it is charming, beautiful, it becomes you exceedingly! But at Chrysaor nobody wears swan's down tufts,—you understand."

"And it is for this, then, that I may be rhododendronised!" exclaimed Chairolas.

"Indeed, I fear so."

"Away, treacherous gift!" exclaimed the prince; and he tore off the fairy ornament. He dashed it to the ground, and left the alcove. The fair Mikra stayed behind to pick up the diamonds: the swan's down itself had vanished, or, at least, it was invisible to the fine lady of Chrysaor.

VII

With the loss of his swan's down Prince Chairolas recovered his self-complacency. No one laughed at him in future. He was relieved from the fear of efflorescence. For a while he was happy. But months glided away, and the prince grew tired of his sojourn at Chrysaor. The sight of the same eternal faces and the same eternal rhododendrons, the sound of the same laughter, wearied him to death. He resolved to pursue his travels. Accordingly, he quarrelled with Mikra, took leave of his friends, and, mounting his favourite steed, departed from the walls of Chrysaor. He took the precaution, this time, of hiring some attendants at Chrysaor, who carried with them provisions. A single one of the many jewels he bore about him would have more than sufficed to purchase the service of half Chrysaor.

Although he had derived so little advantage from one of the fairy gifts, he naturally thought he might be more fortunate with the rest. The pigeon's feather was appropriate enough to travelling (for we may suppose that it was a carrier-pigeon); accordingly he placed it, set in emeralds, amidst the plumage of his cap. He spent some few days in rambling about, until he found he had entered a country unknown even to his guides. The landscape was more flat and less luxuriant than that which had hitherto cheered his way, the sun was less brilliant, and the sky seemed nearer to the earth.

While gazing around him, he became suddenly aware of the presence of a stranger, who, stationed right before his horse, stretched forth his hand and thus accosted him:

"O thrice-noble and generous traveller! save me from starvation. Heaven smiles upon one to whom it has given the inestimable treasure of a pigeon's feather. May Heaven continue to lavish its blessings upon thee,—meanwhile spare me a trifle!"

The charitable Chairolas ordered his purse-bearer to relieve the wants of the stranger, and then inquired the name of the country they had entered. He was informed that it was termed Apatia; * and that its inhabitants were singularly cordial to travellers, "Especially," added the mendicant, "if they possess that rarest of earthly gifts—the feather of a pigeon."

"Well," thought Chairolas, "my good Genius evidently intends to make up for his mistake about the swan's down: doubtless the pigeon's feather will be exceedingly serviceable!"

He desired the mendicant to guide him to the nearest city of Apatia, which, fortunately, happened to be the metropolis.

On entering the streets, Chairolas was struck with the exceeding bustle and animation of the inhabitants; far from the indolent luxury of Chrysaor, everything breathed of activity, enterprise, and toil.

The place resembled a fortified town; the houses were built of ponderous stone, a drawbridge to each; the windows were barred with iron; a sentinel guarded every portico.

"Is there a foreign invasion without the walls?" asked the prince.

"No," answered the mendicant; "but here every man guards against his neighbor; take care of yourself, noble sir." So saying, the grateful Apatian picked the prince's pockets of his loose coin (luckily it was not in his pockets that he kept his jewels), and disappeared amidst the crowd.

VIII

The prince found himself no less courted in the capital of Apatia than he had been in Chrysaor. But society there was much less charming. He amused himself by going out

* Apatia: Greek, "trickery."—Ed.

in the streets incognito, and watching the manners of the inhabitants. He found them addicted to the most singular pursuits. One game consisted in setting up a straw and shooting arrows at it blindfold. If you missed the mark, you paid dearly; if you hit it, you made a fortune. Many persons ruined themselves at this game.

Another amusement consisted in giving certain persons, trained for the purpose, and dressed in long gowns, a quantity of gold, in return for which they threw dirt at you. The game was played thus: You found one of these gownsmen gave him the required quantity of gold—and then stood to be pelted at in a large tennis-court; your adversary did the same: if the gownsmen employed against you dirtied you more than your gownsman dirtied your antagonist, you were stripped naked and turned adrift in the streets; but if your antagonist was the most bespattered, you won your game, and received back half the gold you had given to your gownsman. This was a most popular diversion. They had various other amusements, all of the same kind, in which the chief entertainment was the certainty of loss.

For the rest, the common occupation was quarreling with each other, buying and selling, picking pockets, and making long speeches about liberty and glory.

Chairolas found that the pigeon's feather was everywhere a passport to favour. But in a short time this produced its annoyances. His room was besieged by applications for charity. In vain he resisted. No man with a pigeon's feather, he was assured, ever refused assistance to the poor. All the ladies in the city were in love with him; all the courtiers were his friends; they adored and they plundered him; and the reason of the adoration and the plunder was the pigeon's feather.

One day he found his favourite friend with his favourite fair one—a fair one so favoured, that he had actually proposed and had actually been accepted. Their familiarity and their treachery were evident. Chairolas drew his sabre, and would certainly have slain them both, if the lady's screams had not brought the king's guards into the room. They took all three before the judge. He heard the case gravely, and sentenced Chairolas to forego the lady and pay the costs of the sentence.

"Base foreigner that you are!" he said, gravely, "and unmindful of your honour! Have you not trusted your friend and believed in her you loved? Have you not suffered them to be often together? If you had been an honourable man, you would know that you must always watch a woman and suspect a friend.—Go!"

As Chairolas was retiring, half-choked with rage and shame, the lady seized him by the arm. "Ah!" she whispered, "I should never have deceived you but for the pigeon's feather."

Chairolas threw himself on his bed, and, exhausted by grief, fell fast asleep. When he woke the next morning, he found that his attendants had disappeared with the bulk of his jewels: they left behind them a scroll containing these words—"A man with so fine a pigeon's feather will never hang us for stealing."

Chairolas flung the feather out of the window. The wind blew it away in an instant. An hour afterwards he had mounted his steed and was already beyond the walls of the capital of Apatia.

IX

At nightfall the prince found himself at the gates of a lofty castle. Wearied and worn out, he blew the horn suspended at the portals, and demanded food and shelter for the night. No voice answered, but the gates opened of their own accord. Chairolas left his courser to feed at will on the herbage, and entered the castle: he passed through several magnificent chambers without meeting a soul till he came to a small pavilion. The walls were curiously covered with violets and rose-leaves wrought in mosaic; the lights streamed from jewels of a ruby glow, set in lotos-leaves. The whole spot breathed of enchantment; in fact, Chairolas had at length reached an enchanted castle.

Upon a couch in an alcove reclined a female form, covered with a veil studded with silver stars, but of a texture sufficiently transparent to permit Chairolas to perceive how singularly beautiful were the proportions beneath. The prince approached with a soft step.

"Pardon me," he said, with a hesitating voice, "I fear that I disturb your repose." The figure made no reply; and after a pause, Chairolas, unable to resist the desire to see the face of the sleeper, lifted the veil.

Never had so beautiful a countenance broke even upon his dreams. The first bloom of youth shed its softest hues over the cheek; the lips just parted in a smile which sufficed to call forth a thousand dimples. The face only wanted for the completion of its charm that the eyes should open and light it up with soul; but the lids were closed in a slumber so profound, that, but for the colours of the cheek and the regular and ambrosial breathing of the lips, you might have imagined that the slumber was of death. Beside this fair creature lay a casket, on which the prince read these words engraved—"He only who can unlock this casket can awaken the sleeper; and he who finds the heart may claim the hand."

Chairolas, transported with joy and hope, seized the

casket—the key was in the lock. With trembling hands he sought to turn it in the hasp—it remained immovable—it resisted his most strenuous efforts. Nothing could be more slight than the casket—more minute than the key; but all the strength of Chairolas was insufficient to open the lock.

Chairolas was in despair. He remained for days—for weeks—in the enchanted chamber. He neither ate nor slept during all that time. But such was the magic of the place that he never once felt hunger nor fatigue. Gazing upon that divine form, he for the first time experienced the rapture and intoxication of real love. He spent his days and nights in seeking to unclose the casket; sometimes in his rage he dashed it to the ground—he trampled upon it—he sought to break what he could not open—in vain.

One day while thus employed, he heard the horn wind without the castle gates; then steps echoed along the halls, and presently a stranger entered the enchanted pavilion. The newcomer was neither old nor young, neither handsome nor ugly. He approached the alcove despite the menacing looks of the jealous prince. He gazed upon the sleeper; and, as he gazed, a low music breathed throughout the chamber. Surprised and awed, Chairolas let the casket fall from his hands. The intruder took it from the ground, read the inscription, and applied his hand to the key;—it turned not;—Chairolas laughed aloud;—the stranger sighed, and drew forth from his breast a little tuft of swan's down —he laid it upon the casket—again turned the key—the casket opened at once, and within lay a small golden heart. At that instant a voice broke from the heart. "Thou hast found the charm," it said; and, at the same time, the virgin woke, and, as she bent her eyes upon the last comer, she said, with unutterable tenderness, "It is of thee, then, that I have so long dreamed." The stranger fell at her feet. And

Chairolas, unable to witness his rival's happiness, fled from the pavilion.

"Accursed that I am!" he groaned aloud. "If I had not cast away the fairy gift, *she* would have been mine!"

X

For several days the unfortunate prince wandered through the woods and wastes, supporting himself on wild berries, and venting, in sighs and broken exclamations, his grief and rage. At length he came to the shores of a wide and glassy sea, basking in the softest hues of an Oriental morn in the early summer. Its waves crisped over golden sands with a delicious and heavenly music; the air was scented with unspeakable fragrance, wafted from trees peculiar to the clime, and bearing at the same time the blossom and the fruit. At a slight distance from the shore was an island which seemed one garden—the fabled bowers of the Hesperides. Studded it was with ivory palaces, delicious fountains, and streams that wound amidst groves of asphodel and amaranth. And everywhere throughout the island wandered groups whose faces the prince could distinctly see, and those faces were made beautiful by peace unruffled and happiness unalloyed. Laughter—how different from that of Chrysaor!—was wafted to his ear, and the boughs of the trees, as they waved to the fragrant wind, gave forth melodies more exquisite than ever woke from the lutes of Lydia or the harps of Lesbos.

Wearied and exhausted the prince gazed upon the Happy Isle, and longed to be a partaker of its bliss, when, turning his eyes a little to the right, he saw, from a winding in the shore on which he stood, a vessel, with silken streamers, seemingly about to part for the opposite isle. Several persons of either sex were crowding into the vessel, and already waving their hands to the groups upon the island. Chairolas hastened to the spot. He pushed impatiently through the crowd; he was about to enter the vessel, when a venerable old man stopped and accosted him.

"Stranger, wouldst thou go to the Happy Isle?"

"Yes! Quick—quick, let me pass!"

"Stranger, whoever would enter the vessel must comply first with the conditions and pay the passage."

"I have some jewels left still," said Chairolas, haughtily. "I will pay the amount ten times over."

"We require neither jewels nor money," returned the old man, gravely. "What you must produce is the feather of a pigeon."

Chairolas shrunk back aghast. "But," said he, "I have no longer a pigeon's feather!"

The old man gazed at him with horror. The passengers set up a loud cry—"He has no pigeon's feather!" They pushed him back, the vessel parted, and Chairolas was left upon the strand.

XI

Cursing his visits to Chrysaor and Apatia, which had cost him so dear and given him so little in return, Chairolas tore himself from the sea-shore and renewed his travels.

Towards the noon of the following day he entered a valley covered with immense sunflowers and poppies. Anything so gaudy he had never before beheld. Here and there were rocks, evidently not made by nature;—mounds raised by collections of various rubbish, ornamented with artificial ruins and temples. Sometimes he passed through grottoes formed by bits of coloured glass and shells, intended to imitate spars and even jewels. The only birds that inhabited the boughs were parrots and mock-birds. They

made a most discordant din; but they meant it for imitations
of nightingales and larks. The flare of the poppies and the
noise of the birds were at first intolerable, but by degrees
the wanderer became used to them, and at length found
them charming.

"How delightful this is!" said he, flinging himself under
a yew-tree, which was trimmed into the shape of a pagoda.
"So cheerful—so gay! After all, I am as well off here as I
could have been in the Happy Isle. Nay, I think there is a
greater air of comfort in the sight of these warm sunflowers than in those eternal amaranths; and certainly, the
music of the parrots is exceedingly lively!"

While thus soliloquising the prince saw an old baboon
walk leisurely up to him. The creature supported itself
upon a golden-headed staff. It wore a long wig and a three-
cornered hat. It had a large star of coloured glass on its
breast; and an apron of sky-blue round its middle.

As the baboon approached, Chairolas was much struck
by its countenance; the features were singularly intelligent
and astute, and seemed even more so from a large pair of
spectacles, which gave the animal a learned look about the
eyes.

"Prince!" said the baboon, "I am well acquainted with
your adventures, and I think I can be of service to you in
your present circumstances."

"Can you give me the lady I saw in the enchanted
castle?"

"No!" answered the baboon. "But a man who has seen
so much of the world knows that after a little time one lady
is not better than another."

"Can you then admit me to the Happy Isle?"

"No! but you said rightly just now that you were as
well off in this agreeable valley."

"Can you give me back my tuft of swan's down and my pigeon's feather?"

"No! but I can imitate them so exactly that the imitations will be equally useful. Meanwhile, come and dine with me."

Chairolas followed the baboon into a cave, where he was sumptuously served by pea-green monkeys to dishes of barbecued squirrels.

After dinner the baboon and the prince renewed their conversation. From his host, Chairolas learned that the regions called "the unknown" by the people of Paida were of unlimited extent, inhabited by various nations: that no two of his predecessors had ever met with the same adventures, though most of them had visited both Chrysaor and Apatia. The baboon declared he had been of use to them all. He was, indeed, an animal of exceeding age and experience, and had a perfect recollection of the cities before the deluge.

He made, out of the silky hair of a white fox, a most excellent imitation of the lost tuft of swan's down; and from the breast of a vulture he plucked a feather which any one at a distance might mistake for a pigeon's.

Chairolas received them with delight.

"And now, prince," said the baboon, "observe, that, while you may show these as openly as you please, it will be prudent to conceal the eagle's feather that you have yet left. No inconvenience results from parading the false, —much danger from exhibiting the true. Take this little box of adamant, lock up the eagle's feather in it, and, whenever you meditate any scheme or exploit, open it and consult the feather. In future you will find that it has a voice, and can answer when you speak to it."

Chairolas stayed some days in the baboon's valley, and then once more renewed his travels. What was his surprise to find himself, on the second day of his excursion, in the same defile as that which had conducted him from his paternal realms! He computed, for the first time, the months he had spent in his wanderings, and found that the three years were just accomplished. In less than an hour the prince was at the mouth of the defile, where a numerous cavalcade had been for some days assembled to welcome his return, and conduct him home.

XII

The young prince was welcomed in Paida with the greatest enthusiasm. Every one found him prodigiously improved. He appeared in public with the false swan's down and the false pigeon's feather. They became him even better than the true ones, and indeed he had taken care to have them set in much more magnificent jewels. But the prince was a prey to one violent and master passion—Ambition. This had always been a part of his character; but previous to his travels it had been guided by generous and patriotic impulses. It was so no longer. He spent whole days in conversing with the eagle's feather, though the feather indeed never said but one word, which was—"WAR."

At that time a neighbouring people had chosen five persons instead of two to inspect the treasury accounts. Chairolas affected to be horror-struck with the innovation. He declared it boded no good to Paida; he declaimed against it night and day. At last, he so inflamed the people, that, despite the reluctance of the king, war was declared. An old general of great renown headed the army. Chairolas was appointed second in command. They had scarcely reached the confines of the enemy's country when Chairolas became no less unhappy than before. "Second in command! why not first?" He consulted his demon feather. It said "First." It spoke no other word. The old general was slow in his movements; he pretended that it was unwise to risk a battle at so great a distance from the capital; but in reality, he hoped that the appearance of his army would awe the enemy into replacing the two treasurers, and so secure the object of the war without bloodshed. Chairolas penetrated this design, so contrary to his projects. He wrote home to his father, to accuse the general of taking bribes from the enemy. The old king readily believed one whom a good Genius had so richy endowed. The general was re-called and beheaded. Chairolas succeeded to the command. He hastened to march to the capital, which he took and pillaged; but, instead of replacing the two treasurers, he appointed one chief—himself; and twenty subordinate treasurers—his officers.

Never was prince so popular as Chairolas on his return from his victories. He was intoxicated by the sweetness of power and the desire of yet greater glory. He longed to reign himself—he sighed to think his father was so healthy. He shut himself up in his room and talked to his feather: its word now was "King." Shortly afterwards Chairolas (who was the idol of the soldiers) seized the palace, issued a proclamation that his father was in his dotage, and had abdicated the throne in his favour. The king was removed to a distant wing of the palace, and a day or two afterwards found dead in his bed. Chairolas commanded the Court to wear mourning for three months, and everybody compassionated his grief.

From that time Chairolas, now the monarch of Paida, gave himself up to his ruling passion. He extended his fame from east to west—he was called the Great Chairolas. But his subjects became tired of war; their lands were ravaged

—their treasury exhausted—new taxes were raised for new conquests,—and at length Chairolas was no longer called the "Great," but the "Tyrant."

XIII

As Chairolas advanced in years, he left off wearing the false swan's down and the false pigeon's feather. He had long ceased to lock up his eagle-plume; he carried it constantly in his helmet, that it might whisper with ease into his ear. He had ceased to be popular with any class the moment he abandoned the presents of the baboon. By degrees a report spread through the nation that the king was befriended by an evil spirit, and that the eagle's plume was a talisman which secured to the possessor—while it rendered him grasping, cruel, and avaricious—prosperity, power, and fame. A conspiracy was formed to rob the king of his life and talisman at once. At the head of the conspiracy was the king's heir, Belmanes. They took their measures so well, that they succeeded in seizing the palace. They penetrated into the chamber of the Great Chairolas; they paused at the threshold on hearing his voice. He was addressing the fatal talisman.

"The ordeal," he said, "through which I passed robbed me of thy companions; but no ordeal could rob me of thee. I rule my people with a rod of iron; I have spread my conquests to the farthest regions to which the banner of Paida was ever wafted. I am still dissatisfied—what more can I desire?"

"Death!" cried the conspirators; and the king fell pierced to the heart. Belmanes seized the eagle's plume: it crumbled into dust in his grasp.

After the death of Chairolas, the following sentences

were written in gold letters before the gates of the great academy of Paida by a priest who pretended to be inspired:

"The ridicule of common men aspires to be the leveller of genius."

"To renounce a virtue, because it has made thee suffer from fraud, is to play the robber to thyself."

"Wouldst thou imitate the properties of the swan and the pigeon, borrow from the fox and the vulture. But no man can wear the imitations all his life: when he abandons them, he is undone."

"If thou hast three virtues, and losest two, the third, by itself, may become a vice. There is no blessing to the world like AMBITION joined to SYMPATHY and BENEVOLENCE; no scourge to the world like Ambition divorced from them."

"The choicest gifts of the most benevolent genii are impotent, unless accompanied by a charm against experience."

"The charm against experience is woven by two spirits —Patience and Self-esteem."

On these sentences nine sects of philosophy were founded. Each construed them differently; each produced ten thousand volumes in support of its interpretation; and no man was ever made better or wiser by the sentences, the sects, and the volumes.

⚜ *The Malacca Cane*

by ALFRED DE VIGNY

Alfred de Vigny (1797–1863) was a very disappointed man. He was born too late to die for his hero, Napoleon; he served in the army for fifteen peaceful years, and rose only to a captaincy; his poems and prose had merely moderate success. He was disappointed in his wife, who promptly became an invalid, and in his mistresses, who were unfaithful. He was especially disappointed in his rich father-in-law, who went broke before dying.

The Malacca Cane (*La Canne de jonc*) is an episode from his *Servitude et grandeur militaires* (1835), an analysis of military character. The scene is laid in the "July Revolution" of 1830, when the French people rose against the absolutist regime of the Bourbon King Charles X. Three days of bloody rioting, ("les trois glorieuses") followed, and were ended by the accession of the moderate constitutionalist monarch, Louis-Philippe. The translation is by Morris Bishop.

THE NIGHT OF 27 JULY 1830 was silent and solemn. My remembrance of it is more vivid than that of more dreadful scenes that fate has presented to my eyes. The calm of earth and sea before a hurricane has no more majesty than had the face of Paris in expectation of revolution. The boulevards were deserted. I walked their entire length alone, after midnight, eagerly watching and listening. A cloudless sky diffused over the earth the white gleam of the stars; but the houses were dark, shut, as if dead. All the street-lamps were broken. Some groups of workmen were still gathering under the trees, listening to a mysterious orator who confided to them secret words in a hushed voice. Then they would separate at a run, dashing down narrow black streets. They would lean against little doors in alleyways, which opened like trap-doors and closed behind them. Then nothing further stirred; the city seemed to have only dead inhabitants and plague-stricken houses.

At intervals one would come upon dark, inert forms, which one would recognize only by touch; they were a battalion of the Royal Guards, standing motionless and speechless. Farther on, an artillery battery, surmounted by its lit fuses, like a pair of stars. One passed with impunity before these imposing, somber units; one could circle around them, walk away, return, without receiving from them a question, a gibe, a word. They were inoffensive, without anger, without hate. They were resigned; they were waiting.

As I approached one of the larger battalions an officer advanced toward me most politely, and asked me if the flames which were visible, illuminating in the distance the Porte-Saint-Denis, came from a burning house; he was about to advance with his company to make sure. I told him that they proceeded from tall trees that some merchants were having felled and burned, profiting by the disturbances to get rid of the old elms that hid their shop-fronts. Then, seating himself on one of the stone benches along the boulevard, he began to trace lines and circles in the sand with a malacca cane. That is how I identified him, while he recognized my face. As I remained standing before him, he shook my hand and asked me to sit down beside him.

Captain Renaud was a man of stern, rigorous principles and of a very cultivated mind—a type that abounded in the Guards at that period. His character and habits were well known; those who may read these recollections will picture the serious face to which was attached the *nom de guerre* of Malacca Cane, conceived by the soldiers, adopted by the officers, and accepted indifferently by the man himself. As with old families, old regiments, kept intact in peacetime, take on familiar customs and invent familiar names for their children. An old wound in the right leg prompted the captain's habit of always leaning on that malacca cane with a rather peculiar knob; it attracted the attention of all those who saw it for the first time. He kept it with him everywhere and nearly always had it in his hand. There was, to be sure, no affectation in this habit; his manners were too simple and serious for that. However, one felt that the cane meant a good deal to him. He was much respected in the Guards. Feeling no ambition, and wishing to be only what he was, captain of grenadiers, he spent his time reading, talked as little as possible and then only in monosyllables. Very tall, very pale, melancholy in expression, he bore on his forehead, between the eyebrows, a small but fairly deep scar, which often turned from its normal bluish to black, and sometimes gave a fierce cast to his habitually cold and placid face.

The soldiers were very fond of him, and especially in the Spanish campaign * the pleasure with which they would set out when commanded by Malacca Cane was remarked upon. And in absolute fact it was the malacca cane that directed them, for Captain Renaud would never draw his sword, even when, leading his skirmishers, he would come close enough to the enemy to run the risk of hand-to-hand combat. He was not only well versed in war; he had also an understanding of high European politics under the Empire, so exact that one could hardly account for it. This was at-

---

* France invaded Spain briefly in 1823.—Ed.

tributed sometimes to deep study, sometimes to his possession of influential connections, whom his perpetual reserve
prevented him from revealing. . . .*

There is no profession in which the chill formality of
language and habits contrasts more strongly with the activity of life than does the trade of arms. Therein hatred of
exaggeration is carried far, and the language of a man who
tries to overstate his feelings or draw sympathy for his
sufferings is despised. I knew this; I was on the point of
taking leave of Captain Renaud abruptly, when he took my
arm and held me.

"Did you see the maneuver of the Swiss Guards this
morning?" he said. "It was rather interesting. They did the
'Street-fighting Advance' with perfect precision. In all my
service I had never seen it tried out; it's a parade exercise,
an opera maneuver. But it may have its value in the streets
of a big city, provided that the units to right and left form
up quickly in front of the platoon that has just fired."

At the same time he went on tracing lines on the ground
with the tip of his cane. Then he rose slowly; and as he
walked along the boulevard, intending to draw away from
the group of officers and soldiers, I followed him. He continued to talk to me with a sort of nervous, almost involuntary exaltation which enthralled me. I would never have
expected it from him, who was what is commonly called a
cold man.

He began by making a very simple request. Taking hold
of one of my coat-buttons, he said: "Will you pardon me
if I ask you to send me your breast-plate of the Royal
Guards, if you have kept it? I left mine at home, and I
can't send someone for it or go myself, because they are

---

* A digression on social insincerity is here omitted.—Ed.

shooting us down in the streets like mad dogs. But perhaps in the three or four years since you left the army you have got rid of it. I had also turned in my resignation two weeks ago, for I am very bored with the army. But when I saw the Orders in Council,* I said: 'There's going to be action!' So I packed up my uniform, my epaulets, and my bearskin shako, and I went to the barracks to rejoin those good fellows who are going to get killed at every corner. They would certainly have thought, deep down, that I was walking out on them in a crisis. It would have been contrary to honor, don't you think, entirely contrary to honor?"

"Had you foreseen the Orders in Council," I said, "before your resignation?"

"Lord, no! I haven't even read them yet."

"Well then, what did you have to reproach yourself with?"

"Nothing but appearances; and I didn't want even appearances to be against me."

"That's very admirable," said I.

"Admirable! Admirable!" said Captain Renaud, hastening his steps. "That's the vogue-word now; and what a childish word! I detest admiration; it is the principle of too many bad actions. We hand it out too cheaply, to everybody; we should be on our guard against admiring lightly. Admiration is corrupted and corrupting. We ought to act for our own sakes, not for publicity. Anyway, I have my own ideas on that subject." He stopped abruptly, and seemed on the point of leaving me.

"There is something as fine as a great man," I said; "and that is a man of honor."

* Orders in Council: *les ordonnances*, the King's proclamation of 25 July 1830, abolishing the freedom of the press and annulling the political rights of voters. This precipitated the Revolution.—Ed.

He took my hand cordially. "That is an opinion we share," he said emphatically. "I have practiced it all my life, but it has cost me dear. It isn't so easy as you may think."

At this point the second lieutenant of the company came up and asked for a cigar. The captain pulled several from his pocket and passed them over without a word. The officers began to smoke, walking to and fro, in a calm silence undisturbed by concern for the present circumstances. Neither deigned to speak of the current danger or of their duty, though they were well aware of both.

Captain Renaud returned to my side. "It's a fine night," he said, pointing to the sky with his malacca cane. "I don't know when I'll stop seeing the same stars every evening. There was once a time when I thought I would see those of the South Seas, but I was destined not to leave this hemisphere. No matter; it's lovely weather, and the Parisians are sleeping or pretending to. None of us have had anything to eat or drink for twenty-four hours; that makes one's ideas sharp and clear. I remember that one day, when we were invading Spain, you asked me why I had had so little promotion. I didn't have time to tell you then, but this evening I am tempted to go back over my life, which I was reviewing in memory. You are fond of stories, I recall; and in your retired life you will enjoy remembering us. If you will sit down with me on this parapet of the boulevard, we can talk very calmly; for it seems to me that for the moment they have stopped picking us off from the windows and the cellar-gratings. I'll tell you only a few episodes of my history, and I shall simply follow my whim. I have seen a lot and read a lot, but I am pretty sure that I couldn't write. That isn't my profession, thank God, and I have never tried it. But there is one thing I *can* do—I can make my own life; and I have lived as I had resolved to do, from the time when I had courage enough to do so; and the fact is, that's something. But let's sit down."

I followed him slowly; we went through the battalion, passing to the left of his fine grenadiers. They were standing gravely, resting their chins on their gun-muzzles. Some young fellows were sitting on their knapsacks, being more exhausted than the others by the day's work. All were silent, coolly occupied in cleaning and refurbishing their uniforms. Nothing suggested anxiety or depression. They kept their formation, as after a review, waiting for orders.

When we had sat down, my old comrade began to talk; he recounted, in his own fashion, three important episodes which revealed the sense of his life and explained the peculiarity of his habits and the somber core of his character. Nothing of what he told me has faded from my memory; I shall repeat it almost word for word.

[The first two episodes are here omitted.]

It's funny [he said]. I have never told that story, but this evening I wanted to. Well, no matter; I like to let myself go with an old comrade. All that will give you a subject for serious reflections when you have nothing better to do. It seems to me that the story is not unworthy of such. You will think me very weak or very crazy; that's all right with me. Up to the event, commonplace enough for other men, which I'm going to tell you now—I keep postponing it because it's painful—my love for the glory of armed service had become sober, serious, dedicated, perfectly pure like the simple, unique feeling of duty. But from that day on, other ideas came to cast further shadows on my life.

It was in 1814; it was the beginning of the year and the ending of that dismal war when our poor army was defending the Empire and the Emperor, and when France was watching the combat in discouragement. Soissons had just surrendered to the Prussian Bülow. The armies of Silesia and of the North * had united there. Macdonald † had left Troyes and abandoned the basin of the Yonne to establish his defense line from Nogent to Montereau, with thirty thousand men.

We were to attack Reims, which the Emperor wanted to retake. The weather was dismal, the rain continuous. The day before we had lost a higher officer leading back a troop of prisoners. The Russians had surprised him and killed him during the night and had set free their comrades. Our colonel, who was what is called a tough baby, wanted his revenge. We were near Épernay, flanking the heights that surround it. Evening was approaching; after spending the whole day getting into shape, we were passing near a pretty white château with turrets, called Boursault, when the colonel summoned me. He took me aside while the men were stacking arms, and said to me in his hoarse old voice: "You see a barn up there, on that steep-sided hill? There where that big dummy of a Russian sentry with his bishop's mitre is patrolling?"

"Yes," said I. "I see perfectly the grenadier and the barn."

"Well—since you're an old soldier—you may properly be informed that that is a post the Russians took yesterday, and for the moment it is much on the Emperor's mind. He told me that it is the key to Reims, and he may well be right. In any case, we are going to play a trick on Voronzoff. At eleven o'clock tonight you will take two hundred of your boys, and you will surprise the garrison they have

* I.e., armies of the German-Russian-English coalition against Napoleon.—Ed.

† Macdonald: commander of one of Napoleon's armies.—Ed.

set up in the barn. But, so as not to give the alarm, you will take it with your bayonets."

He took a pinch of snuff and offered me one; then he scattered the rest bit by bit—like this—and then, uttering a phrase with each crumb tossed to the winds, he said: "You understand that I will be over there, behind you, with my body of men. . . . You won't lose more than sixty men, and you will have the six guns they have set up there. . . . You will aim them toward Reims. . . . At eleven o'clock . . . or half past . . . the position will be ours. And we'll sleep till three o'clock to get some rest. . . . We need it, after the little business at Craonne,* which was, as they say, no slouch of an affair."

"That's all I need," I said; and I sent off my lieutenant, my second-in-command, to prepare our evening party. As you see, the important thing was to make no noise. I inspected the arms and had the men remove the cartridges of all the loaded weapons with the ramrod-screw. Then I strolled for some time with my sergeants, while waiting for zero-hour. At half-past ten I had the men put their overcoats over their blouses, hiding the muskets under their overcoats, for in spite of all, as you see this evening, a bayonet is always visible, and although it was a much blacker night than it is now, I couldn't trust the darkness. I had observed the little hedged paths which led up to the Russian position, and I sent up along them the most resolute lads I have ever commanded. (Two of them are still there in the ranks; they remember that action well.) They were used to Russians, and knew how to go after them. The sentries we met as we climbed up disappeared without a sound,

---

* Craonne: scene of a bloody battle fought on 5 March 1814, and of even bloodier battles (of the Chemin-des-Dames) in 1917 and 1918.—Ed.

like reeds that you flatten out with your hand. The one who was standing by the stacked arms needed more attention. He was motionless, his weapon grounded, resting his chin on the muzzle. The poor devil was swaying, like a man half asleep with fatigue, and ready to fall. One of my grenadiers seized him in his arms and squeezed the breath out of him; two others gagged him and threw him into the bushes. I came up slowly; and I admit I couldn't suppress a certain emotion I had never felt in other conflicts. It was shame at attacking sleeping men. I saw them rolled up in their cloaks, under the light of a dark lantern; and my heart beat violently. But suddenly, when the moment of action came, I felt afraid of a weakness like that of cowards; I felt fear of for once feeling fear; and pulling my sabre from under my arm, I dashed in first, setting an example for my grenadiers. I gave them a signal they understood; they leaped first on the muskets, then on the men, like wolves on a flock of sheep. Oh, it was a dumb, horrible butchery! The bayonet pierced, the gun-butt knocked out, the knee disabled, the hands strangled. Cries, half-uttered, were extinguished under the feet of our soldiers; not a head was raised without receiving a mortal blow.

Entering the barn, I had made at a venture a mighty thrust at something black before me; I had pierced it through and through. An old officer, tall and heavily built, white-haired, rose up before me like a ghost. On seeing what I had done he uttered a frightful cry, struck me violently on the face with his sword, and immediately fell dead under the bayonets. I collapsed in a sitting posture beside him, stunned by the blow that had landed between my eyes, and I heard beneath me the dying, tender voice of a boy saying: "Papa——."

I understood then my deed, and I contemplated it with

frantic excitement. I saw one of those fourteen-year-old officers so numerous in the Russian armies then invading us, pupils in a terrible school. His long curly hair fell to his chest, blond and silky like a woman's. His head hung down as if he had merely fallen into a second sleep. His pink lips, open like those of a tiny baby, seemed still fed by his nurse's milk; his big blue eyes, half-opened, had a candid, feminine, caressing beauty. I lifted him up on my arm; his cheek fell against my bloody cheek, as if he were going to hide his head between his mother's chin and shoulder, to warm himself. He seemed to hug my breast in order to flee his murderers. Love for his father, confidence, the peace of delicious sleep dwelt on his dead face; he appeared to be saying: "Let me sleep in peace!"

"So that's an enemy!" I exclaimed. And the paternal feeling that God has planted in every man's heart awoke and stirred in me. I clasped him to my breast, and then I felt pressing against myself the hilt of my sword, piercing his heart, the murderer of that sleeping angel. I tried to lean my head against his, but my blood covered it with broad blotches. I felt the wound on my own brow, and remembered that it was caused by his father. Shamed, I looked about me; I saw only a heap of bodies which my grenadiers were pulling out by the feet and tossing outside, after removing their cartridges. At this moment the colonel entered, followed by his column, whose steps and clash of weapons I had heard.

"Good work, my dear fellow!" said he. "You pulled that off in fine shape. But you're wounded?"

"Look at that," said I. "What difference is there between me and a murderer?"

"Oh, for God's sake, my dear chap! What do you expect? It's our business."

"That's right," I answered; and I stood up to take over my command. The boy fell back in the folds of his cloak; I wrapped him up in it. His little hand, adorned with large rings, dropped a malacca cane, which fell upon my hand as if he had presented it to me. I took it; and I resolved never to use another weapon, whatever might be my future dangers. I didn't have the courage to pull out from his breast my murdering sword.

Hastily I left that retreat, stinking of blood; and when I was in the open air I found strength enough to wipe off my face, dripping red. My grenadiers were in formation; each was coolly wiping off his bayonet on the grass and fixing his flint in the lock. My sergeant-major, followed by the quartermaster-sergeant, was walking in front of the troops, his roster in hand, reading by the light of a candle-end fixed like a torch in his gun-muzzle. He was calmly making the roll-call. I leaned against a tree, and the surgeon came up to bandage my forehead. A heavy March shower was falling on my head; it did me some good. I couldn't check a deep sigh. "I'm sick of war," I said to the surgeon.

"So am I," said a deep voice, which I recognized.

I raised the bandage from my brows, and saw, not Emperor Napoleon, but Napoleon the Soldier. He was alone, dismounted, standing gloomily in front of me, his boots caked with mud, his uniform torn, his hat dripping rain from the brim. He felt that his last days had come; he looked about him at his last soldiers.

He regarded me attentively. "I've seen you somewhere, old *grognard?*" * he said.

At his last word, I recognized that he was using only a banal phrase; I knew that my face looked older than my

---

* *Grognard:* "grumbler," nickname of Napoleon's veterans.—Ed.

years, and that I was well disguised by my fatigues, moustaches, and wounds.*

"I have seen you everywhere, without being seen," I replied.

"Do you want a promotion?"

"It's pretty late," I said.

He folded his arms for a moment without replying. Then: "You are right. In three days, both of us will be leaving the service."

He turned his back on me and remounted his horse, which was held a few steps away. At this moment the head of our column was attacked; shells began to fall on us. One landed in front of my company; a few men started back, with an impulse of which they were ashamed. Bonaparte advanced alone toward the shell, which lay sizzling and smoking in front of his horse; he made his steed sniff at the smoke. We all stood silent and motionless. The shell burst; but no one was hit. The grenadiers were impressed by the terrible lesson; but as for me, I felt something like despair. France was failing him, and for a moment he had doubted his gallant veterans. I felt that I was too well avenged, and he was too well punished for his faults by this abandonment. I stood up with an effort; going up to him, I seized and shook the hand he was holding out to several of us. He did not recognize me; but for me it was a reconciliation between the most obscure and the most illustrious of the men of our century. The drums beat to the charge; next day at dawn we retook Reims. But a few days later, Paris was retaken by others. . . .

[After some reflections, the author resumes his narrative role.]

* A reference to the captain's previous meeting with Napoleon, recounted in an earlier episode.—Ed.

Two weeks after his conversation, which even the Revolution * did not banish from my memory, I was reflecting, in solitude, on modest heroism and on disinterestedness, both so rare! I was trying to forget the blameless blood which had just flowed, and I was rereading, in the history of America, how the victorious Anglo-American army, having laid down its arms and freed the fatherland, was ready to revolt against the Congress—which, too poor to pay off the army, was preparing to dismiss it without a penny. Washington, victorious generalissimo, had only to say a word or nod his head to become dictator; but he did what only he could do—he disbanded the army and resigned. I laid down my book and compared that serene greatness with our own feverish ambitions. I was in a sad mood; I recalled all those pure, martial spirits, without false pretensions or charlatanism, who have loved power and command only for the public good, who have kept their eminence without pride, being unable to turn it against the fatherland or to convert it into gold. I thought of all those men who have made war with full understanding of its real meaning; I thought of the good Collingwood,† so resigned, and finally of the obscure Captain Renaud. At this point I saw a tall man enter, wearing a well-worn blue army overcoat. By his long moustaches and the scars on his coppery face I recognized one of the grenadiers of the captain's company. I asked if the captain was still living; the good fellow's emotion revealed that some misfortune had occurred. He sat down and wiped his brow; when, after a little, he regained possession of himself, he told me what had happened.

* Revolution: i.e., of 1830.—Ed.

† Cuthbert Collingwood: famous English admiral, who appears in an earlier episode of the story, here omitted.—Ed.

During the twenty-eighth and the twenty-ninth of July, Captain Renaud had done nothing but march along the streets, at the head of his grenadiers in column. He placed himself in front of his first squad, and walked calmly through a hail of stones and musket-shots from the cafés, balconies, and windows. When he stopped, it was to close ranks to replace those who fell, and to make sure that his left guides kept the proper intervals and distances from their file-leaders. He had not drawn his sword; he walked with his cane in hand. At first his orders had come through in due form; but whether the aides-de-camp were killed on the way, or whether the staff had not sent them out, in the night of the twenty-eighth to the twenty-ninth he was left in the Place de la Bastille, with no other instructions than to retire on Saint-Cloud, destroying the barricades along his way. This he did, without firing a shot. Arriving at the Pont d'Iéna, he stopped to call the company's roll. He had had fewer losses than any of the Guard companies that had been detached, and also his men were less fatigued than the others. He had been artful enough to provide timely rest in the shade, during those blazing days, and to find in the abandoned barracks the food refused them in hostile houses. The appearance of his column was such that he had found every barricade abandoned, and had had only the trouble of taking them down.

He was, then, standing at the end of the Pont d'Iéna, covered with dust, and shaking it off his feet. He was looking toward the barrier, to see if anything could block the exit of his detachment, and he was designating scouts to send forward. There was no one in the Champ-de-Mars, except two masons lying prone, apparently asleep, and a small boy of about fourteen, barefoot, playing with castanets made of two pieces of broken pottery. From time to

time he would scrape them on the bridge parapet; he came
thus, playing, to the stone marker where Renaud was standing. At this moment the captain was pointing to the heights
of Passy with his cane. The boy approached him, looked at
him with wide, astonished eyes; and pulling a horse-pistol
from his jacket, he took it in both hands and pointed it at
the captain's breast. Renaud deflected the boy's aim with
his cane; the bullet landed in the upper part of the thigh.
The captain fell to a seat on the ground without a word,
and gazed with pity at his singular enemy. He saw the boy,
appalled at what he had done, still holding his weapon in
both hands. The grenadiers were leaning sorrowfully on
their guns; they did not deign to raise a finger against the
little rascal. Some lifted up their captain; others contented
themselves with taking the boy by the arm and leading
him to his victim. He burst into tears; and when he saw
the blood coursing from the officer's wound on his white
trousers, he was horrified by his misdeed, and fainted. Man
and boy were carried off together to a small house near
Passy, where both were still to be found. The column, led
by the lieutenant, had continued on its way to Saint-Cloud,
and four grenadiers, taking off their uniforms, remained in
the hospitable house to tend their old commander. One of
them (the one who was telling me all this) had found a job
as an armorer in Paris; others were fencing-masters; all
brought their pay to the captain, and so far had kept him
from lacking any necessaries. The leg had been amputated;
but the fever was high and alarming, and as he was afraid
of its growing worse, he had sent for me. There was no
time to be lost. I left immediately with the worthy soldier
who had told me all these details, with tearful eyes and
trembling voice, but without a complaint, an angry word,

an accusation. He repeated merely: "It's a great misfortune for us."

The wounded man had been deposited with a little tradeswoman, a widow, living alone in her bit of a shop on a village side-street, with some small children. She had not for a moment been afraid of compromising herself, and no one had thought of bothering her for that reason. On the contrary, the neighbors had hastened to aid her in her care of the sick man. The surgeons who had been summoned had judged that he was not fit to be moved; and after his operation she had kept him on, and had often passed the night beside his bed. When I entered, she came to meet me with an air of gratitude and timidity that I found distressing. I realized how many inconveniences she had concealed through kindness of heart and charitable impulse. She was very pale; her eyes were red and tired. She went to busy herself in a tiny back room visible from the door, and I could see by her haste that she was tidying up the wounded man's narrow quarters and was putting a little coquetry in making them look decent to a visitor. Thus I took care not to move too fast; I gave her all the time she needed.

"You see, sir, he has suffered a lot," she said, opening the door.

Captain Renaud was sitting up on a small curtained bed in a corner of the room; several bolsters propped up his body. He was skeleton-thin; his cheeks were flaming red; the wound on his forehead was black. I saw that he wouldn't last long; his smile carried the same message. He held out his hand and gestured to me to sit down. At his right was a youth holding a glass of sweetened water, which he was stirring with a spoon. He stood up and brought me a chair.

Renaud, from his bed, took him by the ear and said to me gently, in an enfeebled voice: "Look, my dear fellow, I present to you my conqueror."

I shrugged my shoulders; the poor boy lowered his eyes, blushing. I saw a large tear descend on his cheek.

"Come, come!" said the captain, running his hand through the boy's hair. "It isn't his fault. He met a couple of men who gave him a drink of brandy, and paid for it, and then sent him to shoot me with a pistol. He did that just as he might have thrown a marble at a roadside stone. Isn't that right, Jean?"

Jean began to tremble; his expression of pain was so acute that it touched me. I looked at him more attentively; he was a very handsome boy.

"In fact it was a marble," said the shopkeeper. "Look here, sir." And she showed me a small marble of agate, with which the large-bore pistol had been loaded. It was as big as the largest lead bullet.

"That's all you need to take off a captain's leg," said Renaud.

"You mustn't let him talk much," said the shopkeeper timidly. Renaud did not heed her. "Yes, my friend," he said; "I haven't enough stump left to attach a wooden leg."

I squeezed his hand without answering. I was humbled to see that, to kill a man who had seen and suffered much, whose breast was bronzed by twenty campaigns and ten wounds, who had been tested by ice and fire, who had defied bayonet and lance, all that was needful was the escapade of one of those Paris guttersnipes we call gamins.

Renaud answered my unspoken thought. He rested his cheek on the bolster and took my hand. "We were at war," he said. "He is no more an assassin than I was at Reims.

When I killed the Russian boy, wasn't I perhaps also an assassin? In the great war in Spain the men who stabbed our sentries did not regard themselves as assassins, and as we were at war, perhaps they weren't. Did the Catholics and the Huguenots assassinate each other or not? A great battle is made up of how many assassinations? That is one of the questions at which our reason becomes confused and doesn't know what to answer. It is war which is at fault, not we ourselves. I assure you that this little fellow is very nice and kind; he already reads and writes very well. He's a foundling, and was apprenticed to a cabinet-maker. He hasn't left my room for two weeks; he is very fond of me, poor boy. He shows some aptitude for arithmetic; perhaps he could amount to something."

As he was talking ever more painfully and was trying to reach my ear, I bent down. He passed me a small folded sheet of paper, which he asked me to glance at. I recognized a short will, in which he left a sort of insignificant farm to the shopkeeper who had taken him in, leaving it after her to Jean. She was to bring him up. He stipulated the sum for finding him a military substitute; and he designated his little patch of land as a retreat for his four old grenadiers. He appointed as executor a notary of his province. When I had taken the paper, he seemed calmer and ready to doze off. Then he trembled, opened his eyes, and asked me to take and keep his malacca cane. And he drowsed again. His old soldier, shaking his head, took the captain's hand. I took the other; it was cold as ice. He said that his feet were cold; Jean lay down and lent his young breast to warm him. Then Captain Renaud began to pick at the sheets with his hands, saying that he could no longer feel them. That is a fatal sign. His voice was cavernous. He raised a hand painfully to his brow, looked attentively at Jean, and said:

"It's odd! That boy looks like the Russian boy!" Then he closed his eyes, and, clasping my hand with renewed awareness, said: "You see! The brain is going. That's the end."

His glance was different, calmer. We understood the struggle of a stout spirit sitting in judgment on itself, and fighting against the distracting pain. This spectacle, on a wretched couch, was for me full of solemn majesty. He flushed again, and said loudly: "They were both fourteen years old—both of them. Who knows if this isn't that same young spirit which has returned in the other young body to avenge itself?"

Then he shuddered, turned pale, and looked at me calmly, tenderly.

"Tell me," he said. "Couldn't you close my mouth? I am afraid to talk. I feel weaker. I don't want to talk any more. I'm thirsty."

He was given several spoonfuls of water. He said: "I have done my duty. That thought does me good."

He added: "If the country is better off for all we have done, we have nothing to complain of. But you will see——."

Then he dozed off and slept for about half an hour. After that a woman came shyly to the door and indicated that the surgeon was there. I went out on tiptoe to speak to him. I took him into the little garden, and stopped by a well to question him. We heard a loud cry. We ran in and saw a sheet covering the face of that good man, who had breathed his last.

❧ *Morella*

by EDGAR ALLAN POE

Edgar Allan Poe's brief, tortured life (1809–1849) is a case history of the erratic genius unable to accommodate to a world which refused to accommodate to him. Flourishing toward the end of the proper Romantic period, he was Romantic by temperament and in his soaring, hallucinated imaginations, which accorded ill with his exercise of mathematical and scientific rationality. His influence has been enormous—on the school of "art for art's sake"; on the making of "pure poetry"; on symbolism and surrealism; on the practice of literary criticism; on the detective story and the scientific romance.

Morella (1835) is Poe's first rendering of the theme of *Ligeia* and other stories—the survival of a powerful, beloved spirit after death.

Αὐτὸ καθ᾽ αὑτὸ μεθ αὑτοῦ, μονοειδὲς ἀεὶ ὄν.
Itself, by itself solely, ONE everlastingly, and single.

PLATO. *Sympos.* [211, XXIX.]

WITH A FEELING of deep yet most singular affection I regarded my friend Morella. Thrown by accident into her society many years ago, my soul, from our first meeting, burned with fires it had never before known; but the fires were not of Eros, and bitter and tormenting to my spirit was the gradual conviction that I could in no manner define their unusual meaning, or regulate their vague intensity. Yet we met; and fate bound us together at the altar; and I never spoke of passion, nor thought of love. She, however, shunned society, and, attaching herself to me alone, rendered me happy. It is a happiness to wonder;—it is a happiness to dream.

Morella's erudition was profound. As I hope to live, her talents were of no common order—her powers of mind were gigantic. I felt this, and, in many matters, became her pupil. I soon, however, found that, perhaps on account of her Pressburg * education, she placed before me a number of those mystical writings which are usually considered the mere dross of the early German literature. These, for what reason I could not imagine, were her favorite and constant study—and that, in process of time they became my own, should be attributed to the simple but effectual influence of habit and example.

In all this, if I err not, my reason had little to do. My convictions, or I forget myself, were in no manner acted upon by the ideal, nor was any tincture of the mysticism which I read, to be discovered, unless I am greatly mistaken, either in my deeds or in my thoughts. Persuaded of this, I abandoned myself implicitly to the guidance of my wife, and entered with an unflinching heart into the intricacies of her studies. And then—then, when, poring over forbidden pages, I felt a forbidden spirit enkindling within me— would Morella place her cold hand upon my own, and rake up from the ashes of a dead philosophy some low, singular words, whose strange meaning burned themselves in upon my memory. And then, hour after hour, would I linger by her side, and dwell upon the music of her voice—until, at length, its melody was tainted with terror,—and there fell a shadow upon my soul—and I grew pale, and shuddered inwardly at those too unearthly tones. And thus, joy suddenly faded into horror, and the most beautiful became the most hideous, as Hinnon became Ge-Henna.†

* Pressburg: now Bratislava, in Czechoslovakia.—Ed.

† Hinnon, Ge-Henna: synonyms for Tophet, where renegade Hebrews sacrificed children to Moloch.—Ed.

It is unnecessary to state the exact character of those disquisitions which, growing out of the volumes I have mentioned, formed, for so long a time, almost the sole conversation of Morella and myself. By the learned in what might be termed theological morality they will be readily conceived, and by the unlearned they would, at all events, be little understood. The wild Pantheism of Fichte; the modified Παλιγγενεσία * of the Pythagoreans; and, above all, the doctrines of *Identity* as urged by Schelling, were generally the points of discussion presenting the most of beauty to the imaginative Morella. That identity which is termed personal, Mr. Locke,† I think, truly defines to consist in the saneness of a rational being. And since by person we understand an intelligent essence having reason, and since there is a consciousness which always accompanies thinking, it is this which makes us all to be that which we call *ourselves*—thereby distinguishing us from other beings that think, and giving us our personal identity. But the *principium individuationis*—the notion of that identity *which at death is or is not lost forever*, was to me, at all times, a consideration of intense interest; not more from the perplexing and exciting nature of its consequences, than from the marked and agitated manner in which Morella mentioned them.

But, indeed, the time had now arrived when the mystery of my wife's manner oppressed me as a spell. I could no longer bear the touch of her wan fingers, nor the low tone of her musical language, nor the lustre of her melancholy eyes. And she knew all this, but did not upbraid; she

---

* Παλιγγενεσία: palingenesis, rebirth into a higher life.—Ed.

† Poe's erudition was a good deal of a put-on and probably requires no annotation. One wonders why John Locke (1632–1704) alone is qualified as "Mr."—Ed.

seemed conscious of my weakness or my folly, and, smiling, called it Fate. She seemed, also, conscious of a cause, to
me unknown, for the gradual alienation of my regard; but
she gave me no hint or token of its nature. Yet was she
woman, and pined away daily. In time, the crimson spot
settled steadily upon the cheek, and the blue veins upon
the pale forehead became prominent; and, one instant, my
nature melted into pity, but, in the next, I met the glance of
her meaning eyes, and then my soul sickened and became
giddy with the giddiness of one who gazes downward into
some dreary and unfathomable abyss.

Shall I then say that I longed with an earnest and consuming desire for the moment of Morella's decease? I did;
but the fragile spirit clung to its tenement of clay for many
days—for many weeks and irksome months—until my
tortured nerves obtained the mastery over my mind, and I
grew furious through delay, and, with the heart of a fiend,
cursed the days, and the hours, and the bitter moments,
which seemed to lengthen and lengthen as her gentle life
declined—like shadows in the dying of the day.

But one autumnal evening, when the winds lay still in
heaven, Morella called me to her bed-side. There was a
dim mist over all the earth, and a warm glow upon the
waters, and, amid the rich October leaves of the forest, a
rainbow from the firmament had surely fallen.

"It is a day of days," she said, as I approached; "a day of
all days either to live or die. It is a fair day for the sons of
earth and life—ah, more fair for the daughters of heaven
and death!"

I kissed her forehead, and she continued:

"I am dying, yet shall I live."

"Morella!"

"The days have never been when thou couldst love me—

but her whom in life thou didst abhor, in death thou shalt adore."

"Morella!"

"I repeat that I am dying. But within me is a pledge of that affection—ah, how little!—which thou didst feel for me, Morella. And when my spirit departs shall the child live—thy child and mine, Morella's. But thy days shall be days of sorrow—that sorrow which is the most lasting of impressions, as the cypress is the most enduring of trees. For the hours of thy happiness are over; and joy is not gathered twice in a life, as the roses of Pæstum twice in a year. Thou shalt no longer, then, play the Teian * with time, but, being ignorant of the myrtle and the vine, thou shalt bear about with thee thy shroud on the earth, as do the Moslemin † at Mecca."

"Morella!" I cried, "Morella! how knowest thou this?" —but she turned away her face upon the pillow, and, a slight tremor coming over her limbs, she thus died, and I heard her voice no more.

Yet, as she had foretold, her child—to which in dying she had given birth, and which breathed not until the mother breathed no more—her child, a daughter, lived. And she grew strangely in stature and intellect, and was the perfect resemblance of her who had departed, and I loved her with a love more fervent than I had believed it possible to feel for any denizen of earth.

But, ere long, the heaven of this pure affection became darkened, and gloom, and horror, and grief, swept over it in clouds. I said the child grew strangely in stature and intelligence. Strange indeed was her rapid increase in bodily

* Teian: Anacreon, poet of roses and wine and life's transitory delights.—Ed.
* Moslemin: Moslems.—Ed.

size—but terrible, oh! terrible were the tumultuous thoughts which crowded upon me while watching the development of her mental being. Could it be otherwise, when I daily discovered in the conceptions of the child the adult powers and faculties of the woman?—when the lessons of experience fell from the lips of infancy? and when the wisdom or the passions of maturity I found hourly gleaming from its full and speculative eye? When, I say, all this became evident to my appalled senses—when I could no longer hide it from my soul, nor throw it off from those perceptions which trembled to receive it—is it to be wondered at that suspicions, of a nature fearful and exciting, crept in upon my spirit, or that my thoughts fell back aghast upon the wild tales and thrilling theories of the entombed Morella? I snatched from the scrutiny of the world a being whom destiny compelled me to adore, and in the rigorous seclusion of my home, watched with an agonizing anxiety over all which concerned the beloved.

And, as years rolled away, and I gazed, day after day, upon her holy, and mild, and eloquent face, and pored over her maturing form, day after day did I discover new points of resemblance in the child to her mother, the melancholy and the dead. And, hourly, grew darker these shadows of similitude, and more full, and more definite, and more perplexing, and more hideously terrible in their aspect. For that her smile was like her mother's I could bear; but then I shuddered at its too perfect *identity*—that her eyes were like Morella's I could endure; but then they too often looked down into the depths of my soul with Morella's own intense and bewildering meaning. And in the contour of the high forehead, and in the ringlets of the silken hair, and in the wan fingers which buried themselves therein, and in the sad musical tones of her speech, and above all—oh, above all—in the phrases and expressions of the dead on the lips of the loved and the living, I found food for consuming thought and horror—for a worm that *would* not die.

Thus passed away two lustra * of her life, and, as yet, my daughter remained nameless upon the earth. "My child" and "my love" were the designations usually prompted by a father's affection, and the rigid seclusion of her days precluded all other intercourse. Morella's name died with her at her death. Of the mother I had never spoken to the daughter;—it was impossible to speak. Indeed, during the brief period of her existence the latter had received no impressions from the outward world save such as might have been afforded by the narrow limits of her privacy. But at length the ceremony of baptism presented to my mind, in its unnerved and agitated condition, a present deliverance from the terrors of my destiny. And at the baptismal font I hesitated for a name. And many titles of the wise and beautiful, of old and modern times, of my own and foreign lands, came thronging to my lips, with many, many fair titles of the gentle, and the happy, and the good. What prompted me, then, to disturb the memory of the buried dead? What demon urged me to breathe that sound, which, in its very recollection was wont to make ebb the purple blood in torrents from the temples to the heart? What fiend spoke from the recesses of my soul, when, amid those dim aisles, and in the silence of the night, I whispered within the ears of the holy man the syllables—Morella? What more than fiend convulsed the features of my child, and overspread them with hues of death, as starting at that scarcely audible sound, she turned her glassy eyes from the earth to

* Two lustra: ten years.—Ed.

heaven, and, falling prostrate on the black slabs of our ancestral vault, responded—"I am here!"

Distinct, coldly, calmly distinct, fell those few simple sounds within my ear, and thence, like molten lead, rolled hissingly into my brain. Years—years may pass away, but the memory of that epoch—never! Nor was I indeed ignorant of the flowers and the vine—but the hemlock and the cypress overshadowed me night and day. And I kept no reckoning of time or place, and the stars of my fate faded from heaven, and therefore the earth grew dark, and its figures passed by me, like flitting shadows, and among them all I beheld only—Morella. The winds of the firmament breathed but one sound within my ears, and the ripples upon the sea murmured evermore—Morella. But she died; and with my own hands I bore her to the tomb; and I laughed with a long and bitter laugh as I found no traces of the first, in the charnel which I laid the second—Morella.

❧ *The Prophetic Pictures*
by NATHANIEL HAWTHORNE

Nathaniel Hawthorne, the initiator of the psychological novel in America, was born in Salem, Massachusetts, in 1804, of an old New England family. He was deeply imbued with the traditional Puritan doctrines of sin, guilt, and expiation. Such preoccupations blend well with Romantic melancholy and with the Romantic taste for the supernatural and the sensational. Hawthorne died in 1864.

The Prophetic Pictures was first published in 1837. It was probably written earlier; it bears the marks of a Romanticism already on the wane. The author notes: "This story was suggested by an anecdote of [Gilbert] Stuart, related in Dunlap's *History of the Arts of Design*—a most entertaining book to the general reader, and a deeply interesting one, we should think, to the artist."

BUT THIS PAINTER!" cried Walter Ludlow, with animation. "He not only excels in his peculiar art, but possesses vast acquirements in all other learning and science. He talks Hebrew with Dr. Mather, and gives lectures in anatomy to Dr. Boylston.* In a word he will meet the best instructed man among us on his own ground. Moreover, he is a polished gentleman—a citizen of the world—yes, a true cosmopolite; for he will speak like a native of each clime and country of the globe except our own forests, whither he is now going. Nor is all this what I most admire in him."

"Indeed!" said Elinor, who had listened with a woman's interest to the description of such a man. "Yet this is admirable enough."

---

* Dr. Mather, Dr. Boylston: scholarly Boston worthies of the mid-eighteenth century.—Ed.

"Surely it is," replied her lover, "but far less so than his natural gift of adapting himself to every variety of character, insomuch that all men—and all women too, Elinor—shall find a mirror of themselves in this wonderful painter. But the greatest wonder is yet to be told."

"Nay, if he have more wonderful attributes than these," said Elinor, laughing, "Boston is a perilous abode for the poor gentleman. Are you telling me of a painter or a wizard?"

"In truth," answered he, "that question might be asked much more seriously than you suppose. They say that he paints not merely a man's features, but his mind and heart. He catches the secret sentiments and passions, and throws them upon the canvas, like sunshine—or perhaps, in the portraits of dark-souled men, like a gleam of infernal fire. It is an awful gift," added Walter, lowering his voice from its tone of enthusiasm. "I shall be almost afraid to sit to him."

"Walter, are you in earnest?" exclaimed Elinor.

"For Heaven's sake, dearest Elinor, do not let him paint the look which you now wear," said her lover, smiling, though rather perplexed. "There: it is passing away now, but when you spoke you seemed frightened to death, and very sad besides. What were you thinking of?"

"Nothing, nothing," answered Elinor hastily. "You paint my face with your own fantasies. Well, come for me to-morrow, and we will visit this wonderful artist."

But when the young man had departed, it cannot be denied that a remarkable expression was again visible on the fair and youthful face of his mistress. It was a sad and anxious look, little in accordance with what should have been the feelings of a maiden on the eve of wedlock. Yet Walter Ludlow was the chosen of her heart.

"A look!" said Elinor to herself. "No wonder that it startled him, if it expressed what I sometimes feel. I know, by my own experience, how frightful a look may be. But it was all fancy. I thought nothing of it at the time—I have seen nothing of it since—I did but dream it."

And she busied herself about the embroidery of a ruff, in which she meant that her portrait should be taken.

The painter, of whom they had been speaking, was not one of those native artists who, at a later period than this, borrowed their colors from the Indians, and manufactured their pencils of the furs of wild beasts. Perhaps, if he could have revoked his life and prearranged his destiny, he might have chosen to belong to that school without a master, in the hope of being at least original, since there were no works of art to imitate nor rules to follow. But he had been born and educated in Europe. People said that he had studied the grandeur or beauty of conception, and every touch of the master hand, in all the most famous pictures, in cabinets and galleries, and on the walls of churches, till there was nothing more for his powerful mind to learn. Art could add nothing to its lessons, but Nature might. He had therefore visited a world whither none of his professional brethren had preceded him, to feast his eyes on visible images that were noble and picturesque, yet had never been transferred to canvas. America was too poor to afford other temptations to an artist of eminence, though many of the colonial gentry, on the painter's arrival, had expressed a wish to transmit their lineaments to posterity by means of his skill. Whenever such proposals were made, he fixed his piercing eyes on the applicant, and seemed to look him through and through. If he beheld only a sleek and comfortable visage, though there were a gold-laced coat to adorn the picture and golden guineas to pay for it, he civilly rejected the task and the reward. But if the face were the index of any thing uncommon, in thought, sentiment, or experience; or if he met a beggar in the street, with a white beard and a furrowed brow; or if sometimes a child happened to look up and smile, he would exhaust all the art on them that he denied to wealth.

Pictorial skill being so rare in the colonies, the painter became an object of general curiosity. If few or none could appreciate the technical merit of his productions, yet there were points, in regard to which the opinion of the crowd was as valuable as the refined judgment of the amateur. He watched the effect that each picture produced on such untutored beholders, and derived profit from their remarks, while they would as soon have thought of instructing Nature herself as him who seemed to rival her. Their admiration, it must be owned, was tinctured with the prejudices of the age and country. Some deemed it an offence against the Mosaic law, and even a presumptuous mockery of the Creator, to bring into existence such lively images of his creatures. Others, frightened at the art which could raise phantoms at will, and keep the form of the dead among the living, were inclined to consider the painter as a magician, or perhaps the famous Black Man, of old witch times, plotting mischief in a new guise. These foolish fancies were more than half believed among the mob. Even in superior circles his character was invested with a vague awe, partly rising like smoke wreaths from the popular superstitions, but chiefly caused by the varied knowledge and talents which he made subservient to his profession.

Being on the eve of marriage, Walter Ludlow and Elinor were eager to obtain their portraits, as the first of what, they doubtless hoped, would be a long series of family pictures. The day after the conversation above recorded they visited the painter's rooms. A servant ushered them into an apartment, where, though the artist himself was not visible, there were personages whom they could hardly forbear greeting with reverence. They knew, indeed, that the whole assembly were but pictures, yet felt it impossible to separate the idea of life and intellect from such striking counterfeits. Several of the portraits were known to them, either as distinguished characters of the day or their private acquaintances. There was Governor Burnet, looking as if he had just received an undutiful communication from the House of Representatives, and were inditing a most sharp response. Mr. Cooke hung beside the ruler whom he opposed, sturdy, and somewhat puritanical, as befitted a popular leader. The ancient lady of Sir William Phipps eyed them from the wall, in ruff and farthingale,—an imperious old dame, not unsuspected of witchcraft. John Winslow, then a very young man, wore the expression of warlike enterprise, which long afterwards made him a distinguished general. Their personal friends were recognized at a glance. In most of the pictures, the whole mind and character were brought out on the countenance, and concentrated into a single look, so that, to speak paradoxically, the originals hardly resembled themselves so strikingly as the portraits did.

Among these modern worthies there were two old bearded saints, who had almost vanished into the darkening canvas. There was also a pale, but unfaded Madonna, who had perhaps been worshipped in Rome, and now regarded the lovers with such a mild and holy look that they longed to worship too.

"How singular a thought," observed Walter Ludlow, "that this beautiful face has been beautiful for above two hundred years! Oh, if all beauty would endure so well! Do you not envy her, Elinor?"

"If earth were heaven, I might," she replied. "But where all things fade, how miserable to be the one that could not fade!"

"This dark old St. Peter has a fierce and ugly scowl, saint though he be," continued Walter. "He troubles me. But the Virgin looks kindly at us."

"Yes; but very sorrowfully, methinks," said Elinor.

The easel stood beneath these three old pictures, sustaining one that had been recently commenced. After a little inspection, they began to recognize the features of their own minister, the Rev. Dr. Colman, growing into shape and life, as it were, out of a cloud.

"Kind old man!" exclaimed Elinor. "He gazes at me as if he were about to utter a word of paternal advice."

"And at me," said Walter, "as if he were about to shake his head and rebuke me for some suspected iniquity. But so does the original. I shall never feel quite comfortable under his eye till we stand before him to be married."

They now heard a footstep on the floor, and turning, beheld the painter, who had been some moments in the room, and had listened to a few of their remarks. He was a middle-aged man, with a countenance well worthy of his own pencil. Indeed, by the picturesque, though careless arrangement of his rich dress, and, perhaps, because his soul dwelt always among painted shapes, he looked somewhat like a portrait himself. His visitors were sensible of a kindred between the artist and his works, and felt as if one of the pictures had stepped from the canvas to salute them.

Walter Ludlow, who was slightly known to the painter, explained the object of their visit. While he spoke, a sunbeam was falling athwart his figure and Elinor's, with so happy an effect that they also seemed living pictures of youth and beauty, gladdened by bright fortune. The artist was evidently struck.

"My easel is occupied for several ensuing days, and my stay in Boston must be brief," said he, thoughtfully; then, after an observant glance, he added: "but your wishes shall be gratified, though I disappoint the Chief Justice and Madam Oliver. I must not lose this opportunity, for the sake of painting a few ells of broadcloth and brocade."

The painter expressed a desire to introduce both their portraits into one picture, and represent them engaged in some appropriate action. This plan would have delighted the lovers, but was necessarily rejected, because so large a space of canvas would have been unfit for the room which it was intended to decorate. Two half-length portraits were therefore fixed upon. After they had taken leave, Walter Ludlow asked Elinor, with a smile, whether she knew what an influence over their fates the painter was about to acquire.

"The old women of Boston affirm," continued he, "that after he has once got possession of a person's face and figure, he may paint him in any act or situation whatever— and the picture will be prophetic. Do you believe it?"

"Not quite," said Elinor, smiling. "Yet if he has such magic, there is something so gentle in his manner that I am sure he will use it well."

It was the painter's choice to proceed with both the portraits at the same time, assigning as a reason, in the mystical language which he sometimes used, that the faces threw light upon each other. Accordingly he gave now a touch to Walter, and now to Elinor, and the features of one and the other began to start forth so vividly that it appeared as if his triumphant art would actually disengage them from the canvas. Amid the rich light and deep shade, they beheld their phantom selves. But, though the likeness promised to be perfect, they were not quite satisfied with the expression; it seemed more vague than in most of the painter's works. He, however, was satisfied with the prospect of success, and being much interested in the lovers, employed his leisure moments, unknown to them, in making a crayon sketch of their two figures. During their sittings, he engaged them in conversation, and kindled up their faces with characteristic traits, which, though continually varying, it was his purpose to combine and fix. At length he announced that at their next visit both the portraits would be ready for delivery.

"If my pencil will but be true to my conception, in the few last touches which I meditate," observed he, "these two pictures will be my very best performances. Seldom, indeed, has an artist such subjects."

While speaking, he still bent his penetrative eye upon them, nor withdrew it till they had reached the bottom of the stairs.

Nothing, in the whole circle of human vanities, takes stronger hold of the imagination than this affair of having a portrait painted. Yet why should it be so? The looking-glass, the polished globes of the andirons, the mirror-like water, and all other reflecting surfaces, continually present us with portraits, or rather ghosts of ourselves, which we glance at, and straightway forget them. But we forget them only because they vanish. It is the idea of duration—of earthly immortality—that gives such a mysterious interest to our own portraits. Walter and Elinor were not insensible to this feeling, and hastened to the painter's room, punctually at the appointed hour, to meet those pictured shapes which were to be their representatives with posterity. The sunshine flashed after them into the apartment, but left it somewhat gloomy as they closed the door.

Their eyes were immediately attracted to their portraits, which rested against the farthest wall of the room. At the first glance, through the dim light and the distance, seeing themselves in precisely their natural attitudes, and with all the air that they recognized so well, they uttered a simultaneous exclamation of delight.

"There we stand," cried Walter, enthusiastically, "fixed in sunshine forever! No dark passions can gather on our faces!"

"No," said Elinor, more calmly; "no dreary change can sadden us."

This was said while they were approaching, and had yet gained only an imperfect view of the pictures. The painter, after saluting them, busied himself at a table in completing a crayon sketch, leaving his visitors to form their own judgment as to his perfected labors. At intervals, he sent a glance from beneath his deep eyebrows, watching their countenances in profile, with his pencil suspended over the sketch. They had now stood some moments, each in front of the other's picture, contemplating it with entranced attention, but without uttering a word. At length, Walter stepped forward—then back—viewing Elinor's portrait in various lights, and finally spoke.

"Is there not a change?" said he, in a doubtful and meditative tone. "Yes; the perception of it grows more vivid the longer I look. It is certainly the same picture that I saw yesterday; the dress—the features—all are the same; and yet something is altered."

"Is then the picture less like than it was yesterday?"

inquired the painter, now drawing near, with irrepressible interest.

"The features are perfect, Elinor," answered Walter, "and, at the first glance, the expression seemed also here. But, I could fancy that the portrait has changed countenance, while I have been looking at it. The eyes are fixed on mine with a strangely sad and anxious expression. Nay, it is grief and terror! Is this like Elinor?"

"Compare the living face with the pictured one," said the painter.

Walter glanced sidelong at his mistress, and started. Motionless and absorbed—fascinated, as it were—in contemplation of Walter's portrait, Elinor's face had assumed precisely the expression of which he had just been complaining. Had she practised for whole hours before a mirror, she could not have caught the look so successfully. Had the picture itself been a mirror, it could not have thrown back her present aspect with stronger and more melancholy truth. She appeared quite unconscious of the dialogue between the artist and her lover.

"Elinor," exclaimed Walter, in amazement, "what change has come over you?"

She did not hear him, nor desist from her fixed gaze, till he seized her hand, and thus attracted her notice; then, with a sudden tremor, she looked from the picture to the face of the original.

"Do you see no change in your portrait?" asked she.

"In mine?—None!" replied Walter, examining it. "But let me see! Yes; there is a slight change—an improvement, I think, in the picture, though none in the likeness. It has a livelier expression than yesterday, as if some bright thought were flashing from the eyes, and about to be uttered from the lips. Now that I have caught the look, it becomes very decided."

While he was intent on these observations, Elinor turned to the painter. She regarded him with grief and awe, and felt that he repaid her with sympathy and commiseration, though wherefore, she could but vaguely guess.

"That look!" whispered she, and shuddered. "How came it there?"

"Madam," said the painter, sadly, taking her hand, and leading her apart, "in both these pictures, I have painted what I saw. The artist—the true artist—must look beneath the exterior. It is his gift—his proudest, but often a melancholy one—to see the inmost soul, and, by a power indefinable even to himself, to make it glow or darken upon the canvas, in glances that express the thought and sentiment of years. Would that I might convince myself of error in the present instance!"

They had now approached the table, on which were heads in chalk, hands almost as expressive as ordinary faces, ivied church towers, thatched cottages, old thunder-stricken trees, Oriental and antique costume, and all such picturesque vagaries of an artist's idle moments. Turning them over, with seeming carelessness, a crayon sketch of two figures was disclosed.

"If I have failed," continued he—"if your heart does not see itself reflected in your own portrait—if you have no secret cause to trust my delineation of the other—it is not yet too late to alter them. I might change the action of these figures too. But would it influence the event?"

He directed her notice to the sketch. A thrill ran through Elinor's frame; a shriek was upon her lips; but she stifled it, with the self-command that becomes habitual to all who hide thoughts of fear and anguish within their bosoms.

Turning from the table, she perceived that Walter had advanced near enough to have seen the sketch, though she could not determine whether it had caught his eye.

"We will not have the pictures altered," said she, hastily. "If mine is sad, I shall but look the gayer for the contrast."

"Be it so," answered the painter, bowing. "May your griefs be such fanciful ones that only your picture may mourn for them! For your joys—may they be true and deep, and paint themselves upon this lovely face till it quite belie my art!"

After the marriage of Walter and Elinor, the pictures formed the two most splendid ornaments of their abode. They hung side by side, separated by a narrow panel, appearing to eye each other constantly, yet always returning the gaze of the spectator. Travelled gentlemen, who professed a knowledge of such subjects, reckoned these among the most admirable specimens of modern portraiture; while common observers compared them with the originals, feature by feature, and were rapturous in praise of the likeness. But it was on a third class—neither travelled connoisseurs nor common observers, but people of natural sensibility—that the pictures wrought their strongest effect. Such persons might gaze carelessly at first, but, becoming interested, would return day after day, and study these painted faces like the pages of a mystic volume. Walter Ludlow's portrait attracted their earliest notice. In the absence of himself and his bride, they sometimes disputed as to the expression which the painter had intended to throw upon the features; all agreeing that there was a look of earnest import, though no two explained it alike. There was less diversity of opinion in regard to Elinor's picture. They differed, indeed, in their attempts to estimate the nature and depth of the gloom that dwelt upon her face, but agreed that it was gloom, and alien from the natural temperament of their youthful friend. A certain fanciful person announced, as the result of much scrutiny, that both these pictures were parts of one design, and that the melancholy strength of feeling, in Elinor's countenance, bore reference to the more vivid emotion, or, as he termed it, the wild passion, in that of Walter. Though unskilled in the art, he even began a sketch, in which the action of the two figures was to correspond with their mutual expression.

It was whispered among friends that, day by day, Elinor's face was assuming a deeper shade of pensiveness, which threatened soon to render her too true a counterpart of her melancholy picture. Walter, on the other hand, instead of acquiring the vivid look which the painter had given him on the canvas, became reserved and downcast, with no outward flashes of emotion, however it might be smouldering within. In course of time, Elinor hung a gorgeous curtain of purple silk, wrought with flowers and fringed with heavy golden tassels, before the pictures, under pretense that the dust would tarnish their hues, or the light dim them. It was enough. Her visitors felt, that the massive folds of the silk must never be withdrawn, nor the portraits mentioned in her presence.

Time wore on; and the painter came again. He had been far enough to the north to see the silver cascade of the Crystal Hills, and to look over the vast round of cloud and forest from the summit of New England's loftiest mountain. But he did not profane that scene by the mockery of his art. He had also lain in a canoe on the bosom of Lake George, making his soul the mirror of its loveliness and grandeur, till not a picture in the Vatican was more vivid than his recollection. He had gone with the Indian hunters to Niagara, and there, again, had flung his hopeless pencil down the precipice, feeling that he could as soon paint the roar, as aught else that goes to make up the wondrous cataract. In truth, it was seldom his impulse to copy natural scenery, except as a framework for the delineations of the human form and face, instinct with thought, passion, or suffering. With store of such his adventurous ramble had enriched him: the stern dignity of Indian chiefs; the dusky loveliness of Indian girls; the domestic life of wigwams; the stealthy march; the battle beneath gloomy pine-trees; the frontier fortress with its garrison; the anomaly of the old French partisan, bred in courts, but grown gray in shaggy deserts; such were the scenes and portraits that he had sketched. The glow of perilous moments; flashes of wild feeling; struggles of fierce power,—love, hate, grief, frenzy; in a word, all the worn-out heart of the old earth had been revealed to him under a new form. His portfolio was filled with graphic illustrations of the volume of his memory, which genius would transmute into its own substance, and imbue with immortality. He felt that the deep wisdom in his art, which he had sought so far, was found.

But amid stern or lovely nature, in the perils of the forest or its overwhelming peacefulness, still there had been two phantoms, the companions of his way. Like all other men around whom an engrossing purpose wreathes itself, he was insulated from the mass of human kind. He had no aim—no pleasure—no sympathies—but what were ultimately connected with his art. Though gentle in manner and upright in intent and action, he did not possess kindly feelings; his heart was cold; no living creature could be brought near enough to keep him warm. For these two beings, however, he had felt, in its greatest intensity, the sort of interest which always allied him to the subjects of his pencil. He had pried into their souls with his keenest insight, and pictured the result upon their features with his utmost skill, so as barely to fall short of that standard which no genius ever reached, his own severe conception. He had caught from the duskiness of the future—at least, so he fancied—a fearful secret, and had obscurely revealed it on the portraits. So much of himself—of his imagination and all other powers—had been lavished on the study of Walter and Elinor, that he almost regarded them as creations of his own, like the thousands with which he had peopled the realms of Picture. Therefore did they flit through the twilight of the woods, hover on the mist of waterfalls, look forth from the mirror of the lake, nor melt away in the noontide sun. They haunted his pictorial fancy, not as mockeries of life, nor pale goblins of the dead, but in the guise of portraits, each with the unalterable expression which his magic had evoked from the caverns of the soul. He could not recross the Atlantic till he had again beheld the originals of those airy pictures.

"O glorious Art!" thus mused the enthusiastic painter as he trod the street, "thou art the image of the Creator's own. The innumerable forms, that wander in nothingness, start into being at thy beck. The dead live again. Thou recallest them to their old scenes, and givest their gray shadows the lustre of a better life, at once earthly and immortal. Thou snatchest back the fleeting moments of History. With thee there is no Past, for, at thy touch, all that is great becomes forever present; and illustrious men live through long ages, in the visible performance of the very deeds which made them what they are. O potent Art! as thou bringest the faintly revealed Past to stand in that narrow strip of sunlight, which we call Now, canst thou summon the shrouded Future to meet her there? Have I not achieved it? Am I not thy Prophet?"

Thus, with a proud, yet melancholy fervor, did he almost cry aloud, as he passed through the toilsome street, among people that knew not of his reveries, nor could understand nor care for them. It is not good for man to cherish a solitary ambition. Unless there be those around him by whose example he may regulate himself, his thoughts, desires, and hopes will become extravagant, and he the semblance, perhaps the reality, of a madman. Reading other bosoms with an acuteness almost preternatural, the painter failed to see the disorder of his own.

"And this should be the house," said he, looking up and down the front, before he knocked. "Heaven help my brains! That picture! Methinks it will never vanish. Whether I look at the windows or the door, there it is framed within them, painted strongly, and glowing in the richest tints—the faces of the portraits—the figures and action of the sketch!"

He knocked.

"The Portraits! Are they within?" inquired he of the domestic; then recollecting himself—"your master and mistress! Are they at home?"

"They are, sir," said the servant, adding, as he noticed that picturesque aspect of which the painter could never divest himself, "and the Portraits too!"

The guest was admitted into a parlor, communicating by a central door with an interior room of the same size. As the first apartment was empty, he passed to the entrance of the second, within which his eyes were greeted by those living personages, as well as their pictured representatives, who had long been the objects of so singular an interest. He involuntarily paused on the threshold.

They had not perceived his approach. Walter and Elinor were standing before the portraits, whence the former had just flung back the rich and voluminous folds of the silken curtain, holding its golden tassel with one hand, while the other grasped that of his bride. The pictures, concealed for months, gleamed forth again in undiminished splendor, appearing to throw a sombre light across the room, rather than to be disclosed by a borrowed radiance. That of Elinor had been almost prophetic. A pensiveness, and next a gentle sorrow, had successively dwelt upon her countenance, deepening, with the lapse of time, into a quiet anguish. A mixture of affright would now have made it the very expression of the portrait. Walter's face was moody and dull, or animated only by fitful flashes, which left a heavier darkness for their momentary illumination. He looked from Elinor to her portrait, and thence to his own, in the contemplation of which he finally stood absorbed.

The painter seemed to hear the step of Destiny approaching behind him, on its progress towards its victims. A strange thought darted into his mind. Was not his own the form in which that destiny had embodied itself, and he a chief agent of the coming evil which he had foreshadowed?

Still, Walter remained silent before the picture, communing with it as with his own heart, and abandoning himself to the spell of evil influence that the painter had cast upon the features. Gradually his eyes kindled; while as Elinor watched the increasing wildness of his face, her own assumed a look of terror; and when at last he turned upon her, the resemblance of both to their portraits was complete.

"Our fate is upon us!" howled Walter. "Die!"

Drawing a knife, he sustained her, as she was sinking to the ground, and aimed it at her bosom. In the action, and in the look and attitude of each, the painter beheld the figures of his sketch. The picture, with all its tremendous coloring, was finished.

"Hold, madman!" cried he, sternly.

He had advanced from the door, and interposed himself between the wretched beings, with the same sense of power to regulate their destiny as to alter a scene upon the canvas. He stood like a magician, controlling the phantoms which he had evoked.

"What!" muttered Walter Ludlow, as he relapsed from fierce excitement into silent gloom. "Does Fate impede its own decree?"

"Wretched lady!" said the painter, "did I not warn you?"

"You did," replied Elinor, calmly, as her terror gave place to the quiet grief which it had disturbed. "But—I loved him!"

Is there not a deep moral in the tale? Could the result of one, or all our deeds, be shadowed forth and set before us, some would call it Fate, and hurry onward, others be swept along by their passionate desires, and none be turned aside by the PROPHETIC PICTURES.

A Romantic Storybook

Designed by R. E. Rosenbaum.
Composed by Kingsport Press, Inc.,
in 11 point linotype Janson, 3 points leaded,
with display lines in Palatino.
Printed letterpress from type by Kingsport Press,
on Warren's Olde Style India, 60 pound basis,
with the Cornell University Press watermark.
Bound by Kingsport Press
in Interlaken AL3 book cloth
and stamped in All Purpose gold foil.
End papers are Weyerhaeuser Carousel Text.